Tulle Little, Tulle Late

Kimberly Llewellyn

BERKLEY BOOKS, NEW YORK

THE BERKLEY PUBLISHING GROUP
Published by the Penguin Group
Penguin Group (USA) Inc.
375 Hudson Street, New York, New York 10014, USA
Penguin Group (Canada), 90 Eglinton Avenue East, Suite 700, Toronto, Ontario M4P 2Y3, Canada
(a division of Pearson Penguin Canada Inc.)
Penguin Books Ltd., 80 Strand, London WC2R 0RL, England
Penguin Group Ireland, 25 St. Stephen's Green, Dublin 2, Ireland (a division of Penguin Books Ltd.)
Penguin Group (Australia), 250 Camberwell Road, Camberwell, Victoria 3124, Austraila
(a division of Pearson Australia Group Pty. Ltd.)
Penguin Books India Pvt. Ltd., 11 Community Centre, Panchsheel Park, New Delhi—110 017, India
Penguin Group (NZ), Cnr. Airborne and Rosedale Roads, Albany, Auckland 1310, New Zealand
(a divison of Pearson New Zealand Ltd.)
Penguin Books (South Africa) (Pty.) Ltd., 24 Sturdee Avenue, Rosebank, Johannesburg 2196, South Africa

Penguin Books Ltd., Registered Offices: 80 Strand, London WC2R 0RL, England

This is a work of fiction. Names, characters, places, and incidents either are the product of the author's imagination or are used fictitiously, and any resemblance to actual persons, living or dead, business establishments, events, or locales is entirely coincidental. The publisher does not have any control over and does not assume any responsibility for author or third-party websites or their content.

TULLE LITTLE, TULLE LATE

Copyright © 2006 by Kimberly Llewellyn
Cover design by Lesley Worrell
Cover illustration by Kim Johnson
Book design by Stacy Irwin

PRINTING HISTORY
Berkley trade paperback edition / August 2006

Berkley trade paperback ISBN: 0-425-21132-0

An application to register this book for cataloging has been submitted to the Library of Congress.

PRINTED IN THE UNITED STATES OF AMERICA

10 9 8 7 6 5 4 3 2 1

Watch out . . .
HERE COMES THE BRIDE

Mom reaches up and rips Celie's tiara from my scalp, along with a good clumping of hair roots. But some of the roots stay attached to my head, keeping me leashed to the tiara like a rabid mongrel. Mom plows ahead. With her firm grip on the headpiece, she totters over toward the dresser. I'm yelping and have no choice but to be dragged along.

"Nina! Quit moving!" Brooke snaps. "I almost had it! What the hell did they use to sew this thing, dental floss? I'm gonna have to rip a hook! I got no choice!"

Brooke yanks me back into place. I feel her take hold of the bustle of the gown, followed by her foot slamming into the small of my back so she can brace herself.

"On the count of three . . ."

Mom loses her grip on the tiara, which now dangles from my hair. With her free hand—God forbid she put down her drink—she tries to detangle the tiara, while Brooke's foot slips down lower and kicks me.

"Yeow!"

That's when a long, drawn-out, deep, guttural wail rolls through the air, making the very walls of the house tremble.

Mom, Brooke, and I freeze in our godawfully tangled position.

I draw my gaze to the doorway.

Celie is standing statuelike, her hinged mouth loosely dangling somewhere around her size-eight sternum. Although the rest of her Botox-poisoned face is generally still expressionless, she's obviously disgusted by the sight before her . . .

For Cheryl Anne Porter

Acknowledgments

I'd like to thank all my favorite codependents, enablers, and co-whores who've helped me become the fabulously maladjusted individual I am today.

ONE

I tried to contain myself but I escaped.

My troubles actually began a month ago, gawdawful troubles that led me to the predicament I'm in now. See, at this very moment, I'm standing alone in the middle of a cream-and-mauve decorated bedroom, wearing a gloriously white Vera Wang wedding gown with an Alençon lace–sheathed bodice and oversized satin rosettes on the sleeves. The shade of white matches my complexion perfectly and the entire ensemble fits me surprisingly well.

But I'm indulging in a full-blown panic attack, which comes complete with all the bells and whistles, including the uncanny inability to expand a lung for a single breath, not to mention rivers of sweat gushing down my prettily made-up face.

At least the wedding gown looks fabulous.

Trouble is, it's not my wedding gown.

"Damn it. What am I doing in this thing?" I demand of my reflection in the full-length mahogany mirror.

Here I am, an up-and-comer in the joyful cocktail hour called life, suddenly reduced to slipping into another woman's wedding gown on the sly. In said-woman's own home. While her over-catered bridal shower carries on downstairs in the formal parlor at the foot of the grand staircase.

Nina Robertson, what did you get yourself into now?

I smear my sweat-soaked palm across my forehead to mop up the damp foundation makeup mixed with perspiration. Following that exercise in futility (the only exercise I've done in the last month, mind you), I unconsciously wipe my hands on my wedding gown's full princess skirt drowning in tulle fabric.

Correction: my *cousin's* wedding gown.

But that's to be discussed, dissected, analyzed, and chopped to bits with a hacksaw a little later on. The only thing I can focus on now as I labor for air is how inconceivable it would seem that my current dilemma and hysterical state of mind could have possibly started because of one little word.

Sperm.

Okay, about a month earlier . . . the day I went into full-sperm labor . . .

The morning had started out like any other, maybe even a little better than most. It had been a bright, cheery New England late-spring day, a happy Saturday morning in May, not too hot, not too cool. The kind of day where you open all your windows, fully intent on having spring fever tackle you and giddily wrestle you to the ground.

Okay, so I didn't get a case of spring fever, because that would mean love was in the air here in Salem, Massachusetts, or at least a flurry of pheromones, which was clearly not the case for me.

Instead of spring fever, I had a case of spring cleaning to do. Armed with a bucket of sudsy water and sponge, I was ready. But then I'd made the mistake of doing a one-armed swoosh over a pile of useless paperwork and junk, pushing it to one end of the counter of my too small kitchenette in my too small apartmentette.

That's when the innocent little white envelope peeked out and reared its ugly head from under the morning mail.

The invitation to the bridal shower for Celie, my dear sweet cousin from hell.

I snatched up Celie's invitation. I couldn't stop the lump of angst swelling in my throat. The tearful lump actually proved to be a good thing in that it blocked up any chance of an impromptu crying jag.

Not only had my own cousin purchased what I considered my dream wedding gown (she'd seen the ad for the little Vera Wang number I'd ripped from *Bride* magazine), she even stole my dream "wedding color" and used it for her own. An unusual color combination that the bridal industry had dreamed up, a cross between royal blue and purple, lovingly known as *royple*.

I opened the envelope to see—printed in royple ink—the day, date, and time of this soiree.

I had exactly one month to completely change my life. To make it so fabulous that I'd be the envy of everyone at the bridal shower to the point that even Celie's own mother would forget about the guest of honor because she'd be so blinded by my sudden beauty and career success and svelte figure.

Yeah. Right. One month.

I felt my lower lip tremble.

Yes, I knew this day would come ever since I'd first heard of Celie's engagement. I was happy for her. Honest. Maybe it would get her off my back. She's really competitive with me and loves to rub things in my face. So goes the rivalry between two cousins who'd been pitted against each other by the family since birth. Not that I ever cared; I was always too busy doing my own thing.

We were born around the same time; we're the same height at five foot four, both with chestnutty hair and blue eyes. Although we came from the same family, Celie had taken this competition thing to heart the same way an enemy does when heading into battle.

I guess it's no wonder. The topic of who was prettier, smarter, or more talented has been an ongoing subject of debate during reunions, weddings, holiday parties . . . you name it. Several years ago, the banter shifted into high gear on who would be the first to marry. This ultimate competition began during one of our traditional Memorial Day weekend family backyard barbecues and has continued ever since.

The discussion goes something like this:

"Celie's eyes are a lighter blue—she gets that from our side of the family, and she can cook," one auntie always argued while sitting at the picnic table.

"Oh, but Nina's such a . . . 'bright' girl," another auntie would offer my mother in a consoling manner as an afterthought.

My mom would nod apologetically and return to tapping the keg perched on ice in the corner of the backyard. "You know, she got her sense of humor from her father, God rest his soul."

My father's not dead. But he did walk out on us about a million years ago. Ever since then, my mother's been praying for God to literally *rest* his soul for what he did to us. Nothing fancy. Something swift and painless, like a run-in with a bus.

You gotta remember, this all started way back in the eighties and into the nineties, a mongrel time for young women like me. (I just hit the big three-uh-oh a few months back; Celie was right behind me.) Too young to be a yuppie, not exactly a Gen-X-er. The best I could call women around my age is Generation "O." As in Oprah. She served as our guide, our goddess, our guru. A beacon of light in the dark murky waters of finding oneself.

Although finding yourself didn't happen too easily "B.O." (Before Oprah), at least we had the aunties to help with hunting down the perfect "boys" to set us up. All the while, my mom would be right there, complaining it was a lost cause.

"Why do you women obsess over finding a man anyway?" she'd always yell. "They either die or defect anyway! Your father did, God rest his soul."

"Ma, please, Dad's not dead."

"I know. And yet every day, I keep praying; God! Rest his soul! The bastard!"

Fast forward to the bridal shower invitation . . .

I'm not sure if much has changed between Celie and me since then. Yes, I was a grown woman today—or so I told myself—and I've never really given in to the petty childhood rivalry with Celie. In fact, I've put it all behind me. Countless times. Unfortunately, Celie hasn't, and I wished I could think of a way to end this fruitless competition once and for all. It would come to me, I knew it would.

As I gazed down at the bridal shower invitation, I noted Celie's gorgeously scrawled handwriting at the bottom.

I'm going to love seeing you there! Looking forward to it! Love, Celie.

With my keen eye (my vision: 20/20; hers: 20/25, by the way, ha!), I knew what her sweet message was really saying.

Translation:

Can't wait to see you so I can rub this in your face, and ohhh, I'm going to enjoy every minute of it. Eat shit and die. Love, Celie.

I recognized this underlying encryption, because I did something in the same vein to her when I'd sent out my own engagement party invitations, only I tried to be kinder about it. My message was to be translated as: *Can we end the rivalry once and for all?*

Yes, that's right, I'd been engaged briefly before, which explained why I never got to officially wear my dream gown, but that's for later. Still hurts to think about it, which is another reason I really did want this "milestone rivalry" between us to cease and desist. As far as milestones went, I wasn't achieving any and I didn't need Celie reminding me.

No, I was no longer in my twenties. No, I wasn't married. And no, I didn't even have a prospect in the works. No, I hadn't exactly been shimmying up the corporate ladder at the ad agency where I work anywhere near as fast as I could have been. Hey, I thought I'd be married, popping out puppies eventually, and I would have traded in career for motherhood anyway.

Yes, in fact, I still shared a tiny apartment just north of Boston with my friend Brooke. Yes, my biological clock was ticking. Loudly. And incessantly. Yes, I was still struggling to make ends meet. Yes, I still occasionally had what appeared to be "irrational tendencies," like investing in a pair of sky-kissing stems by Prada instead of that retirement plan I'd been meaning to start.

Then again, an investment is an investment. I simply chose to invest in my short-term future of looking amazing for when I met Dr. Right, right down to my toes, is all.

With my own milestones at a complete standstill—actually they'd gone into reverse when my fiancé bagged out on me—I had to find some aggressive way to end my nagging problem with Celie.

That's when the idea of sperm crossed my mind.

I suddenly realized that the only thing I could do on such short notice, to end this rivalry once and for all, would be to show up at the bridal shower knocked up and waddling about with my shirt untucked. This would be very doable since I would probably be ovulating in the next couple of days! Then again, you never know with my wacko-tempermental ovulation cycles. Okay, so maybe the untucked shirt and waddling part would be a bit overly dramatic, but still perhaps, *doable*.

Maybe the fumes from the bucket of cleaning solution got to me, but getting pregnant in time for this shindig seemed like the perfect answer . . . actually the answer to lots of my dilemmas. Perhaps I'd be rushing things, but why wait for the milestones to happen in a painstakingly slow, particular order when I could take destiny by the testes and create my own fate at that very moment?

A minute later, I was surfing the Internet in search of a sperm bank. I never realized they delivered! Amazing! Who knew?

I was so engrossed in my search for sperm, I didn't even hear my apartmentette-mate come home, until I felt a tap on my shoulder.

"Hi! Watcha doing?"

"Oh! Ah, ordering sperm off the Internet." I tried to answer casually and stared back at the computer monitor, as if this were an everyday occurrence. Brooke had seen me do worse, so I knew she wouldn't be too surprised.

"Why? What's happened this time?"

"I've got my cousin Celie's bridal shower next month and I need to be pregnant by then."

"Oh, I should have guessed. Why do you let her get to you like that?"

"Do I want washed or unwashed?" I asked without answering her question. I kept with my perusal of a sperm bank's web site with the slogan, "Fresh, Never Frozen." It detailed donor information, shipping options, and various types of sperm I could order. "Well? Washed or unwashed?" I repeated impatiently.

"Washed or unwashed . . . what? What are you talking about?"

"The sperm!"

"I don't know," Brooke said, then paused thoughtfully. "I'd say washed, right? I mean, it should be clean."

Brooke's transparent response indicated she was humoring me and treated this with all the falsified seriousness she could muster. I wasn't buying her feigned sincerity.

"Oh, forget I asked . . . what do you know about sperm anyway?"

"I know I've choked down enough of the stuff to want it to be washed. How about you?"

She had a point. I growled with indignation. I hadn't exactly been swimming in a sea of semen lately, so I surely was no expert. Keeping her advice in mind, I read the web site for further clarification.

"Well, it says here, one type is for uterine processing, one's for cervical processing," I said aloud.

I frowned in confusion. *Uterine? Cervical?*

Where's the type for *vaginal*?

"Nina, come on, seriously. I know you were ready to start a new life and get married. I've been living with you long enough to know when you're really upset. I know how bad you've been aching to have a baby."

"Bad? You don't know the half. My ovaries are no longer on speaking terms with me."

"Still, don't you think you're jumping the gun by ordering cyber-sperm on-line? This isn't about Celie at all, now is it? You know what this is really about—"

"—fifteen million critters per unit. Two units per vat. You think thirty million's enough? I'd better order two vats. I hope they take a credit card. Ohhh, there's overnight delivery!"

"I mean it, you don't want to do it this way."

"Don't I?" I finally turned and peered up into Brooke's clear ice-green eyes as she hovered over me. "It's too hard going the traditional route. I mean the whole dating thing is so excruciating—"

"Which you haven't done since your breakup with—"

"Brooke, please—"

"Jeremiah."

Jeremiah.

The lump in my throat, which had just started to deflate, ballooned right back up again. I let out a shaky sigh, hoping the menacing tears won't make good on their threat.

Brooke was right, I hadn't dated at all since Jeremiah broke it off. He and I had only been engaged for a few months, but it still smarted if I thought about it too hard.

As a blushing-albeit-brief bride to be, I'd managed to accomplish a lot in that short time. I had selected the wedding gown, the bridesmaids, and flowers. Jeremiah and I even scouted out the perfect location; a quaint manor house nestled in the woodsy hills of New Hampshire, about two hours north of Boston.

Since our breakup six months ago however, I'd simply been attempting to live on an emotionally even keel to try and get over the guy's jumping ship. I figured maintaining a calm, structured life would keep me from snapping in two. Of course, that all ended when I got Celie's invitation.

"Face it, before Jeremiah, I did enough dating to last me two lifetimes. I need to move on. Take the next step to another phase of my life. With or without him."

Or any guy for that matter!

"So a vial of sperm and a turkey baster is your next step?"

"Why not?"

"Because I know you. And I know you wouldn't want to raise a kid who never has a dad around."

"My mother did it."

"She had no choice. Your father walked out on her twenty years ago. In this case, your child would never know the father because the poor kid had been smeared onto a petri dish. Either way, you know what it feels like with no dad and you wouldn't purposely do that, it's not your style."

Did she *always* have to be right? Brooke had this amazing intuition and incredible insight into people. Because of her talent, dating happened naturally for her. It made her life so easy; when it came to men, she treasured the hunt. She simply sensed what a particular man wanted in a woman, and she became that woman; it was a God-given gift.

I only knew that she never got stuck home on a Saturday night with a bag of sodium-encrusted popcorn, a two-liter of warm Diet Coke, and a not-so-good movie on basic cable. Yep, my date nights lately included only one man: Orville Redenbacher.

I let Brooke's words sink in and eventually came to my senses. No, going into full-sperm labor just to shut up Celie didn't sound like the fantastic idea I'd originally thought. I also noted the little disclaimer on the web site; something about your OB/GYN needing to set up an account first. So much for going the turkey baster route. I shut down the computer.

"So, what do I do?" I asked, dejected.

"You go to this bridal shower with your head held high. Don't let her see you so bugged."

"I'll need your support. Come with me."

"What? And crash the bridal shower?" she asked with dramatic disdain.

"Please? Do this for me?" I shot her my best dead-serious imploring look. The one she never could turn down.

"There'll be food, right?" she asked.

"Yup."

"But wouldn't that be rude? Wouldn't Celie get all ticked off at you?"

"Uh-huh."

Brooke broke into a full, satisfied grin.

"Aw, what are friends for?"

"Thanks, Brooke! I mean how bad can it be?"

Little did I know that a seemingly straightforward bridal shower would lead me to having a total meltdown while ensnared inside a bridal gown that wasn't technically mine.

TWO

Reality bites . . . I've got the teeth marks to prove it.

The impending bridal-gown incident fast approaches . . .

Okay, so the next month flies by, which always happens when a foreboding day looms. You know, like a major operation, a court sentencing, or an execution date set for a public hanging. And Celie would love nothing more than to witness me hanging by my own Versace belly-belt for all her guests to see. Yes, in this case, the foreboding day is Celie's bridal shower.

"Never let 'em see you fret" is my motto for this day. And I'm not wearing a belly-belt as I opt for a simple crisp white DKNY shirt, with a pair of sensible gray pumps and gray skirt. Oh, I might add here, the length of my little skirt falls somewhere in the vicinity of "mini" and "hoochie." I keep my shoulder-length hair down and free. Okay, so maybe I added some highlights to these chestnutty tresses, but my hairdresser, Chloe, said it would add depth and richness to my color. And having my new-cropped layers "pulsing" around my shoulders gives my hair more "swing" . . . those are all Chloe's words.

Brooke's late from working at a catering job and has to meet me at the shower. Till then, I'll do my damnedest to hold my head up high and glide with confidence up to the front door of Celie's home. The house is more like a large white monstrosity flanked by Corinthian, phallic-like columns, situated on the top of a meticulously landscaped hill in Marblehead, a quaint sea-side town immersed in maritime history and dripping with hard, cold cashola. I mean, where else would you see a leopard-print designer license plate with the letters "PRNCSS" on a grown woman's Lexus?

The town has more yacht clubs per square foot than the colored marble chips on the mosaic terrazzo floor of Celie's grand foyer. Hell, here in Marblehead, you can't walk more than two feet along its shoreline without stubbing your toe on a boat slip to someone's yacht.

As for the town's landlubbers, Marblehead also has its share of wealthy golf aficionados. When a rich Marblehead business-man says he recently bought a new set of clubs, he's referring to *country* clubs.

This might be a good time to add that Celie's family is "new" money . . . so it really doesn't count, now does it? And since she's not a third generation born in Marblehead, she really isn't a "Header" in the true sense of the word, no matter how hard she tries to pass herself off as one. She was born in Woonsocket, Rhode Island.

But I take the newish opulence in stride as her mother—my Auntie Carolyn—greets me at the front door and ushers me in. She propels me in the direction of Celie, who's holding court and surrounded by her entourage of doting bridesmaids, or should I say, sentinels.

Celie's first unspoken dig had been *not* asking me to be a bridesmaid. Fortunately, her attempt to dis me backfired in that I'm actually relieved not to be part of the bridal pack during her six-month engagement. It's only six months because she's following the southern tradition where a society girl wouldn't be caught dead engaged for longer than that . . . it tain't fittin'. While Celie is a northerner through and through, she always likes to cover all the etiquette bases nationwide.

As for me, the idea of wearing a royple bridesmaid gown instead of my Very Vera Wang would have hurt too much anyway.

After I draw in a deep breath, I float across the off-white, sunk-in parlor's carpeting and sail into Celie's arms, air kissing my way around her. She hugs me back, puckering her plum-painted lips and sucking up all the good airspace by my ear.

"Nina! Sooo glad you made it! I'm so happy we'll have this day together with the wedding just a few weeks away!"

Translation:

Unlike you, I'm almost done with the engagement part and plan to see this wedding through.

"Yes! Congratulations!" I cry out too emphatically. "Oh, and you remember my friend, Brooke, right? She'll be along today, too. I hope you don't mind."

Translation:

If you're not careful, I may just pull trailer-trash antics on your ass by performing social faux pas right up through to your wedding day. Be afraid, be very afraid.

Celie's expression remains frozen as if to mentally process the information about Brooke's crashing her shower. I know she's doing a brain scan of Emily Post's etiquette book on how to handle this proletarian snafu. After a contemplative moment (I think it's contemplative, but I can't tell. She's not knitting her brow like she usually does when socially thrown off guard), she pastes on a dazzling smile and nods. But there's something different about her expression today. If only I could place it. Something that goes beyond her thin lips and overbleached incisors. I'll figure it out, I'm sure.

"Why, of course I don't mind if Brooke shows up. No problem," she says, interrupting my speculation of her frozen facial features. "I'm sure there's plenty of food. We'll find a place for her. Now tell me, how's the dating going? I've been so worried about you. Why haven't you called? I could have used your help on accessorizing for the upcoming big day."

Celie says all this without taking a breath.

Translation:

I'm not going to show how it still bugs me that some man I'd dated five years ago dumped me because he experienced love at first sight with Brooke. After all, I'm getting married . . . just keep her away from my fiancé. Did I mention in the last five minutes that I'm getting married and you're not? In your dream wedding gown?

Touché. I handed her one terrific serve, which she managed to graciously volley back into my court.

I wax poetic about the offers of dates pouring in and how I simply can't decide who to date. I then complain how my skyrocketing career has kept me so busy lately, I haven't had a moment to think about squeezing any more into my already crammed social calendar. I graciously follow up with an apology for not calling.

When have I *ever* called her?

Celie nods again with a smile, but still looks a little—I don't know—blank. No brow-knitting. Then I realize she hasn't got that tiny vertical line carved in her forehead from years of knitting her brow too much. I always like to see that line because it reminds me how the etchings on her face started before mine. It hits me about what's going on. I grit my teeth.

Botox.

Oh, she's good. I drag my expression away from her immovable fixed features. I don't want her to catch me staring.

"So, have the rest of your guests arrived?" I ask, ready to change the subject. I glance about the room at the other ladies ohhhing and ahhhing over a new Fabergé egg perched on the new mantel, apparently a new acquisition with their new money.

Celie pauses and says, "Well, your mother's here. By the punch bowl. She seems to really be enjoying the mimosas." She only offers a half-smile and her tone is pleading as she enunciates the word, *mimosas.*

Translation:

Your mom's already dipping in the sauce. Pleeeeease babysit her and make her behave herself!

"Right, oh, I could use something to drink . . . I'll go see her," I say just in time for the next round of aunties from the future groom's side of the family to come waltzing into the formal parlor.

I brace myself to see my mom. Over the past two days, she has left me seven messages and I meant to call her back. Honest. But a woman like me needs to psyche herself up for such an event. Not that my relationship with my mom is bad. It's just, um, tense, at times. Just your typical mother-daughter-why-don't-I-have-grandkids-by-now relationship.

I guess it's kind of embarrassing for her since she's the only member of the Razzle Dazzle Red Hat Divas Club who hasn't got a wallet full of photos of grandkids to show off to the other "red hats." Every month, Mom dons some crazy new red hat she's created, trying to outdo the other divas, and together they "lunch" and watch fashion shows. It's got something to do with a poem about when you get old, you plan to wear the color purple with a big red hat. I only know it's very important to her.

I make my way through the crowd saying hello and air kissing nonfamilial relatives until I reach the mahogany Chippendale sideboard in the formal dining room. I note it's decorated with a silver candelabra, porcelain vase teeming with white roses, royple-colored linen napkins (of course), Waterford crystal goblets, and a matching Waterford crystal punch bowl.

"Hi, Ma," I say and sidle up to her. I reach for the ladle in the punch bowl and load up my mimosa.

"Oh, hi, baby. I got a head start . . . cheers." She lifts her goblet to mine and clinks our glasses. "Ten bucks says your cousin can't go five minutes without mentioning she got down to a size eight."

I laugh. "I'm not taking that bet, not when I know I'll lose."

"Gawd help me, but if I hear her talk about her low-carb diet one more time and being a size eight, I'll kill myself. I mean you're about the same size she is right now, but you don't go running around rattling off the numbers every chance you get."

"Ma, I never heard you talk about her like this."

She harrumphs. "Must be the mimosas. It happens when I drink the good stuff."

She holds her goblet up to the light of the Mikasa crystal chandelier and inspects the swirling orange liquid as if her keen eye can detect the quality of champagne in there.

"I'm just surprised to hear you say such a thing about Celie, is all," I say.

"Oh, I'm sorry, baby. It's just that even I have my pain threshold. Your aunt's been calling me every day upset over something about this wedding. Then again, at least she calls me."

My mom tilts her jaw at me in a hurt manner and takes another healthy gulp of her champagne and orange juice.

I try to ignore the pang of guilt over not returning her phone calls. "Sorry, Ma. This past month has been rough, and I knew I'd see you here," I offer, but she's only half listening as she refills her goblet. "Brooke's coming today," I add.

"Oh, I didn't realize she was close with Celie."

"She's not. I'm making her tag along."

"Didn't an old boyfriend of Celie's drop her for Brooke a few years ago?"

"Yeah, kinda."

"I always liked Brooke."

In the background a few bridesmaid's break out into squeals of delight over the bridal cake in the shape of a wedding gown, complete with lace ribbons made of frosting. Celie can be heard complaining how her wedding gown practically fell off her and required three alterations to make it small enough to fit her. Because, you know, she's a size eight now. She then goes on to say she had no choice because size eight was the tiniest size they could produce on such short notice. What's a girl to do?

My mom checks her watch. "Ahhh, five minutes on the nose."

Celie's weight goes up and down just like the rest of womankind, me included. Unlike her, though, I don't worry about the tag on my clothes. I'm an old-fashioned kind of girl. I prefer to have my day completely ruined due to the cruel number on the bathroom scale.

As far as scale numbers go, I also try to follow the old weight guidelines from the airlines; a flight attendant who's five feet tall should be one hundred pounds. Add five pounds for every inch over that. Now, for me, at five-foot-four, getting down to a weight of a hundred twenty pounds is a little far-reaching. But I did get down there once. About ten years ago. After a bout of a Montezuma's Revenge–type flu. But the new weight didn't take.

As far as ideal weight, yes, I tend to fluctuate, yet I continue to try. Yes, I still resort to the occasional appetite suppressant washed down with a latté for breakfast, a birth control pill washed down with Diet Coke for lunch. As for dinner, I often meet up with my friends, who prefer the term, "co-whores" over "cohorts" any day. I'd then have a cocktail, usually a Sex on the Beach, followed by some sex on the beach . . . if I had my way.

O.T.O.H., Celie prefers to run around in search of big skirts with bigger prices, but with small-sized tags. I guess she doesn't realize that today's designers are making their clothes run bigger than ever before. They finally figured out that a woman will buy a garment on the sole basis that the tag says, "Size . . . (you fill in the blank)."

Designers have long since given up the snotty attitude of producing only small-sized clothes so that their brand names would find their way onto only the slimmest of hips, guaranteeing a fabulous look every time. The bottom line won out and their clothes can now be found on the bottom lines of all women of all sizes.

The bridal industry does something similar by making their gowns run enormous where a size ten is reclassified as an eight. Why not? It'll keep the bride gushing, right? Besides, that's where the real money is made . . . they hold hostage your too-large gown and force you into excessive, expensive alterations. What a racket! Celie is merely fashion's latest unsuspecting victim.

Poor thing. Someone should tell her.

I'm only in the know about this because of my insatiable appetite for reading up on fashion and trends in magazines and trade rags, like *Women's Wear Daily*. I tend to be "magazine" smart over "book" smart. It makes sense. Magazines are much more up-to-date. In fact, reading is part of my job as an assistant account executive at Avalon Advertising and PR. Working in advertising is something that I really, really like, but have been neglecting lately.

That whole baby plan, remember?

"And to think we have to go through all this hullabaloo again for the *trousseau* tea," my mom remarks.

"The true-*what*?" My thoughts leap from saddle bags to tea bags.

"*Trousseau*. An old Canadian tradition. We all come back for tea in a few weeks to see the rest of the pre-wedding gifts on display, and to view her honeymoon wardrobe and lingerie all laid out."

Honeymoon wardrobe? Lingerie?

In a reflex my lips pucker.

But we're not in Canada. We're in Marblehead, Massachusetts. I mean, gawd! Will her sex toys be laid out, too? Her vibrator? Motion lotion? Her fiancé's thong underwear with the cartoon of an elephant on the front panel, its trunk to provide the perfect place to house his—

"Package."

"What?" I ask. Apparently, my mom kept talking while I took a mental inventory of what's to come. I shudder.

"I said it's part of the package. She paid for a catered shower, *trousseau* tea, and bridesmaid's luncheon. Celie likes to follow tradition."

Tradition.

Isn't it bad enough she's following every single tradition from here to the Mason-Dixon line, but she's also got to follow traditions as far north as the Arctic?

The thought of going through this again makes me groan.

"I don't know why we bother with the hoopla. You know what I always say. Men either die or defect on you." Mom swallows some orange champagne.

More giddy squeals come from the bevy of girls surrounding Celie, who's engrossed in providing details of her upcoming wedding. Did I mention, in the past two minutes, she's a size eight?

In the midst of her conversation, she speaks the phrase, "Vera Wang," and nods proudly. She repeats the designer name. I can only watch her as the diamond-studded words roll from her plum-colored lips and hang in the air like glittery fairy dust.

She's obviously describing my wedding gown.

A knot hardens in the pit of my stomach and I suddenly feel the need for solitary confinement in the nearest bathroom.

Where the hell is Brooke when I need her?

"Hey, Ma, I'm not feeling so good. If Brooke shows, tell her to come find me, arrright?"

Leaving my mimosa, I make a beeline to a guest bath tucked by the dark paneled library at the back of the house. The bathroom door's locked. My hardening abdominal knot quickly turns to nausea and I need the reassurance of a porcelain bowl by my side. I head through the crowd and without calling too much attention to myself, I grab the railing of the ornately banistered circular staircase à la *Gone with the Wind* and climb the steps two at a time.

After reaching the landing, I make an abrupt turn to head

toward the hall bathroom. But before I get there, I notice something in Celie's parents' master bedroom. I stop dead in my tracks and peer in astonishment through the bedroom door.

The Very Vera Wang.

My wedding gown, in all its opulent glory, is hanging from a planter hook in the ceiling. The midmorning sun streams through the window, highlighting the alabaster white lace and showcasing its beauty for anyone fortunate enough to pass by.

My mouth drops in awe. All the while, I swear I hear a chorus of angels harmoniously break out into song, accompanied by a harpsichord, its heavenly music swirling around me. What can I say? The dress sings to me. It always has. From the moment I ripped the ad from *Bride* magazine so many months ago to the one time I plucked the sample dress from the rack at Becca's Bridal Boutique.

I never did get to try it on.

I remember why, too.

In fact, I'll never forget the life-altering moment I found the dress.

I had the gown in my very clutches at the precise second my cell phone rang. Noting Jeremiah's telephone number on the caller ID, I, of course, picked it up to share my good news; I'd found my treasure. Only, he'd called to tell me his bad news.

There would be no wedding.

I shake the memory from my mind.

I still can't think about our breakup too much, although I know I'll have to let nature run its course eventually. What I mean is, I'll have to face the grief of that moment . . . someday. I'll have to look the beast right in its cold and calculating eyes and fully feel the anger and hurt. But not today.

Believe me, I've tried. But each time I attempt to face it, I retreat big time, and go shopping instead. I guess I'm still in the denial phase.

But whatever phase I'm in, now's still not the time to reflect on such a lousy memory . . . not with the work of art hanging before my very eyes.

I levitate toward the gown. I'm still mesmerized by it and unaware of what I'm doing, including the drool seeping from the corner of my mouth. Even my abdominal knot of nausea recedes. The mere presence of the gown tames my savagely anguished soul (as anguished as I'll allow). With an outstretched hand, I trace the swirling lace on the bodice, then gingerly finger the satiny rosettes on the sleeves.

As I view the garment, I finally acknowledge a small piece of unfinished business from my past.

I never got to try on my gown.

I never got to know what it felt like to have the lace against my skin.

Let's face it. Women need closure. I'm no exception. Not trying on the gown at the boutique that day left a small, but important chapter of my life open just a crack and unresolved. I just never realized it until now.

All I have to do is slip into the gown, see what it feels like, and be done with it. I'd have this whole thing out of my system in one fell swoop. And I would come closer to the closure I've been so desperately needing all these months. Then, and only then, could I actually move on with my life.

Ever know that feeling of seeing a single piece of chocolate left behind? All alone. Crying out your name. You just think about it and think about it and think about it until you can't stand it anymore, until you just cram it into your mouth so you don't have to look at it anymore. I mean, if you eat the damn thing once and for all, then you no longer have to face the idea of giving into temptation, right?

To me, at this very moment, the gown is as tempting as one mother-sized piece of chocolate. How can I resist? Ohhh, I just have to take a bite.

Hurriedly, I close the bedroom door, strip down to my bra and panties. I then pluck away at the dainty hooks along the back of the dress, unfastening it as I go.

With a gentle tug, I pull the gown free from the plump, pink satin hanger. As it falls into my arms, I gasp with delight and hug it to me hard. I smell its newness and indulge in the guilty pleasure. Life's too short not to take advantage of this opportunity.

I slip into it, and with shuddering breaths, hook up the backside high enough to hold the bodice in place.

Good God, it's everything I dreamed about!

Okay, it's a teeny bit loose on me, but I don't care. I frolic around the room, losing myself in the moment, feeling the dress on me, from the shoulders, to the false padded cups, to the waist of the full skirt to—

Something catches my eye. Something that's sparkling in the sunlight. Something on top of the long white lacquered dresser.

The tiara.

I can't help myself! I dash over, grab the headpiece, plunk it on top of my head, and dig the combs into my scalp to set it into place. I turn back around and stand before the full-length mirror in the corner of the room. I gape in astonishment.

I now see what I would have looked like had I become Mrs. Jeremiah Stone, wife to the famous tough-as-nails, globe-trotting journalist known for his trailblazing tactics to uncover international travesties in all four corners of the world.

And, according to my daydreams, I would be by his side for support, at least sometimes. Other times, I'd keep my little advertising job just long enough for Jeremiah to come home from a dangerous international assignment to make wild passionate love to me, which leads to my staying home and having his baby. Of course, this occurs repeatedly.

But the daydreams don't end there.

Soon, the kids and I (along with a nanny and tutor) would meet up with Jeremiah and follow him to the ends of the earth. We'd keep a flat in London. A villa in the south of France. Perhaps an unpretentious palace as a stopover somewhere in the Middle East.

At night, Jeremiah would come home, and I would ask, "How was your day, dear?" He'd fill me in on how he'd reported on some guerrilla warfare, or risked life and limb to reveal an injustice to mankind *somewhere* (who can keep track?). Then he'd tell me how he'd managed to finish things up in time for a pow-wow with Geraldo, live on CNN via satellite, just prior to coming home for dinner.

That about wraps up the daydream.

I stare into the mirror, at the wedding gown and all the fantasies and hopes it represents, and realize those hopes are dashed.

Then the age-old question hits:

What are you going to do with the rest of your life?

Cue the panic attack . . . right . . . about . . . now.

I break into a hot, clammy sweat. Facing the rest of my life is like having my toes curling over the edge of a great black chasm with a pit of snakes at the bottom (I totally stole that from Indiana Jones) and due to the cannibalistic pygmies after me, my only hope of survival is to jump.

The very thought of facing the unknown causes my chest to constrict and I fight for air.

I want things to go back to the way things were! I want to go back to knowing where my life was headed!

I want to go back to being engaged! To digging through the racks of gowns to find my very own Vera!

I want to go back to knowing what my future holds in store for me!

Gawd, I just want to go back to picking a china pattern!

The fear of the unknown—being my uncertain future in this case—completely freaks me out. And I realize my troubles of late don't stem from Celie. Not at all. She's merely been a gauge by which I've been subconsciously measuring my life.

Quite frankly, I haven't been measuring up. Not even to my own standards. It's not Jeremiah's fault. It's not even Celie's fault. It's mine. I've been so rigid in my views on how things should be in my life, and how they are (not) going, I left myself totally unprepared for "what if." It's as though I've kept my life on hold, waiting for my future to fall into my lap.

Maybe my mother was right. A woman's gotta take care of herself. After all, men either die or defect on you. I recall her saying those words once while on the phone talking about my breakup with Jeremiah when she didn't know I was around. I didn't want to believe them at the time. But with my father not around and Jeremiah off on other adventures, my mom's prophetic words come back to haunt me.

I desperately gasp for air.

"Nina? You up here?"

I hear Brooke's voice bellowing up from the stairway. Oh, shit! I can't let her see me in this thing. She'll know I've gone totally bonkers. Since the full-sperm-labor incident, I've worked hard to convince her that "I'm perfectly fine . . . honest." I can't have her find out how I've been lying through my teeth. I reach around my backside to unfasten a few hooks on the bodice.

Apparently, hooks are much easier to fasten than to unfasten.

"Nina?" Brooke pops her head in the door, her light green eyes widen in horror. "What the fuccaya doin'!" she squeals.

"I—" I begin to say, twirling about like a dog chasing its tail while I try to undo at least one hook on my backside. This would be a good time to be double-jointed. *Oh, hell.* "I don't know what I'm doing!" I shout back.

"Omigawd! Celie's gathering up a crowd to come up here and see the dress!" Brooke hisses.

"What?" I'm horrified.

"She wants to show the gown to some out-of-town relatives! Did you know she's down to a size eight? Apparently, so are you!" she yells. She's referring to the slightly loose fit of the altered gown. I know this because I see her pointing at the bodice during one of my twirls to get out of the damn thing.

"Augh! Just help me out of this!" I continue to rotate.

"Oh, man, Nina!" Brooke crosses the bedroom and lunges toward my waist. "Stay still!"

"Please Brooke, get me out of here—" I finish my last twirl, until she grabs hold and spins me away from her to get to the hooks in the back.

"Suck it in so I can get at 'em better!"

I stand upright, suck in (again, thank God I didn't go the turkey baster route), and look up at the doorway to view the last person I want to see.

"Whadda ya doin'!" Mom yells through a drunken slur.

She's weaving in the doorway, grabbing the frame for support.

I momentarily panic because I think she's bracing herself for a heart attack, but really, she's just steadying her drink.

"If yer faddar ever saw you now! Gawd resht hiss soul!"

"Aw, Ma! Now's not the time! Just keep a lookout for Celie, arrright?"

"Nina! Stop squirming!" Brooke shrieks from behind me. "You actually hooked yourself to a piece of lace!"

"Nina, iff yah don't get atta that dresh, yer ash is grash!" Mom starts to march into the room, but stops to sip from the goblet to keep it from sloshing over the sides. "Speakin' ah which, that dresh ish better than what you were wearing. I swear, Nina, if your miniskirt wuz any shorta today, your mookie woulda been hanging out."

"Ma! Just tell me if Celie's coming up! Is she?" I ask in a feverish pitch. I have to know.

I hear giddy voices echoing from the bottom of the stairs, and they're getting louder. Oh, hell, she's coming.

"Lishen, young raydy, I been puttin' up with Celie's mutha's crap for thirty years. If I gotta do it, you gotta do it. Cripes, take that fing off yah head!"

Mom reaches up and rips the tiara from my scalp, along with a good clumping of hair roots. But some of the roots stay firmly attached to my head, keeping me leashed to the tiara liked a rabid mongrel. Mom plows ahead, and with her firm grip on the headpiece, she totters over toward the dresser. I'm yelping and have no choice but to be dragged along.

"Nina! Quit moving!" Brooke snaps. "I almost had it! What the hell did they use to sew this thing, dental floss? I'm gonna have to rip a hook! I got no choice! Brace yourself!"

Brooke yanks me back into place. I feel her take hold of the bustle of the gown, followed by her foot slamming into the small of my back so she can brace herself.

"On the count of three, Nina, I'm gonna just rip!" she squeals.

Mom loses her grip on the tiara, which now dangles from my hair. With her free hand—God forbid she put down her drink—she tries to detangle the tiara, while Brooke's foot slips down lower and kicks me.

"Yeow! Brooke! What the fuccaya doin'?" I yelp.

That's when a long drawn out, deep, guttural wail rolls through the air, making the very walls of the house tremble.

Mom, Brooke, and I freeze in our godawfully tangled position.

My gaze goes to the doorway.

Celie is standing statuelike, her unhinged mouth loosely dangling somewhere around her size-eight sternum. Although the rest of her Botox-poisoned face is generally still expressionless, she's obviously disgusted by the sight set before her.

It's at this point, a few things become painfully clear to me. I'm quite sure that:

The rivalry between us is over,

I could never be more humiliated, and

Brooke's foot is permanently lodged up my ass.

THREE

Pardon me, boys, is this the "chattaranga" choo-choo?

∝

"I can't believe Celie called off the entire wedding on account of you," Brooke murmurs for the twenty-fourth time in the last twenty-four hours as she pulls her Saturn into the parking lot to Ironworks Gym.

"I can't believe it either," I say.

Apparently, humiliation knows no limits. Sure, it's pretty bad to catch someone else in your wedding gown. I could understand why Celie would be upset, especially when she witnessed Brooke attempting to rip apart the hooks in the back. But for Celie to call off her entire wedding really did seem like overkill, a bad case of histrionics.

She'd ranted and raved that I'd tainted her gown. She screamed how the whole thing meant her marriage was destined for disaster. All because a woman who was still single, as Celie duly noted, had stepped into her bridal world and "used up" all the good energy of the gown. Namely, me.

The idea of Celie calling off the wedding irks me worse today than yesterday. Especially the part when she said she couldn't get married because she couldn't wear the gown as it had been—ahem—so defiled. From all my diseases apparently. She then went on to say, she'd never find another gown in time for the wedding anyway. She wrapped up her tirade with announcing how this whole mess was a sign not to get married.

Why is it that when women become engaged they suddenly turn all-righteous, pious, and holier than thou?

And why is it that if you're not doing what they're doing at that particular moment in time, then you're treated like a second-class citizen? Or like some foreign body that needs to be dislodged from their life? It was just a few months prior that Celie had been single, too. So what turns a woman like Celie into a virginal white wedding bride worthy of a halo?

Oh, just wait until she has her first baby. I can already guess she'll transform into one of those maternal breastfeeding Madonna-types the moment she spurts out her placenta. Who is she kidding?

But more than her mere vainglorious attitude bugs me. I don't know, but something doesn't sit right with me about the whole thing. Something—some sort of variable—is at play here, and I can't figure out what.

What I did was bad. It's true. Rotten, in fact. Lousy. Self-centered. Self-involved. I shudder at my own behavior. Deplorable. Absolutely deplorable. I had indeed suffered a case of temporary insanity, all at Celie's expense.

But even *my* shortcomings don't seem reason enough for Celie to call off her wedding, especially when she'd come so close to winning our marriage race. I wrack my brain as I mentally replay yesterday afternoon's fiasco. Even today, I still can't keep the memory of Celie from flashing through my mind, her scratchy screams clawing through me like fingernails on a chalkboard.

"You bitch! You ruined my wedding!" Celie had yelled.

Translation:

"You bitch! You ruined my wedding!"

No more pleasantries stuffed with evil-intended innuendo. No more nice-weather-we're-having chats sopping with an undercurrent of tension. The time came for Celie to put her Emily Post façade aside and call a spade a spade.

"Come on, let's go." Brooke interrupts my obsessive thinking. "Unity's teaching a yoga class and should be wrapping up soon. I told her to meet us in the Jacuzzi. She'll know what to do with you."

I sigh. Poor Unity. She always gets stuck keeping Brooke and me from falling to pieces during any one of our crises. She often starts with her deep breathing techniques and moves quickly into the glowing ball of light that starts from our toes, to our ovaries, and finally up to our head. And only then does she address our problem-du-jour.

"I'm not so sure if Unity can help this time. No amount of metaphysical mumbo-jumbo can help me out of this one or patch together Celie's wedding. You heard her. It's over."

Brooke turns off the ignition. "I still can't believe—"

"Yeah, yeah, I know. You still can't believe she called off the entire wedding because of me. I was there, remember?"

We both hop out the car, grab our gym bags from the back seat, and trudge toward the gym entrance.

"Don't worry, a nice session in here will do you good." Within minutes, we're in our little designer brand, dry-clean-only bathing suits that scream "overdressed" for this place. We pass the lap pool full of serious swimmers and head straight to the Jacuzzi.

I dip my toe into the hot-but-soothing whirlpool as I examine the water's condition today. Since the sudsy-like froth forming along the edges isn't brown, I slowly immerse myself. Brooke sinks in next to me.

"Ahhhh. Now this is what I call a workout," she says through a moan. She leans her head against the edge of the small whirlpool. The foamy froth closes in and forms a crown of suds around her scalp.

As we wait for Unity's arrival, each burning bubble skitters and pops against my skin, while the heat of the water invades my taut muscles. It feels good, especially since it's the only sensation other than humiliation that I've felt in the past twenty-four hours.

"Ahhh-hem."

I open an eyelid and look up in time to see our yoga friend, Unity, standing before us by the Jacuzzi's edge. She has on a black one-piece bathing suit that makes her already reed-thin willowy torso look about the width of a surgical thread. She crosses her arms in front of her sculpted chest and shifts onto a pelvic bone she would probably argue was a hip.

"Would it hurt you guys just once to actually *take* my yoga class?" Unity's voice is as soft and whispery as an early-sixties version of Jackie Kennedy.

"But we're in no shape to exercise," I answer lightly. "Don't you remember what happened the one time we tried yoga? You ended up throwing us out 'cause we kept talking and giggling in the back of the class."

"You were interrupting the others. Why is it that your only idea of a workout is doing a biceps curl to lift a chocolate martini to your lips?"

"That's not true. I also do a lot of jumping . . . to conclusions!" I high-five Brooke in midair over my wisecrack.

"I'm just saying, if you take yoga a little more seriously, you might get some benefit out of it."

"No way," Brooke announces. "That big sweaty guy will get in front of me again. Whenever he'd *down-dog* onto his floor mat, he'd pass major-league gas. I was always stuck downwind of his Van Yasha Flow!" She scrunches her face and fakes a gag reflex.

"I'm only saying it wouldn't kill you guys to actually work out once in a while. They call this place a *gym* for a reason."

"What flew up your *sitting-bones* today, *chattaranga* girl?"

I haven't seen Unity this uptight since she quit her spiritual drumming class. She dated the instructor and, when their relationship encountered disharmony, he told her to go beat off to a different teacher's drum.

Unity uncharacteristically slouches her lean, lithe form in response to my inquiry.

"I'm sorry. I just got word that my newest yoga video release might get hung up. The production company might not get it done in time for the annual video review in *Shape* magazine."

"Sorry to hear that. It'll work out for you, it always does. Now come *down-dog* your ass in here and relax with us."

Unity obliges. Once she settles into the vibrating vat of froth, she turns to Brooke. "So what's the crisis? You said you two got yourselves into hot water at Celie's bridal shower."

"Nina thought it would be fun to sneak into Celie's bridal gown. Only she got stuck. Then she got caught by Celie. So did I . . . trying to rip her out of the damn thing."

Unity squeezes her eyes shut. "Tell me you didn't, Nina. A bridal gown is a sacred thing. It represents a whole new life." She opens her eyes wide and sets her gaze on me. "Wearing a white wedding gown is like a ceremonial purge."

"Oh, there was plenty of purging going on, that's for sure," I remark. "Celie purged all over the place, then she purged Brooke, my mom, and me right out of there."

At that, Brooke and I proceed to give Unity a blow-by-blow account of the bridal gown fiasco at Celie's own shower.

"But what brought all this on?" Unity asks me.

"Remember my full-sperm-labor episode last month? Apparently, I had a relapse. Seems some residual psychosis didn't get out of my system, and it regurgitated itself at the shower."

"So you're still on your sperm kick?" Unity questioned.

"Look, about needing sperm so bad," Brooke cut in, "I know you have issues with immediate gratification, so if you still want semen that bad, I can hook you up—"

"Oh, right, with who?"

"How about Reggie, who lives down the hall from us?"

"Reggie the cleavage-peeker?"

"Granted he's a little older . . ."

"Older? That guy wreaks of impending death. We're talking an aromatic mix of Brut and expired Geritol. He smells bad enough as it is. I couldn't imagine what affect it would have on the odor of his sperm," I joke.

"Sometimes you gotta overlook sperm odor," Brooke volleys back seriously.

"Easy for you to say, she-who-considers-sperm-a-food-group," I remark.

Unity tries to stifle a laugh but ends up snorting foam out her nose.

Brooke glares at her. "Hey, at least I get protein a natural way."

Unity's laughing expression turns to surprise. "What's that supposed to mean?"

Brooke scoffs. "Oh, come off it. I've seen all your so-called supplements and health pills. Cripes, you make the entire *Valley of the Dolls* look like a pothole."

"Me? I'll have you know, everything I take is all natural! Right down to Primrose oil . . . unlike your antidepressants or whatever your drug-of-the-month club membership has you on."

"Hey." Brooke points a soggy finger at her. "I need those antidepressants. Ever since I volunteered for that experimental birth control pill last year, I've been bipolar. Before that, I was just polar."

"Arrright, you two. I'm the one with the crisis, remember? Now can we please get back to the reason why we're here?"

"Why *are* we here?" Unity asks.

"If you two are done with the fang-fest, I'll tell you." I pause, and they listen with exaggerated earnestness. "See, when I was hung up in Celie's wedding gown, something occurred to me. I always figured by the time I reached thirty I'd have certain things in my life. Well, I'm six months into thirty, and I've got none of them."

"Like what?" Unity asks.

"Oh, I don't know, a marriage, maybe?"

"It's not your fault that Jeremiah bailed."

"Not technically, but still, I'd invested so much into him . . . do I have a marriage certificate to show for it? No. Am I anywhere near to having a baby? No. I got nothing. On top of it, I realized I've ignored investing in myself by passing up promotions and by not building a career. Or having a hobby. Something—anything—that I can call mine."

"Finding a true soul mate takes time. Sometimes an *entire* lifetime," Unity explains. "In fact, it can take *several* lifetimes to achieve. Each life is a learning experience till the day you die. Then you come back and do it all over again until you get it right. Believe me, I know."

But I don't want to hear Unity's metaphysical rationale as to why I wasn't getting it right in *this* lifetime. The moment I got engaged to Jeremiah, I made such a public announcement about it that every available male within five counties whited me out of their "available" list.

"Well, I resent that the future *me* in my future *life* is gonna have what I want today. My need for immediate gratification is dictating that I demand it all now."

"I don't blame you, but getting it all now is a tall order."

"I'm tired of being in reactive mode, trying to adapt to others' conditions. Jeremiah decided he couldn't commit to me because there's a whole world out there waiting for him to explore and report on, so I'm the one stuck with the reluctant single status."

My future flashes before my eyes, which includes sharing a villa with my mother at her retiree village and attending weekly whist parties with forty other ladies vying for the attention of the four males on oxygen tanks, but still alive, in the rec hall. It ain't pretty. My thoughts then settle on an image of myself wearing purple, with a big red hat, surrounded by other big red hats. Instead of bar hopping, I'm teahouse hopping.

"No," I blurt out in response to my own obsessive thoughts. "I've made a decision. I want to grab life by the cajones and change my current condition right now. I was taught that if you're a good girl, you get rewarded. Well you don't. You get squashed like a bug. And I'm gonna do something about it."

"How do you suppose to do all that?" Brooke asks.

"That's where you guys come in. I don't know where to begin and I need your help."

"I'll call Prancing Wolf," Unity offers, "he'll know what to do with you. He can do a reading, look into your future—"

"Thanks, but no, having a homosexual spiritual guide might work for you, but I want to go the secular route for this."

"What you need," Brooke pipes up, "is a carefully laid-out plan. Something that works for you, that you can manage easily."

"A plan, huh?" My thoughts zero in on the countless marketing plans and production schedules I assist the account executives with at the ad agency. *Grrr.* "Just what I need . . . to add more planning to my agenda."

"I mean it. You need, like, a task list. Broken down into bite-size pieces. Shoot. If my boss and I didn't do it for all the catering jobs, we'd go bonkers."

As I warm up to the idea, I nod slowly. Brooke's reasoning starts to mold and take shape in my brain. After all, as an assistant account executive I'm awful good at making marketing plans at work. Why not apply the skill to my personal life?

"Hmmm. I think you're onto something. I mean, if I were a product at the ad agency, I'd make myself a marketing plan. I can do that." Excitement courses its way through me.

See, this is why I hang with these girls. I'm usually so mired in my own dilemma-of-the-day, I can't see the obvious. It's as if I'm too close to the situation to be objective about the answer. But once Brooke planted the seed by suggesting a plan, she was talking my language.

I merely need a marketing plan. One with all the bells and whistles. One that will put me on the road to success as of yesterday.

"Okay, so if you were your own client, what would you do first with a marketing plan?" Brooke asks me.

"Well, let's see. I'd look at features and benefits. And build the brand from there. Then I'd have to promote myself, you know, get my big fat assets out there. Display the goods."

"Okay, and what do you want to work on first? Career? Relationships? Finance?"

"Yes," I answer, till Brooke gives me the "I'm-serious-here" look.

Hmmm. I have to think about this. *Where to start, where to start.* I have so many places I need to begin.

"Career. And men. And finances. And kids. In that order, but also simultaneously. Now."

Brooke groans. "Well, it's a start. At least you prioritized. Sort of."

"Actually, I'll kill off two birds with one stone with the first two. For both, I'll have to consider personal brand positioning, brand identity, and target audience. Choose a creative strategy to show off my best features—whatever they are. Really button down the details."

The three of us sit amid the burning bubbles and discuss the steps to get my career where it should be.

We then move on to the need to cast my dating net wide across the gene pool while focusing on highly concentrated areas of men. This means I'd be dating my brains out in search of candidates for "Mr. Right." But we all agree that I should also have the occasional boy-toy to fill in any dead times, someone to romp around with, yet have no emotional attachment.

"How do I find a boy-toy?"

"Just by putting yourself out there. Take your *assets* and throw it on 'em. It's all about your attitude. Believe me, you put out the vibes, the men will catch on and will beg you to let them be your boy-toy." Brooke nods for emphasis.

"They'll just know?"

"Oh, yeah. It's in your confidence. Don't just sing along to a tune, *harmonize* it. Don't sit in a corner, sit *dead center*. And don't walk . . . *strut*. You just gotta *chicka boom* your way into a room. And when I say that, I mean you do it so slow and sultry, you'd make Mae West look like a sprinter." Brooke slowly and seductively shimmies her shoulders while singing *chicka chicka boom chicka boom*, in a throaty catlike purr.

"I can do that," I tell her with growing confidence. "I can *chicka boom* with the best of them. And I'll have those boy-toys at my beck and call today, if I want to."

Yes, I'll have my boy-toy. And all subsequent goals will follow. Personal goals like fixing my financial stability, which is as shaky as a needle-thin stiletto heel right now. Other goals eventually include the pitter-patter of little tax deductions. But honestly, and most importantly, I would finally spend the rest of my life with the man of my wet dreams.

I drive my Honda along the endless winding driveway to Avalon Advertising and pull up to the large mansion that has been refurbished into a business employing more than a hundred people. Unlike the big city ad agencies of New York or Boston or Atlanta, Avalon Advertising is tucked away amid the ocean-lined woods of a small seaside town just north of Boston. Mr. John Avalon likes to keep to his long-time New England roots; that's why he's set up shop right where he grew up. He also wants to create an atmosphere where clients feel a wealth of pampering and employees feel comfy.

Too comfy, I fear, when it comes to my own situation. I'd snuggled into my little adorable, semicreative job too well and fell into career hibernation. Or severe coma, in this case.

But no more coma for me.

In my new blue designer suit straight from the clearance rack of Filene's Basement, I'm ready to put out the vibe that I've gone corporate. I'm dressed so sharp I fear I'm gonna cut someone to the bone. But I remind myself of my new mantra for work: build my personal brand and promote my features and benefits and stick my assets out there. Finally, I have something in my life I can work on in a proactive manner. And not behave in reactive mode all because I've been waiting to live out some Cinderella fairy tale.

I'm now on a mission to get back on track and in the mainstream. I want job advancement to occur faster than the speed of light. And I know just where to start; the opening for the position of "Account Executive of Special Projects" that HR posted recently. I didn't bother to seriously consider the job until the Jacuzzi meeting with my co-whores, Brooke and Unity.

Minutes later, I career down the long hall full of doorways leading into private offices and head toward my bay, a fancy marketing term for "open air" cubicle. Every employee gets an office, unless you're deemed, "support staff."

Translation:

Meaning "me."

Up to four people can share bays scattered throughout the mansion. Oh, the bays are nice enough, with fancily framed Impressionist prints on the walls and mahogany-colored desks and cabinets, but these "common" areas were for "common" employees. You know, those like me, who are discovered to have no burning career aspirations.

Until now, that is.

I tuck my purse in a drawer in my bay, stride back to the little kitchen to drop off my insulated, leopard-print lunch bag, and ready myself to embark on this new journey.

I march back down the hall and with all the confidence, drive, and determination I can muster, I head toward my boss's office. I square my shoulders and ready myself to burst in there and make my demands in such a commanding manner, he'll have no choice but to recommend me for the account executive position.

Yep. Any minute now and I'm going in there.

Any second now and I'm gonna make my move.

Just another moment and I'm—

"Nina! You comin' in or are you gonna hang outside there for another ten minutes?" Ray's voice bellows through the partially ajar door.

Translation:

Get your ass in here.

I jolt momentarily and collect my wits. I mean, I'd be happy to walk in, explain to him its been a pleasure working with him, then scale up along the corporate ladder, only my legs are buckling out from under me. I crumble against the wall.

With my back still braced against the wall and knees wobbling, I remain rooted to the carpeting and smile casually at passing fellow employees who, by the way, are *not* in blue business suits. After all, this is advertising, where you're paid *not* to be the status quo. Only, I'm in account services, and we see clients almost daily, so we have to dress like we *do* give a damn. But today, my suit is squeezing the life out of me.

By now, my spine has turned to rubber, and I have to inch along the wall the way a suicidal employee does while standing along the scrawny ledge of a skyscraper before jumping. I guess it's probably the same feeling I'm experiencing right now. Slowly, I crane my neck and poke my head into Ray's office.

"You busy?" I ask.

"Always," he snaps without looking up from the paperwork on his desk. His computer is perched behind him, not turned on, and not wiped of its dust ever since Ned, the Network Security Administrator guy put it there last year.

He then raises his gaze and watches me expectantly. His silver hair is impeccably combed and goes well with his perfectly groomed graying mustache and beard. His look comes complete with heavily rimmed glasses and a paisley bow tie adorning his crisp white shirt. Definitely a man of the old school with only a few years to go before retiring.

While ninety-nine percent of the staff has barely celebrated their thirtieth birthdays and the rest are still sopping wet behind the ears—where a "long-time employee" means longer than six months—the upper echelon of senior staff still remains the old-boy network. That's why he's a director, the highest you can go without being "partner," so to speak.

"Got something on your mind?" he asks and returns his gaze to some letter he's drafting by pen. This means of course, that in a half hour, the handwritten letter will find its way to my in basket to be formally typed. I don't mind. I type fast and I like working on the computer. I break my grip of the doorjamb and slink toward the guest chair and sit. I'm sweating so fiercely from my suit and hosiery that my toes feel like they're steeped in ricotta cheese.

"I, uh, decided something and thought you should be the first to know," I begin.

"So have I. I've come to a decision and I'll let you be first to know, too."

Intrigued, I sit mute. I mean, usually, I'm the last to know anything, which means I get the least amount of time to meet deadlines. I work a lot of late nights that way.

"Uh, you go first," I gesture to him. It'll give me time to work up the courage to tell him I don't plan to work with him anymore, as much as I like him. I already know he'll take it personally. He takes everything to heart at work. He's an advertising man.

"I'm leaving." He holds up his hand-scrawled letter.

I stare in astonishment at the paper dangling in the air and read the writing. The word *resignation* pops out at me.

He's going to resign? I'm shocked. After all, Ray's been a fixture around here since, well, forever. I mean, he helped build Avalon Advertising since its infancy. In fact, rumor had it that Ray had been hanging around these parts so long that they had to build the mansion around him and give the guy a job as a tax write-off.

And now he's leaving? Just like that?

"Yeah, just like that," he says.

Apparently, I verbalized my disbelief loud and clear. With my right hand, I close shut my slack-jaw mouth. And blink hard, just to be sure I didn't take a right turn into la-la land.

"You're quitting?" I ask.

"Retiring," he corrects. "It's time and I don't want to waste another minute." He shakes his head and hands me the letter to be typed. I take another quick glance just to be sure, and there it is, in black and white. Yep, he's retiring.

"Did something happen, Ray? What is it?" I ask.

I can't stop the thought that maybe a terminal illness has afflicted him. Or perhaps he butted heads once too often with one of the other three big wigs—the Trinity as I affectionately call them. You got the owner, the VP of Creative, and the VP of Account Services. Under those guys come all the Directors, duly labeled, the Six Kings. Of course, verbal altercations would break out whenever analytical types wrangle with creative types, but I never thought I'd see the day that Ray would leave.

"Nothing's wrong. Everything's right, in fact. Too right, and that's what's wrong." He frowns at his desk before pivoting his chair and staring out the window to the leafy maples soaking up the early summer sunshine outside.

"Oh, well, no wonder you're leaving. It makes sense. Everything's going well and we all know what a disaster that can be."

He pivots back around and crosses his arms over his chest. "That's just it. I've got everything I wanted and I'm not happy. I've cut throats over the years to get to where I am today. And still, with all those so-called rewards, I've got nothing." He shakes his head in disgust. "Nothing! Except discontent and boredom." He returns his attention back out the window.

Not sure what to do with this, I gaze down at his desk. That's when I notice *Ad Age* open to a large article featuring an older woman. The title mentions her marriage to a Wall Street mogul. It doesn't take a genius to wonder if Ray got a good slap of reality today.

"Did you know her?" I ask.

When he looks back, I point to the publication and read the article title. "Marcia Cate weds on Wall Street."

"Did you know her?" I repeat.

"Know her? I should have married her. Years ago."

Ray? Marry someone? To think this confirmed bachelor wanted to shack up with someone?

"Wow." I look at the black-and-white photo of the older attractive woman on the pages. "So, what happened?"

"She and I used to work here together. A long time ago."

"And?"

"Remember all those throats I said I cut over the years? Let's just say I was an equal opportunity offender. She never spoke to me again, well, except to break our engagement. She turned out to be a real shooting star. The *Journal* still loves her today. Writes her up all the time."

"Don't let some rivalry affect you now. You've had a great career, Ray."

"It's not my career. It's my life." He scratches the gray hairs along his bearded jawline. "Seeing her here made me realize I missed out on an entire lifetime of memories with the only woman I ever loved. I gave that up all because I wasn't about to let anyone get in the way of my career. Least of all, a woman." He folds up the magazine and tosses it aside.

I can't believe he's telling me all this. But he's pretty shaken up and obviously needs to vent, even if it is only to little ol' me.

"I'm sorry. So, what are you gonna do now that you're retiring early?"

"Not sure." He settles into the office chair and laces his fingertips in the back of his head. "Maybe get a little place overlooking the water in Maine. Do a little writing up there. Cultivate a garden. Yeah, I always wanted a garden."

His wistful look spirals back to reality. His expression hardens and he looks at me expectantly. "And, what's your news?"

But I'm still spinning from his announcement, so I take a sec to gather my thoughts. I take a deep breath.

"I want the new AE position," I blurt unceremoniously.

Ray cocks his head to one side. "A promotion? Why now?"

"Why *not* now?"

"Look, you're a great kid and you'd be terrific at it, but I'm just surprised. You've always been—"

"A perpetual entry-level junkie? I know. But it's time to change that. What do you think?"

"You saying you want my help? My blessing?"

I nod. He takes a moment, as if to size up the situation. His eyes narrow in a devious way and he grins.

"Looks to me like I got a chance to rectify my past and help someone for a change, now don't I? At least before I'm outta here."

I merely smile. "Can I take that as a yes?"

"Whoa, it's not that easy. I talked to the VP of Account Services about this new job. It's still a junior position technically, you know. Only a small step up. The person's gotta be flexible, handle any odd projects that come his, er, her way. In other words, it's got a catch to it."

"Catch?"

"A couple catches."

"A *couple* catches?"

"The full title is Account Executive of Special Projects for good reason. You'd be handling smaller accounts, and some very *delicate* situations."

Delicate, huh?

I smile to myself. I get the feeling Ray's referring to Delicate Delights, a chocolate maker looking for an agency to help them with their new line of dark delectable treats. It would be a small account, but Avalon has been wanting to round out its client base to include more food products in their repertoire of print ad campaigns. Visions of delicate chocolate samples dance in my head. Why hadn't I decided to do something like this sooner?

"I can do *delicate*. You know that," I assert with a wink.

"Well, with any sweet deal, there's only gonna be more catches." Ray groans like a big ol' woolly bear, interrupting my chocolaty notions. "I just heard someone else in-house has decided to go for the position, too."

"And who is that?"

Who could possibly manage chocolate as well as me?

"Chad Gorham. Claims he finds being a media buyer not gratifying and wants to make the jump to Account Services."

"Chad Gorham?"

A different set of visions invades my mind. Images of "sleazes" and "bags." This is what Chad Gorham reminds me of. A regular snake charmer, that one. He begs, borrows, and steals his way through this company. And if those mild techniques don't work, he resorts to his own ruthless cunning.

I don't know why Chad has to slither his way through his day. It takes hard work to viciously "hack" your way through getting the job done. Toss in his womanizing and cut-throat ambition, and you got yourself one mean-spirited guy. He feeds off other people's misfortune and has cut his teeth on enough unsuspecting employees to help him get ahead fast, which would explain his excessive incisors. And the VPs who make up the Trinity couldn't love him more. I didn't want his fangs anywhere near my sweet account.

"But Chad's only been here for, like, nine months!" I gasp.

Granted, nine months is a lifetime in this racket, but it's worth a shot to complain. After all, my four-year anniversary is just around the corner.

"Yeah, and since day one he's expressed the desire to get ahead." Ray shoots me an accusatory look.

Touché.

"Hey, I may not have expressed an interest in climbing the corporate ladder, but I'm still a company girl. And now I'm saying I'm ready."

"You sure you want this?"

"Hell, yeah!"

"Then let's do it!"

FOUR

When life gives you lemons, throw
them at whoever is making life sour for you.

❦

Ray makes a quick phone call and minutes later, he and I head toward the offices of the Trinity. We stop by the desk of John Avalon's secretary, Marilyn. You can't miss her, she's the bleach blonde with the water-balloon-sized breasts and wearing John's engagement ring on her finger. We ask to see him. Her baby blue wide-set eyes blink momentarily, her black lashes long as tentacles winnowing up and down as she does so.

Finally she nods and indicates to go on in. She returns to her reading, a French cookbook, I note. I heard the story how she'd mentioned to John that she'd like to take a cooking class, and so he paid for her to go to France last month. Usually, I'd find something like this annoying, but she's so damn sweet, it's hard not to like her.

We pleasantly nod thank you and go on in. My sights settle directly onto the four men sitting at the mahogany conference table (real mahogany, by the way). John Avalon sits at the head of the table, with the other two members who make up the Trinity, Paul and Harry. Chad sits down one side.

I know the Trinity likes Chad because of his corporate guile and antics. But I also know why else they like him. He's a *Gorham*. And the Gorham name pulls a lot of weight on the north shore of Massachusetts, not to mention the rest of North America. His family comes from such old Bostonian wealth, some people refer to them as the "other Kennedy's." The connections Chad would have toward obtaining future accounts for Avalon would be priceless to the agency. And Chad was looking to make a name for himself in the advertising world, probably to start up his own empire one day, I assume.

John Avalon waits for us to sit before he smiles at both Chad and me.

"I understand you both are interested in the AESP position. While this is a dilemma for the two of you, it has a silver lining for us."

He pauses to pour a tall glass of water from the silver pitcher and adds a slice of lemon. "You see, the Account Executive of Special Projects is just above a junior position, not a big jump. Think of it as still playing in the minor leagues. You'd be going to bat for smaller, unique clients, sometimes for short-term campaigns. It's something we're exploring as a way to branch out, increase our stats, and provide a training ground for employee advancement within the agency. In fact, we already have two clients lined up. That's where you two come in."

"You're going to hire two AESPs?" Chad asks. He's fondling his tie as if rearing to go.

"No, but the two clients have agreed to allow Avalon Advertising to take on their marketing and advertising for a minimum cost to them in lieu of our having to gear up for a new business pitch and competing with other agencies. We already have other new-business pitches on deck, which has eaten up the time of Creative, not to mention our budget."

"So, are you looking to divide the duties of the AESP between the two of us and incorporate them into our existing jobs?" I ask. After all, Chad had piped up, so I better, too.

"Good thinking, but no. We decided to let your own work speak for itself. Chad, you'll take on one client; Nina, the other. We can see how it goes at the end of the month."

"Do we have to work with each other?" I choke on the words and swallow back the big chunks of disdain in my tone.

"No. In fact, you'll both be up at bat, both on your own, reporting to your current directors. In fact, we can announce who gets the promotion at Avalon's Annual Spring Fling Gala in a few weeks." John smiles at his own genius. "We'll also announce it in the business section of the papers, send it to *Ad Age*, as part of our newest branching-out campaign. Let the business world know we're here to pinch-hit for smaller clients as well."

"Hey, maybe Nina and I should go to the ball together, show that although there's competition, we're really a team," Chad offers.

"Interesting idea." John nods with approval.

"Very interesting. Strength in numbers," Harry agrees.

"Then it's settled," Chad announces.

"No!" I shout. Okay, so the word explodes from my lips before I could edit it. "I mean, I'm all for healthy, spirited competition along with teamwork, but—but—but I'm already going with someone."

Now, I know that they know that I know that they know all about my fiasco with Jeremiah. They couldn't miss it. The stock price of Kleenex skyrocketed in direct proportion to my usage of their tissues due to my crying jags at the time. So it comes as no surprise when a few bushy eyebrows get raised upon hearing my announcement. But their interest in this information could work to my advantage. They saw me in pieces over my breakup, now they can see how well I bounce back. Even if the alleged bounce-back is a full-blown unadulterated fabrication.

I feel my cheeks cooking at my own lie. But worse, I feel Chad's hot angry glare on me. I can tell he hates my rejection even though I have a valid reason for not allowing myself to be caught up in his tentacles. No way could I show up on his arm the night of the ball. I'd be dead meat.

"Well then, if you're going with someone, then you're going with someone. Now if that's all, I look forward to seeing how you perform in time for the Spring Fling Gala. Any questions?" John settles his gaze on Chad and me.

"Ah, yeah. Who are the clients?" I ask.

John smiles. "Well, I was going to let your directors talk to you about that, but since you asked . . . we've assigned Jason Hart to Chad."

"The golf pro?" Chad's eyes widen.

John nods. "He's looking to launch a line of golf attire, you know, polo shirts, hats, golf shoes, and then wants to open a chain of shops. As I said, you'll be working with your director closely on this." John angles his head toward Harry. "Harry will fill you in on the details. We're looking for a hole-in-one from you, Chad."

I breathe a sigh of relief I didn't get the golf pro; that guy's a Boston native, so his wild reputation is pretty well known, and well documented in papers like the *Globe*. Between swinging golf clubs by day and swigging Jack Daniels by night, he'd give me a run for my money. Poor Chad, I think to myself. He's finally met his match. He may be happy about it now, but just wait. I don't see how he could BS or connive his way to success with this one.

"And Nina, we've assigned Jackleen Liquori to you."

Thee Jackleen Liquori?

That's when my own eyes widen. But not in delight. More like in shock. Disbelief. And yes, even in horror.

"Excuse me? Did you say Jackleen Liquori? The crazy movie star lady? The one who pulled a 'Zsa-Zsa Gabor' on that IRS agent last year?"

I couldn't have heard him right. I mean, this came out of left field. I'd heard rumors that the agency had been kissing up to the golf pro lately to get his business, but Jackleen Liquori? I hadn't even heard she'd gotten out of jail. I sit stunned. Don't know what to think. Don't know if I should laugh or cry. So I just sit there, praying I won't pee myself.

"Nina?" John searches my eyes to get a response.

I round my mouth to sound a vowel, to enunciate anything to show I could pull myself together at the news. Come up with some witty, sports-related pun. To show I'm one of the guys. Finally, I manage to say what I truly think.

"What? No chocolate?"

"It was awful, I tell you, just awful." I groan to my apartmentette-mate, Brooke, but my stare remains fixed on my bedroom ceiling. Brooke's been sitting with me in my bedroom, patiently listening to the horrors of the day. "Can you imagine? I have to baby-sit Jackleen Liquori to get the promotion! She got a supporting role in a movie. She's coming here to Salem to film most of it."

"Huh. I didn't even know she got out of jail," Brooke says.

"That's what I said! I'm usually more on top of these things, what with all the magazines I read. I should have seen her parole announced in *People* or something!"

Because of my new duties, I quickly realize that my long leisurely weekends with my mags will soon be a thing of the past. I'm meeting the star herself this Saturday morning, the only time she can squeeze me in. I already miss my favorite activity of devouring magazines. All because of one Jackleen Liquori.

"Can you believe this? The last I knew, she got arrested for tax evasion or something. And when the IRS guy came around to confiscate her office documents, she jumped him and wrestled him to the ground. Clawed him to bits, too."

"That old lady, what a hoot," Brooke says. "It still makes me laugh."

I sit up and watch Brooke chuckle over the thought. In her hands, she's fiddling with a pair of pink furry toy handcuffs. The sex toy tells me she's working on one of her erotic gift baskets she sells over the Internet. It helps with extra money when things are slow at the local caterer where she works. The baskets include her own homemade shortbread penis cookies and even chocolate peeny pops on a stick. She's really good at it, too, and business has been taking off by leaps and bounds. Of course, it's mostly for bachelorette parties, something I'll probably never have at this rate. Hell, I can't even conjure up a date for the Spring Fling Gala next month.

The Gala.

I look forward to the Spring Fling every year. It always falls on the final Saturday prior to the summer solstice and first day of summer. It's to say good-bye to the cold of winter and rain of spring and gear up for a great summer. In reality, it's for Avalon Advertising to showcase its clients along with its shooting stars, and to gather together every top "name" in the industry from the *Wall Street Journal* to *Vogue* magazine and have everyone party their brains out. As for me, if I don't find a date, it looks like this little Cinderella will be forced to go with Prince Cut Throat—one Chad Gorham.

I shake off the stray miserable thought and refocus on the original miserable thought that must take priority right now.

"'Mean Jackleen' Liquori is an absolute terror. Did you know she tore through something like four personal assistants in six months? And she showed up naked under her mink coat at someone else's movie premiere because she felt as though she should have gotten the part of the aunt? Then she bitch-slapped a member of the paparazzi . . . who happened to be her nephew! Gawd, I'm hosed. I'll never beat out Chad for that position."

I realize that taking on a drunkard golf pro seems really, really tame about now. Why did Chad have to catch the break?

"Even if you don't get this promotion, don't worry, there'll be others."

"Oh, I don't think so," I say in a full-blown sulk. I sit up on my bed and play with the tassel on my pink bed pillow.

"C'mon, you're just getting started. Why so fatalistic? I know you're trying to play catch-up with your life, but it's one little job promotion. Surely another's right around the corner. Why worry so much?"

I didn't know what to say. Or how to say it. Hell, my best defense against failure had always been to avoid success. I was saving my success for wedded bliss. Fat lotta good it's done me.

"Jobs do come up at the agency, but to be honest, they're never something I'd be really good at."

"Excuse me? And I suppose you think if you sat at some piano right now, you'd be able to play Mozart off the bat? You've got to start somewhere. No one starts a new position perfect at it. And you're good at your job right now, right?"

"That's why this junior account executive position is perfect for me. When I first saw the posting, I had actually thought it looked interesting. But I never thought to go for it, probably out of habit. And now, I can't think of anything but. And I want it right now. More than anything. Well, except for the whole Jackleen part."

"Gosh, Nina, at first, I thought you might be afraid of failure, but you're really afraid of success."

"Wouldn't *you* be? I mean, I thought Jeremiah and I were a success. I hate being wrong. I hate that I failed our relationship. I don't want to fail at anything else."

"You didn't fail the relationship. Jeremiah did. And just to prove it, I'm taking you out with me this Friday night."

With my two hands, I form the letter T indicating a time-out. "Whoa, not-so-smooth change of subject. What do you mean, this Friday night?"

"That's right. You heard me. I got invited to a loft party and was told to bring along a couple friends. You and Unity are coming with me."

"Where?"

"Boston."

"Oh, no, you don't. I'm not going slumming in Boston on Friday. I'll end up in some gay club, bookended by a couple gay guy-friends of yours who are prettier than me. No way."

"That only happened to you once. Okay, twice."

"Doesn't matter anyway. I've got to be up at the crack of dawn Saturday morning to meet my ex-con movie star client."

"I'll make sure you're awake in time Saturday. Besides it's not a big all-nighter. Just a gathering at a friend's house."

"What's the friend's name?"

"Can't recall, oh, okay, so it's more like a friend of a friend. And not just a gathering, more like a theme party."

"I'm too old for theme parties."

"Gimme a break! It'll be fun."

"Well, what's the theme?"

"Pimp-and-ho."

"You got to be kidding. Aren't those passé by now?"

"Heck no. You know that trends in this country start in California, then head across the country, hitting the east coast a few years later. So, technically, we're right on schedule. We're not behind at all."

"Speaking of behinds, I'll have to work on mine if I'm gonna be out meeting men at my age."

"What? You just turned thirty!"

"Yeah, and my birthday cake had so many candles on it, the damn thing required scaffolding to keep it from collapsing under the weight! Not to mention getting my first gray hair."

Brooke stares up at my head, scrutinizing it for grays.

"I didn't get the gray hair up there, arrright?"

She sets her gaze back on me. "Nina, what you're having is a pre-ejaculatory quasi-midlife crisis. We're all gonna have it. You're just freaking out about it ten years sooner than most everyone else. Until then, you need to be distracted so you won't get so upset."

"A distraction, huh? I've been distracted my entire life. What makes you think I need another one now?"

"Because I need the distraction, too." She sinks more deeply into the wicker chair. "I had a realization today and I didn't like it. Not a damn bit."

"What happened?"

"I was supposed to hook up with someone next weekend. And we were chatting on-line, and I made some remark about KC and the Sunshine Band. He then remarked something about them being old. So I asked him how old he was."

"Tell me."

"Twenty-three. I mean, he knows I'm thirty and doesn't have a problem with that, but I've been doing a little number-crunching in my life lately."

"And?"

"It occurred to me that the men I date are either single twenty-somethings with the maturity of a seedling or over-forty-five and divorced. They're usually carrying more baggage than a sky cap at Logan Airport. Very rarely do I see men in between."

I note the solemn look on her face and I don't like where this is going. I've only been checking the "single" box in my magazine surveys for a handful of months and didn't really want to hear any bad news.

"And?" I ask more slowly.

"I figured it out. The men in between the age of twenty-five and forty-five are still married. Usually with kids. And their marriages haven't fallen apart yet."

"You sure about this?"

"Yeah, take today for instance. This afternoon, I worked at a catered office party. There I was, assembling the luncheon, and this beautiful man, about thirty-five is talking to me." Brooke starts fidgeting with the furry handcuffs as a gleam lights her eyes at the gorgeous memory.

"So, what happened?" I asked.

"Well, I'm thinking, God, I'd love for him to ask me out. But he won't because the gold band around his finger tells me I got to wait another ten years for his marriage to go belly up before I even have a chance with him. But by then, I'll probably feel too old to have a baby, and he won't want one anyway because he'll have three kids in private school and couldn't face starting over with the whole diaper thing."

The handcuffs slip from her fingers and drop to her lap. She rubs her temple to tame what looks to be an onslaught of a migraine.

"Um, what about the twenty-somethings?" I ask feebly.

"Student loans," she whines. "They're not looking to get married, or have babies. Hell, they can't even get a decent job or move from home, let alone afford a serious relationship."

Brooke's sobering news shocks me, along with her emotional reaction to it. In fact, I've never seen her like this. I've got to do something to help her. She's been so good to me, always rationalizing my erratic behavior, that I need to reciprocate by keeping a stiff upper lip. This is all way too new for me to get depressed just yet.

"Well then, there's only one thing left to do."

"What's that?"

"In a word, *boy-toys*. And lots of them."

Brooke cocks an eyebrow. "You think?"

"Why not? Look, we've already discussed this. And it's time to put our plan in action. Hey, if we have to wait around ten years for these men's family lives to fall apart and divorce, we might as well enjoy ourselves. And don't worry about their wives, they'll all be freed up to go and marry the guys they secretly wanted to marry in the first place."

"Oh, you're really catching on to this whole 'rationalize your way through anything' skill. You do me proud."

"I learned from the best. So, let's do it. Let's head for this pimp-and-ho party and get distracted as hell. Find us boy-toys to hold us over."

"It makes sense. Just because we're waiting for the right man to come along, doesn't mean we can't have fun with all the wrong ones in the meantime!"

"Maybe I'll even find a date in time for the Spring Fling Gala. But just promise me one thing. Don't do any more number-crunching, okay?"

Which is why, that following Friday, I find myself wobbling along a sidewalk in stripper heels in some rundown neighborhood on the outskirts of Boston, tightly clutching my little sequin purse on a chain. I tug at my fluorescent pink miniskirt with slits up to my armpits to keep it from twisting and riding up my backside. It's my own fault really. I was the one who said the pink would go well with the black fishnet stockings I found at an S&M shop. My hair is teased à la Big Eighties and my lips are painted a bold engorged-labial-pink. Oh yeah, I'm feeling the whole distraction thing now.

But Unity and Brooke walk right beside me, looking just as ridiculous, clutching their own purses. Brooke merely pulled something out of her closet of club clothes for this shindig. And Unity simply put on head-to-toe black, right down to her own painted black lips.

I wish I could say where we were exactly, but Brooke drove and got lost so many times, my head is still spinning. Then again, with the elevator-slut-heels I have on, the air is pretty thin up here and could be causing the lightheadedness.

We already survived Brooke's lousy parallel parking job, and now we make our way down the street in search of the loft party. I start looking around for a warehouse, or renovated factory in the neighborhood.

"Okay, here's the address. Yep, sixteen ninety-four Pangloss Street." Brooke stops in front of an unassuming, decrepit, white house with a worn wrought-iron fence around it.

I stumble to a stop beside her.

"I thought you said it was a loft party."

"It is."

She points to a tiny lit window tucked inside the peak of the house's roof. Faint music and girlie squeals emanate from the opened window.

"That's not a loft. That's an attic. We're going to spend a Friday night in an attic, Brooke."

"It sure beats going to bed early to get up in time for a has-been ex-con movie star, now doesn't it?"

"I'm not so sure."

Then again I haven't been sure about much in my life lately. And as I gaze up at this house before me, I realize how fitting this whole scenario is. While I've been preparing to live a "loft" kind of lifestyle, I realize I've been stuck in a stuffy old attic, metaphorically speaking.

"Oh, hell, let's go in. We're on a mission, so assume the missionary position."

The three of us adjust our bra cups to jut out the flesh and fix our skirts before we march, or rather, totter, up to the front porch and knock.

"Who is it that invited you again?" I ask Brooke.

"I still forget, but I assume it was some guy."

"Will you recognize him if you see him?"

"I hope so."

I hear Unity angrily chanting under her breath. "So help me, Brooke, you better hope that my soul mate is in some parallel universe tonight, because if I passed him up all for a pimp-and-ho party, I swear—"

The front door flies open. A young guy fills up the door frame. He's wearing a red velvet fedora with a red feather and a long purple trench coat. I can't help but think he should be at my mother's Red Hat Divas club instead of here. He sweeps us in, hands us warm beer in plastic cups, and ushers us upstairs so he can move on to fraternize with the next group of victims who happen to knock on the front door.

Speaking of the term, *fraternize*, I can't help but notice the average age of the party-goers was, well, that of a fraternity.

As we reach the top of the stairs to the attic space, I look around to the clusters of pimped-out guys and ho-to-the-hilt gals chatting amid the low rafters. Some sort of techno-house-music plays in the background.

"This is a college party," I snap at Brooke.

"How was I supposed to know that?" she snaps back.

Unity chants louder. "I'll bet half these kids have mothers who are still lactating!"

"Are they even housebroken?" I add.

"Hey, guys, come on. Can we just keep an open mind about this? We'll stay for a beer or two and get out of here, okay? Remember, we're just here for a distraction, and a boy-toy, if we're so inclined."

If Brooke hadn't thrown those words in my face, reminding me it was my idea to get distracted with a boy-toy tonight, I'd have done an about-face right then and there.

"Okay, a beer or two, and then we can say we did this."

But Brooke is looking past me and her face lights up. Obviously, she's recognized the guy who must have invited her. She starts to say hi, until the guy swoops her into his arms and carries her off.

Unity sighs and her thin shoulders droop. "I have to pee. I passed a bathroom downstairs, I'll be back."

I nod, and before I can say anything more, my two co-whores disappear from sight. I take a sip from the plastic cup of the warm beer plunked into my grip earlier. I don't know why I'm drinking it. I don't even like beer. I rotate around amid the growing crowd decked out in feather boas and pinstriped suits donned with large gold medallions and search for some sign of Brooke. Nothing. I glance around one more time, until I happen to look to the tiny window in the peak of the roof.

And there he is.

Your average, everyday, ordinary Adonis.

My eyes pop out, ping toward him, then ricochet back into my sockets. But during this brief moment, I manage to scope his heavenly body up and down and sideways. Twice.

Gawd, how he makes a pimp look so good. He's got a black leather jacket on that caresses the length of his torso, just to his hips. His denim jeans absorb onto his skin more intimately than massage oil (oh, I wish I were a bottle o' oil right now!). While this guy could make a trash bag look good, my focus diverts from the clothes, to the man.

My gaze follows the contours of his jawline and pauses to visually mount the Adam's apple defining his throat, before the vision disappears into the layer of leather. The hair? Longish. Unkempt. And dark. The eyes? Devilish and gray in the dim light, not to mention appearing a little more world-worn than the drunken rugrats littering this place. The nose? Straight and sharp. Like I said, pure Adonis.

While I drool, he sits casually, overseeing the crowd, as if king of this domain.

A girl in vinyl hot pants and a sequined bandeau approaches him and leans in close to whisper something in his ear. She drapes her arms around his neck and dangles there like a sexual bling. She finishes whispering into his ear. He prizes her with a broad grin. A minute later, she heads downstairs. Another minute later, he rises and follows. The man is a walking superlative.

He brushes past me. When his skin strikes mine, his body-electric touch radiates into my shoulder, and I gasp. Noisily. His eyes lower to mine and he dips his head in apology for having gently pushed against me.

That's when he smiles. A brilliant, one-hundred-watt smile and I have to squint to see through the glare. I smile back into his pearly wattage, ready to say something so witty, so profound, that he'd have to stop and strike up conversation with me . . . and forget all about the other 'ho he was following downstairs. I would *chicka boom* my way into his arms.

But apparently a thick wad of cotton somehow clumped itself into my throat, because a whole bunch of nothing comes out of my mouth. A moment later, all six feet of uninterrupted masculinity disappears down the stairs and out of sight. So much for *chicka boom.*

Brooke sidles up beside me and digs her nails into my arm. She points down the attic stairs to my Adonis.

"Oh, dear God, who was that?"

"No freakin' clue."

"Holy shit, where'd he come from?"

"No freakin' idea."

"Nina! You just had a *moment* with him and you don't know who he is?"

"No freakin' clue."

"Augh! Then go after him! Hellooo! We just had a boy-toy discussion recently, remember?"

Her words snap me back to reality.

"But I don't even know his name!" I say and point to the stairwell. "Besides, he followed some girl out. A girl about ten years younger than me with nipples pointing ten inches higher than mine."

Brooke's male friend appears beside her. "The guy's name is Dante. Don't see him too much these days."

"Dante, huh?" I ask. "What's his last name?"

"Don't know. Always just been Dante, as long as I've heard of him."

Dante. I like that. Very ethereal. Celestial. And sexy as freakin' hell.

I couldn't begin to imagine what sex would be like with a guy like that . . . or rather the *consequences* of sex. This guy's so hot, he'd melt the condom. And where would that leave me? To have his beautiful children, that's what.

I can't help the onslaught of fantasies of romping around with Dante. To be honest, my sex life has been on the thin side lately. Model-thin, in fact. Okay, more like emaciated. Anorexic. Third-World skinny. Admittedly, I'm famished for a little carnal knowledge.

And I want nothing more than to devour every piece of that eye candy. No, not just the candy, but the whole candy *store*. We're talking from his Penis Butter Cup to his Lickers Bar, nuts and all. My own yummy bear. Not just M&Ms, but S&Ms. Almond-oil Joy. Sugar Daddy. Mr. Goodbar gone bad.

"Hey!" a kid in a vintage Hawaiian shirt and his hair slicked back yells up the stairs. "They're towing at the end of the street!

Anyone with a car out there better check to see if you're in a tow zone!"

Brooke curses. "Oh man, I didn't even check to see if I parked legally. Did you see any yellow strip on the curb? A street sign?" she asks me.

"No, I don't remember. I'll go check for you."

What else is there for me to do? The Adonis has disappeared so I have nothing keeping me here. I hold open my palm and wait for Brooke to produce her car keys. I know she's thrilled; now she can spend a little more quality time with the guy she's with, if only she could remember his name.

I carefully maneuver my way around couples loitering on the stairs and head out the front door. I teeter-totter along the sidewalk, each step causing a little more pain in my feet. These shoes were not made for walking, that's for sure. But with each step, comes a different set of footsteps behind me. Now, I don't know how a simple set of footsteps could come across as ominous, but I do know that it's enough to raise the hairs on the nape of my neck. I walk faster. So do the footsteps.

"Hey! You got the time?" a deep voice bellows out.

I turn. A guy's walking toward me. I can't make out his features with the streetlight's glare behind him. But I do see him joined by another guy who suddenly appears from behind a van. Immediately outnumbered, I shake my head no, that I don't have the time, and resume walking. I keep Brooke's keys tightly between my fingers, so if I get jumped, I might have a chance at carving out their faces.

"We only need the time!" the second guy calls out.

"I don't have the time!" I shout over my shoulder.

Fine time to realize that strolling along in a rundown neighborhood in striptease clothes might not be such a good idea.

Wouldn't want to give the wrong impression, now would I? But full-blown panic and fear hasn't quite set in, after all, they only asked for the time.

"Sure, you got the time. I know I got the time. How 'bout it?"

Okay, the fear comes avalanching down now. Getting to the car and locking myself in and driving for help might be my only option here.

As sore as the feet are, I do my best to break into a run, but in these heels, it's more like shuffling along the pavement. I hear the other footsteps coming faster, too. What the hell was I thinking? Apparently, I wasn't thinking at all. I still can't think straight now either, not with my heart pumping hard and the blood noisily roaring through my ears.

I hear the two men catching up but I stay focused on trying to find Brooke's car. Before I do, I feel a beefy paw grip onto my arm, halting me in my stilettoed tracks.

FIVE

One knight's stand

❧

"Look pal, I said I don't have the time!" I snarl. I try to pull away from the stranger's grip, but it's no good. His fingers dig more tightly into my skin.

"Oh, I think you do have the time," he snarls back.

But then I hear an even bigger growl of a motorcycle coming from behind them. Hell, they brought backup, I fear. The motorcycle's wail pierces the air as it rumbles up along the sidewalk and collides into one of the two men. The taller one who has his filthy mitts on me, loses his balance, and sends me flying before he falls to the ground. I stumble back and land hard against a telephone pole.

The large round headlight on the motorcycle momentarily blinds me before I see a faint outline of a man straddling the bike. The man uses his booted leg to knock the other guy to the ground. The bike rumbles toward me, its guttural groan fills the air around us.

"You all right?" he asks. He's got on a helmet, but I can tell from the lush tangle of hair peeking out from underneath, it's my Adonis.

I nod. "I think so."

He tilts his head over to one side. "Hop on!"

I hesitate, until I see the two guys staggering to their feet. It's all the motivation I need. I stumble over to Dante and as unladylike as possible, I straddle the back of the bike and hug him hard. He passes me a helmet. With one hand he grips my calf and positions my leg where it should be on the bike so I won't burn myself on the tailpipe. But it's too late. He's already left scorch marks.

"I have to return the car keys to the party!" I shout over the screaming engine.

He nods in understanding. He takes off down the sidewalk, pulls a U-turn onto the road and heads back toward the house. I see the two guys standing dazed by the side of the street. I breathe a sigh of relief.

As we approach the house, Brooke is making her way down the front stairs from the porch. She's got her cute guy-friend by the hand and watches in awe as the Adonis and I rumble up to the curb.

"You might wanna call the cops on those two over there." My leather-clad man kicks his head in the direction of the down-for-the-count thugs. "Till then, keep an eye on 'em."

"They just tried to mug me and who knows what else!" I yell in explanation while sitting on the back of the bike with my inner thighs straddling this guy's outer thighs. My arms are squeezing him tight. Too tight for a gal riding a bike that's well, *idle*, for the moment. I don't wanna get off. I mean, *I want to get off* with this guy, no doubt, but I don't want to get off this bike.

My head says to behave and leave him, but my butt cheeks are clinging fiercely to the leather seat and screaming that they want to stay put. Then again, it could just be the vinyl from my pink mini sticking to the seat.

"I guess this is where I have to leave you . . ." I say through a sigh.

"How 'bout I take you for a ride instead?" He revs the bike's throttle, sending a thunderous growl through the air.

How can I resist?

"You don't have to ask me twice." My butt cheeks remain firmly rooted to the bike's seat and cheer. I turn toward the stairs. "Hey, Brooke! Catch! Don't worry about me. I'll find my own way home." I toss the car keys in her direction.

Brooke catches the keys midair, then waves as the motorcycle pulls out into the street, speeds up, and takes off down the road.

"Where are you taking me?" I shout over the noise.

"Home."

"You don't know where I live."

"So tell me."

"I live up on the North Shore, but I don't want to go home."

"Then we'll hit the beach."

"At this time of night?"

I immediately regret what I just said. Nothing says "old fart" like questioning an activity meant to be fun, unusual, and spontaneous.

"When else would you go to Kelly's Roast Beef?"

"Of course!"

Kelly's Roast Beef is open during the day, too, but there's just something special about their seaside shack food that tastes extra special after a wild night, when the clubs close and you're starving to death.

Quickly, we make our way to the ocean and fly down the main drag alongside the sea wall before stopping at Kelly's. With the getup I'm in, I stay by the bike parked along the wall while he joins the lines of hungry patrons across the street. He comes back with a pile of food and my small Diet Coke; a D.C. is all I could manage in this tight skirt.

He sets the food and drink up on the wall. With almost no effort, he hoists me into the air to set me on the wall as well. This is good because I had no idea how I would scale the wall in these godforsaken clothes. I swing my legs up and over until my butt pivots and I'm facing the darkness of the sand and rhythmic beat of the black ocean waves. Overhead, a formation of lights dot the sky and twinkle down on us. I have no idea how or why I'm here and I don't care.

Dante hops up onto the wall next to me. He hands me the soda.

"Thanks for helping me out tonight."

"Like I had a choice," he says, pretending to sound irritated. "Anyway, you're welcome. The name's Dante."

"I know. I'm Nina."

"Nina. Neeeh-naah. Got a ring to it. So what were you doin' outside alone instead of inside at the pimp-and-ho party tonight, Neeeh-Naah?"

The way he wraps his tongue around my name sends my senses careening. I gulp a large lump of lust down with my diet soda.

"Me? Nothing, really. I was gonna move my friend's car for her. Didn't get far though."

"Good thing I showed when I did. The way you were dressed, and out walking alone, you were asking for trouble."

"You know my getup was for the party. I wasn't *asking* for *anything*," I retort, irritated that he thought I'd somehow deserved to be jumped because I went out in skanked-out clothes just to move a car.

"Yeah, but those guys didn't know why you were dressed like that. So, who'd you know at the party? Where'd you come from?"

"I didn't know anyone. My friend did. I sort of got abandoned right around the time you left." I also recall his leaving hot on the trail of a woman. "Say, when you left, um, weren't you leaving with someone?"

"You keeping tabs?"

"No," I refute way too quickly. "I just, noticed, is all. I hope you didn't leave her abandoned to come and help me."

"No. I'll get back to her later."

Disappointed, I answer with a bleak, "Oh."

Apparently women are just accessories to him.

"So, I guess I oughta ask. What's a nice girl like you doing in a place like a pimp-and-ho party?"

"Getting distracted," I answer absently. I take a slurp of my D.C., then play with the soda straw, drilling it in and out of the hole of the cup's plastic lid. I realize the action could be viewed as copulatory, so I immediately stop.

He takes my cup away, removes the lid, pours out a small amount of the soda onto the sand below us, and places the cup and lid between us. From inside the depths of his leather jacket, he pulls out a flask-sized bottle of rum and pours a healthy dollop, and I do mean *healthy*, into my cup. He reattaches the lid and casually hands it back to me. I merely stare in awe as I continue slurping on the now-stiff drink.

"So, Neeeh-naah, what are you getting distracted from?" he asks before tossing a french fry into his mouth. Then he pops one in my mouth.

"I need a distraction from life, I guess. Things have been too, er, quiet, and my friends decided we needed to shake things up, you know?"

"Yeah, I know what that's like. You get all restless. Like you're willing to do anything to break away from everything," he says and keeps to his task of tackling his roast beef with a robust bite. In the light of the street lamp, I can see a droplet of special sauce snuggled contentedly into the corner of his mouth. I do everything in my power not to lick it away. Cause if I start licking him now . . .

"So, you decided to do something crazy, huh?" he asks, but pauses to take a long gulp of straight rum. "Like walking the streets, looking to get mugged?" He's teasing and leans over to nudge me.

"What can I say? I'm a natural-born streetwalker. Apparently I missed my calling in life." I straighten my legs to show off my CFM heels.

"Nice gams," he says and lays a hot palm to my thigh.

He looks me square in the eye, the lamplight dances against his irises. He's so beautiful to look at, he makes my bones ache, not to mention a few other important body parts. At his touch, a full constellation of sexual emotions erupt within me. Talk about your big bang theory. By now, I'm intermittently chewing on my straw and sucking up the rum and D.C. like there's no tomorrow. He then hooks a finger onto my fishnet stocking and inspects them closer.

"Going fishin'?"

"Oh yeah, and it seems I found my catch."

His smile broadens, but then he pulls away and kicks back another hard gulp of rum.

Oh man, did I really have to say that? It's one thing to be a witty smart-ass with my co-whores, but it's another when bantering with a guy I just met. What if he doesn't like it? A woman's satire and sarcasm can exude confidence and intelligence, which can turn off a man. Will he end up being the one who got away?

"Yeah, and I took the bait. Hook, line, and sinker," he answers.

His playful response leaves me relieved. Okay, so he's not intimidated by my genius, wit, and wisecracking charm.

"Now that I'm hooked, tell me what really brought you out tonight. You tired of being a good girl? Needing to test drive your alter ego, Neeeh-naah?"

The timbre of his voice slides smoothly into my ear canal the way the rum soothingly heats the back of my throat. He sucks me into his sexual undertow. I try to remain calm, and not answer right away. I try to remember my goals: seriously date my brains out (not just him), have a few playful romps with some boy-toys (not just with him), and advance my career (not just advance on him).

The last goal about my career haunts me. I'm supposed to get up early in the morning. But the way things are going, I'm going to end up watching the sunrise from this very spot. I now understand why my good friend Brooke wanted me to work on one shortcoming at a time. Juggling all my inadequacies simultaneously can get awful hard awful fast.

Yes, I gotta get up in the morning to meet one notorious Jackleen Liquori, but with my head clouding up from the rum now heating the blood to my temples, further notions of Jackleen get real woozy. I decant the liquidy thought of her out of my head and pour myself into something a little more indulgent; the hefty hunk of he-man beside me.

"You really want to know what brought me out here tonight? I mean, you really, really want to know? Dressed like this? Skulking around the streets of Boston?"

I know it's the rum talking. Then again, did he actually have rum in that bottle? Or did he really slip some aphrodisiacal truth serum into my cup?

"Yeah, I want to know. I wouldn't have asked if I didn't."

"Short version? Social life, too quiet. Sex life, even quieter. Career might as well be a deaf mute. I'm looking to rectify all that."

The glint in his eye isn't wasted on me. It prods me on. With the floodgates of my back story open, I just let the information flow.

"For instance, careerwise . . . tomorrow morning, I'm meeting with *thee* Jackleen Liquori to help straighten out her reputation. On a Saturday, mind you!"

"The old movie star? I thought she was in prison."

"That's what I said! But she's made parole and is in town filming some movie on the streets of Salem. I'm serving as her PR person . . . which translates that I'm really her glorified baby-sitter. I have to stick to her side to make sure she behaves herself while filming, or it's back to the big house for her. My career depends on it."

I shudder involuntarily.

"Sounds cool enough. What about the social life?"

"The social life . . . well, you can see for yourself." I point to the bright pink mini. "Yep, that's me, the pimp-and-ho party girl!"

And I must be a party girl as this rum is going straight to the old noggin.

"And?" he asks.

"And?" I ask back.

"What about the sex life?"

Needing to shut up, I kill the last of my rum-spiked soda as a pathetic diversion to the question. With a final gulp, my throat burns, and I realize most of the rum settled to the bottom of the cup. Things are looking more fuzzy and suddenly, I'm feeling reckless. I swallow the last of the burning liquid, along with any residual inhibitions.

"My sex life, huh? Yeah, that could use a kick start."

I laugh heartily at my adorable little motorcycle joke. But inside any joke, a painful truth is always lurking.

"It's a lot to cover in twenty-four hours, rectifying so much in such a short time."

"It's my *modus operandi*. When I want something, I want it all *now*. It's my one tragic flaw."

"Sounds like you're accomplishing your tasks. To summarize, we got the career covered tomorrow morning," he says and counts on his finger.

"Mmm. Career covered."

"And we got the social aspect covered, with the party tonight." He keeps counting on his fingers.

"Mmm. Social covered."

"So that leaves just one thing left."

"Mmm. One thing left." I register his words and through the liquory haze, I hear him loud and clear. I look up into his eyes. "How we gonna cover that? I'm supposed to be dating my brains out to do that."

"Not necessarily."

He leans in and lays the most warm, sensual lips onto mine. The mingling of rum and male sensuality tingle my mouth. His kiss tastes of the night, and of danger, which now becomes my new favorite flavor. With his lips pressed against mine, I can feel his physical restraint, holding back an unchecked need. A need I'm more than willing to fulfill.

His lips part, demanding more of me. I open my mouth to him, taking him in, toying with his tongue, his teeth, the heat of his mouth. Sheer electricity shivers its way down my spine, radiating white-hot fingers of heat to the tips of my nipples, to my oh-so-sensitive hot spot, down to my curling toes. Hell, if the old floodgates weren't completely flooded before, they're absolutely gushing open now!

I sink into his kiss, and feel his firm hand grip possessively around my neck. A regular caveman-like gesture, but if he wants to drag me by my brunette locks and haul me back to his cave, then it's all right by me.

I'm in the middle of that nonfeminist thought when I have the most intoxicated clarity of my life. I want the romp. The whirlwind affair. I want the romantically forbidden fling stuffed with sex.

Not the ordinary kind of great sex either, but the kind that leaves you gasping for breath. That wears rug burns on your knees, nail scratches permanently scarred on your thighs. The dangerous kind where you're terrified you'll get caught any minute. Where you may lose your job. Go to prison even. End up on the evening news. Or the TV show, *Caught On Tape*. A good old-fashioned $9^1/_2$ *Weeks* kind of lusty affair that only comes once, okay maybe twice, in a woman's lifetime.

And . . . I want it *now*.

I tear myself from his kiss.

"I don't know if we should be doing this. I don't even *know you.*"

Translation:

Take me now or else!

The devilish glare in his eye, which I've already grown accustomed to, emblazons his face. He looks around like a wild exotic animal scheming on how to lean in for the kill. In one fell swoop, he grabs my leg and slips off one heel. I groan in response, partly because of his searing touch, but also because it feels so freaking good to get the damn thing off.

After easing up my other leg and sliding off the other heel, he gives me a trust-me smile and bounds off toward his bike. A second later, he returns, a small rolled blanket from the bike's knapsack tucked under his arm.

With the same self-assuredness as before, he clamps his hands onto my hips and eases me to the sand. The sand feels funky between my fishnetted toes, but at this point, I really don't care. I grab my purse just before we hightail it down toward the beach's shore. We saunter along ocean's edge, blanketed by the night.

We playfully romp around under the pilings groaning under the weight of the dilapidated wharf that they support. We stroll toward a jetty of rocks slicing the surf. Just beyond, I make out a silhouette of an abandoned shipwreck leaning on its side like a beached whale on the sand. I recall the incident happening during a blizzard last winter.

"Okay," I ask, winded by all this, "I basically spilled my guts to you. So what's your story?"

"Isn't one."

"Come on, not fair. Spill it."

He hooks an arm around my neck and snuggles me into his steel pecs.

"You want me to spill it, huh?"

"Fair's fair. You talked about getting restless and wanting to break away. So what does one do when one gets restless, hmmm?"

He chuckles low and his rumbling chest resonates against my cheek.

"When I get restless, huh? Let's see. For me, it means getting out of 'Dodge' for a while. You know, go places. Take the old bike and just take off . . . instead of just talking about it like most poor slobs.

"Oh, a regular wanderer are you?"

"Is there any way else to live?"

"I like to think so. That's why I'm working so hard to put all my ducks in a row."

"Hey, whatever suits you. But speakin' of suits, that's not exactly the kind of life I could get all amped-up about."

"No?"

He shakes his head.

"So tell me more."

"Don't keep in touch with my family. We mutually disowned each other. We didn't exactly see eye-to-eye on things. They say I got my priorities mixed up. After that, I toured Europe a while on a café racer. A *Buell*, to be specific."

What is it about family that drives us so crazy? Hell, I've disowned my own mother a thousand times. But for now, I keep to the goal of learning anything else I can about Dante.

"Okay, family life accounted for and a travel hobby, to boot. What about a job? How do you make ends meet?"

"I run a few raves to get by. Clean ones. Got a little savings. Got paid for some work on motorbikes I did in Germany. Don't need much more than that."

"Ok, career accounted for enough." I brazenly go in for a kill of my own. "What about sex life?"

"Darlin' you're about to find out."

I realize we're coming up on the old shipwreck, a fairly large boat that used to take partyers out on Boston Harbor cruises. I look up at the dark immense structure encrusted with old barnacles.

"Care to go on the cruise of a lifetime?" he asks.

I pause to consider his question. I've been ready to embark on something like this for way too long, but didn't have the courage until now. I know I can do it, right? Hell, I'm thirty! I should have had tons of one-nighters by now. I know I've got what it takes.

I mean, I'm sure I still got it . . . I just forgot where I put it. It'll come to me somehow, or else I might not get to come at all.

I answer him with a resounding yes.

The blanket tucked under his arm never exactly makes it to the sand to be neatly laid for a tender, romantic interlude. Instead it falls to a heap at our feet. No time for much else. Not with the leather jacket getting tugged off. Or shirts getting ripped apart and cast aside. Or belts a-flying and zippers unzipping faster than a rip cord.

With my black lace bra still intact, the neon pink mini scrunched up around my waist, and his pants still regretfully perched on his lean hips, we pause only long enough to entangle arms and indulge in a heart-stopping kiss. And only after that did we stop our assault on each other long enough to brace my backside against a leaning pole, hidden in the shadow of the wreck.

His hand, tracing my inner thigh, courses a treacherous path of destruction up my leg, cupping me at the V, making me gasp.

"Oh, I have to take these fishnets off! Help me. Now! Hurry! Peel 'em!"

"Honey, I intend to peel you like an orange and suck the juice right out of you."

With deft fingers Dante strips me clean of the vexing hosiery. His mouth skillfully works mine. And with the hardened ridge of him pressed against my pelvic bone, it's another sensual assault on the senses. A clear case of coital attraction.

Why is it that the moment he tears my bra to get to a nipple straining against the lace, the pencil-neck-geek in me decides to spar with the more primal, banal sensual goddess in me?

And like my panties, I'm torn. I don't know whether to continue as we are or stop us dead in our tracks. I have good reason.

"Wait! We can't do this," the geek in me yelps and I clutch back my breast, already aching and missing his mouth the minute I pry him off me.

He sucks in a breath but then starts nibbling on my collar bone. "We can't do this?" he asks between kisses. "Cause it feels like we are."

"I mean, we can't because we don't have a condom."

He curses. "No condom?"

"No, it's over there in my purse!"

His expression twists into one of solemn surprise.

"Wow, you really are hell-bent on rectifying your sex life tonight, huh? You came equipped and everything."

"Well, not exactly. My friend gave it to me a long time ago and I tucked it into a little pocket inside my purse. I'd forgotten it was in there it's been so long. It must have been in there since forever. I'd say at least since—" I stop my number-crunching and gawk at him. "Oh, just forget how long it's been in there for. But I do have to ask one thing."

"What's that?"

"Do condoms have expiration dates?"

"Never kept one long enough to worry about it."

Before I can call him on his remark, he breaks away to retrieve my purse. I'm immediately distracted by the chance to admire his delightfully delectable buns. I have to take in a good gulp of fresh air. I didn't realize I stopped breathing.

After he returns with my purse, I rummage through the pockets to get to the only thing that's keeping me from carnal bliss. *Voilà!* I hold up the condom. Now nothing or no one stands in the way of my romp of a lifetime . . . except maybe me.

SIX

The body may be a temple, but
there ain't no services this morning.

❧

The noise of what sounds like wailing sea lions in heat blasts into my ear and wakes me from a sound sleep. I try to open an eye to see what the hell is going on, but don't have to. I recognize the horrible noise. It's not sea lions mating, it's Brooke blowing her brains out on her damn kazoo. In my ear. Loudly. At the crack of dawn.

She blows her mating call on it again.

"Arrright! You kept your promise and got me up. Now get the hell out of here!"

She breaks into a kazoo version of "Twinkle, Twinkle, Little Star." I sit up and cover my ears. "Brooke! Please! My brain is hemorrhaging out my ears!"

That gets her to stop. Now if only I can get my bed to stop spinning like a Tilt o' Whirl.

"Oh, shit," I whine. "I'm still drunk. What time is it?"

"Six."

I want to cry. I can't function for the rest of the day still in-toxicated and living on two hours of sleep.

"So what time did you roll in last night?" Brooke asks.

"Four."

"This morning? Omigawd! What happened with you?"

"I need coffee." I hold a pounding temple to keep it in place. Last night's events barely unfold and refuse to come into focus. "Oh, I really need coffee."

"That good, huh? I want to hear all the details. Oh, and speaking of details, those two losers who harassed you last night disappeared before the cops came. But police cars were out pa-trolling the neighborhood the rest of the night. I'm just glad you're all right. Come on, get up. I already made a pot of java. Hit the shower, guzzle some diesel-strength caffeine, and tell me everything before I head out for my run!"

I groan. Why does Brooke insist on going running at the crack of dawn three times a week?

I can't do this today. I just can't.

I cover my head with the blanket.

My blood's still thick with rum, the sediment of alcoholic sludge clogging my arteries. But with Brooke pulling down the blanket and prodding me on, I get up, and barely make it to the shower. Several minutes later, hardly awakened by the cool wa-ter that pelted me, I scuff down the hall to the kitchenette in a robe and slippers in search of caffeine.

Brooke presents me with a steaming mug. Gratefully, I take it and sip.

"So, I got worried about you last night. It felt like forever to finally fall asleep."

"I'm sorry. I didn't mean to keep you up worried all night."

"Oh, no. I wasn't up all night. I crashed by eleven-thirty. But it still felt like forever."

"That's some concern." I smile and take another sip.

"So, what did you do last night? What kind of trouble did you get yourself into?"

"Honestly? I'm not sure. It's all still kinda fuzzy, but I know it was wonderful."

Brooke's face drops. "Holy shit, you slept with the gorgeous guy last night, didn't you?"

"I think I sorta, kinda, mighta did."

"Where? When?" she cries.

"On the beach, on the way home. Oh, God, what have I done?" Unable to hold up my head, I let it fall and thump onto the table. The coolness of the Formica against the throb actually feels good. "We used protection and everything, but what do I know about this guy? Could I be infested with some disease?"

"Oh, well, a while back, I did read an article about all the diseases you can get from having sex with strangers. There are tons. So I stopped right away."

"Having sex?"

"Reading."

"Oh, Brooke, what am I gonna do?"

"You're gonna do what the rest of us have had to do. Get ready for work and pray a bunch of semen doesn't run down your leg in the middle of a business meeting."

I raise my head off the table and look her square in the eye.

"How do we do that?"

"Do what? Prevent semen leakage?"

"No, manage to work semen into every conversation?"

"Hey, it's your fault the subject came up. I wasn't the one out slumming last night."

Just then, Guy-With-No-Name appears in the kitchen, scoops up Brooke, and kisses her. I give her a confused look.

"You just said you weren't out slumming last night."

"I wasn't. I was *in* slumming."

Guy-With-No-Name nods a cheery good morning to me and whisks Brooke off back to her bedroom. All the while, she's shouting things like, "We'll discuss this later!" and "I want details!" and "Get ready for work already!"

I return to my mug of coffee and my unsettling thoughts. First, I have to deal with Jackleen Liquori today. A Saturday. On my day off.

Second, I have to deal with the constant thoughts about Dante and what happened last night. But the worst, most sobering thought I have is, I don't know if I'll ever get to see him again.

Turner Street. Turner Street. Turner Street. Where the hell is it?

I'm finagling my Honda down a narrow Salem street in search of Turner. I already passed Pickering Wharf, Customs House, and Pig's Eye Pub. I've been down Turner before, I just know the street is down here. But it's been so long, I can't remember how far down. I keep looking.

Jackleen is supposed to be shooting a scene on Turner Street today, seven o'clock sharp, right at sunrise just outside the House of Seven Gables, a famous Salem tourist spot. The day and time of the filming is an unusual arrangement, and goes against guild rules, but it's the only one the film company could work out with the city. I won't get into the heavy compensation to all parties involved.

Jackleen's playing a high-priestess witch who happens to look gorgeous for her age—she had it written into her contract—in a movie called *Cacambo!* It deals with lost love and an ancient curse. Her character's helping to lift the curse so the star-crossed lovers can be together and live happily ever after.

At least it works in the movies.

I approach a couple of large trucks hogging up the road and slowly maneuver my way past. The side of the truck reads, Palladium Productions. Turner Street must be up ahead. Thank God, because I'm almost late as it is.

But as I'm about to take the right, Turner Street's blocked off. With a growl, I drive straight and have no choice but to parallel park near a small tourist shop with T-shirts and seashells for sale in the window. I grab my purse and briefcase, hop out, and squint into the blinding sunshine, which worsens my throbbing head. I steady myself on the curb and get my bearings.

Unable to face wearing a skirt this morning, I opted for a crisp white shirt, sensible trousers, and matching jacket. I had to. I didn't have anything else that would go with the comfortable, smart shoes I have on today after the painful skyscrapers I wore last night.

Oh, God. Last night!

Images flash through my sensitive mind. The memory of two slick bodies entwining, groping, clinging, and pumping invade my senses.

Great, the ol' brain has to kick into high gear and fuzzy memories become crystal-clear details right now. Last night had been wonderful. Dante's very touch had sent me into carnal overdrive. His hands had covered every inch of me and I let him. But he wasn't alone in this. I did my share of groping; on his thighs, his abs, his manhood—

Manhood?

Oh, hell. Did I really just call it his manhood?

But it was. It really, really was one-hundred percent, prime-choice-cut *manhood.*

I know what I'm talking about, because I held, stroked, and writhed against it before he and I consummated our lust, right there on the beach, under the stars, against the pole in the leaning shipwreck.

Speaking of wreck, that's how I feel. He left me wrecked for anyone else. Physically wrecked, because no one has or ever could compare to him. Emotionally wrecked, because I have no method, means, or opportunity to see him again. We were two shipwrecks that passed in the night.

I can still feel his final kiss full on my lips when he said good-bye. I made him drop me off at the corner of my street. Didn't want the roar of the motorcycle to wake the entire apartment building; I'd never hear the end of it.

As for Dante and me, for some reason, the idea of seeing each other again didn't come up. We both recognized the night for what it was and saw no need in dragging out the scenario. He knew I merely looked to rectify my situation. I knew he was supposed to be with another girl that night. He'd get back to her, he said. And so he probably has.

Is it possible to get sexually addicted to someone? To their eyes? Their smell? Their skin? Their breath? Their sex? Because that's how I feel. When it comes to Dante, I still got a major raging craving.

I shake off the perilous thoughts. Sobering up won't be easy this morning if I'm gonna have to endure these flashbacks to flesh. I pull myself together, suck in my gut, stick out my chest, and march to the rhythmic throbbing still going on in my temples. After walking down Turner, I dodge film cameras and lights, pass a table full of pastries that trigger the nausea I thought I squelched, and look for Mean Jackleen Liquori.

I'm about to ask the help of a young girl wearing a headset and carrying a clipboard who just burst out of a trailer. But before I reach her she starts balling her eyes out. She runs up to another woman with a makeup case and starts wailing, "I can't take her anymore! I'm through! I'm not paid enough to put up with her shit!" The other assistant tries to console her, but the headset girl breaks free and makes a mad dash to another trailer. The other follows.

I hold down my nausea. I reflect on the scene that just unfolded before me and shake my head. I know where this is going. I turn and look back at the trailer she just came out of. On the door reads the sign: JACKLEEN LIQUORI.

Oh, it just keeps getting better and better.

I ease my way to the trailer and knock. After a "Come in, dammit," I open the door and step in.

Her back is to me. She's rummaging through makeup items, a pack of cigarettes, and a few pieces of costume jewelry in search of something on her lighted dresser. Around her mirror are tucked a few photos of her and other stars, like Merv Griffin, and Johnny, along with a still shot of her gig on the *Love Boat*.

"Ah, here it is."

She reaches for a gold lighter and lights up. Through her

swirling boa of smoke, she looks into the mirror and acknowledges my reflection. In the light, I'm surprised by what I see. Her features are softer than I imagined. Blue eyes that pierce. Blond shoulder-length hair frames her face, not to mention her perfectly arched eyebrows. Her lips are just as arched. Her skin, flawless. Granted, I'm sure she's had her share of nips and tucks, but I honestly believe what I'm witnessing might be what people refer to as star quality. Dressed in a creamy goddess-like robe for a costume, she's lucent in the light.

Her long lashed eyes look me up and down. "You look like shit."

"I feel like shit."

Oh, that would still be the rum talkin'.

"Glad to hear it. Doesn't leave me anyplace to go with you, now does it?" She smiles to me and turns. She holds out a hand to shake. "Jack-LEEN Liquori. Are you that little girl they were supposed to send from the ad agency?"

"Yes, I'm Nina Robertson," I say and shake her hand.

"What you are . . . is late. Showing up late and looking like shit. That's two for two."

"They blocked off the street, I couldn't get down here."

"Why don't you make it easy on us both and tell me why you weren't here early. Doesn't show much love or adoration, not to mention respect, for your client."

I just don't have the energy to suck up to the woman. I could already see the promotion flying out the window. But I wouldn't give it up without a fight. And apparently a migraine. But honesty seemed to be the best policy with this woman.

"I'm late because I'm hung over. Was out all night, in fact."

"My kind of girl." She smiles again, then frowns. "But do it on your own time."

"It *was* my own time."

"Not when it interferes with *my* time, or it interferes with your performance. I like to consider the eight hours of sleep you require before working for me as a requisite from now on. Believe me, you'll need it."

"I'm here now. It won't happen again. Last night was a once in a lifetime—never mind. Maybe we should just get started."

I hoist my briefcase onto a small table with a bench for a seat. I need to keep her promotional appearances in order (as her publicist quit). I need to keep her perfectly clothed and coiffed (as her personal stylist quit). Finally, I need to keep her well behaved (as her parole officer quit). I need to do all these things at least until she rebuilds her entourage.

On top of this, I'm to interview her for her vision of a new line of clothes and wigs she's been wanting to create and sell on the shopping channels. Hey, she's actually paying the agency well for this kind of attention, and she can afford it, despite her run-in with the law and court fees.

"Let's see," I begin. "I suggest we review your guest appearances here in town to promote yourself and this movie. Tomorrow is a luncheon at Wellesley College. Then, after that, you've got a mall appearance at—"

But it's awful quiet. I look up. She's staring intently in the mirror at her perfectly applied lipstick. Is she even listening? Before I can ask, a knock on the door interrupts. Jackleen answers with, "Come in, dammit!"

A different person, this time a guy with a headset, pokes his head in.

"We're ready for you, Ms. Liquori," the young man says. "I just love your work. I'll be watching, if you need anything."

Jackleen turns to him and gives him an endearing smile.

"Thank you, baby-doll-dahling. Be a sweetie and tell them it'll be just a moment more?"

The young man agrees and after he shuts the door, Jackleen shuts off the charm. I sense a little reverse chauvinism going on. I do recall her occasional *rendezvous* with young lovers she'd collect during her travels.

"I'm on. We'll go over my schedule later. If you'd like to watch the filming, they have a section set aside. You can leave your things on the table for now." She gathers her robe and waits for me to get the door for her. I oblige and follow her out the trailer.

The scene they're filming takes place on the edge of the property of the House of Seven Gables, a landmark made famous by Hawthorne in his novel of the same name. But for this movie scene, the characters have the ocean bay in the background and the Gables off to the side. Right in the middle, Jackleen effortlessly acts her heart out as the ever-endearing, but meddling, witch.

The minutes turn into more than an hour; the standing and waiting is exhausting. I have the rest of the day to go. This is definitely the not-so-glamorous part of Hollywood. Just as the director yells cut and to take a break, Jackleen takes off to discuss her creative input with the director. She points to me, then holds up ten fingers. It's not that she's saying she'll be about ten more minutes, she's making sure I'll be ready to go in ten minutes. I nod back in understanding.

At the end of the street, a low throaty rumble fills the air. A few people stop to look. Others go about their work on the set. As for me? My heart dips in recognition.

Dante.

I twirl around and look. At the end of the street, behind the row of wooden road barriers, the motorcycle rolls into view and stops. The rider removes his helmet and hangs it on the back of his bike. He doesn't move, but rather, sits and watches. His gaze spans the locale until his eyes settle on me. He smiles.

Before I start melting onto the pavement, I go to him. I try to walk casually while I nonchalantly drag my fingers through my hair to primp for him. Sort of a waste of time with my little Annie Hall look today. But I don't care. I approach him and stop at the large wooden road barrier between us.

"Morning," he says.

"Hi."

"Nice monkey suit. Almost didn't recognize you without fishnets," he teases.

"And I almost didn't recognize you with clothes on." I bat my eyelashes at him, but I do it with confidence.

"So, you were telling the truth. You really are stuck working on a movie set this morning."

"Yeah, so, what are you doing here?"

"Came to see you."

"You did? How'd you find me?"

"Not too many caravans of movie production trucks in the city. Just asked around. Hope it's okay."

"It's more than okay," I admit. "I never expected you to show up."

"Neither did I." His deep tone once again proves he's got the sexiest voice in the universe. "But I'm glad I came. So what are you doing?"

"Right this second? Oh, just hanging around. A whole lot of nothing goes on during a film apparently. But I'm meeting with

Jackleen to go over her PR and promotional gigs in a few minutes. They just wrapped up a scene. It's not going well for me. She hates women, and loves men."

"So, is doing all this nothing helping to rectify your career situation so far?"

"It's helping to worsen my sore feet, I know that much."

"Maybe I can help in that department. Now get over here and kiss me."

He leans his bike over just enough to lean his body over the barrier separating us. In a reflex I do as he demands. I brace my hands on the barrier and kiss him right back. He tastes just as fine as I remember. For the moment, I forget everything but him.

"Come for a ride," he says in a hoarse, low whisper.

"Oh, I can't," I answer, breathless. I grip the wooden road barrier between us harder and force myself not to catapult my ass over it and take him up on his offer.

"They won't miss you. We'll be gone five minutes."

"No, really, I—"

He nods and pulls back. "I get it. You're on the clock." He grins at me, that same bright, devilish grin. "That's what good girls do."

"Hey, I resemble that remark," I tease. "But honest, I have a job to do here, and it may not seem too important to someone who's used to coming and going, but it's what I have to do."

"You're right. I don't sit still long enough to know what it's like." He looks to all the staff running around like squirrels getting their work done before the next shoot. Then he looks down at his bike. "But I do think I like it better on this side of the fence."

"How can you be sure? How do you know unless you try?"

"I've been known to set up camp, but never for the long

haul. Got too many road trips to take. Not too keen on convention, you know?"

"Wow, I'm totally trying to 'do convention' and you're totally rejecting it. Now there's two opposites."

"And there's a fight if I ever saw one," Dante says, distracted
by some fracas behind me.

"What?"

He nods over to someone or something over my shoulder. I
follow his gaze and watch the scene play out on the other side of
the set.

There, Jackleen is stalking off, raising her fists into the air.
The director follows behind her. She's stops and turns to yell
something at him, I don't know what, she's out of earshot. The
director yells something back. She thrusts her hands on her hips
and squabbles again. He squabbles back. She raises her hand as
if to slap him, but shows visible restraint. She then breaks into
tears and dashes toward a Mercedes convertible with its top
down, parked on the side of the road.

"Oh, no. Please, not now. What is she doing? Oh, some
baby-sitter I turn out to be!" I start to go after her, but before I
make it more than a few steps she's already peeled off down the
street in the convertible, almost taking out one of the road barriers.

I turn back to Dante to say I'll take the ride from him after
all, but he's already got the helmet out waiting for me.

"Oh, hell! This could be the end of it for me! And I just
got here!"

Dante revs up the bike and we take off in pursuit of Jackleen.

"Does she know where she's going?" Dante calls out to me.

"I don't think so. This is not good! This is so not good."

"Hang on!" Dante angles the bike and swerves between the traffic on the narrow street as we head back toward Pickering Wharf.

"What is she doing? She's still on probation! She'll go back to jail if she screws up. And it'll be my fault!"

Suddenly, at the next major intersection by Engine House Pizza, the convertible stops. Well, not *at* the intersection, per se. More like, *in* the intersection.

Cars behind her skid to a halt and begin to beep. She doesn't move. The light overhead turns red. The cross traffic is unable to proceed and a gridlock quickly ensues. Dante motors along in between cars to get to Jackleen.

I hop off and race to the driver's side. Jackleen has her hands still on the steering wheel, her head pressed against her forearms. My stomach knots; my kind of luck, the woman probably had a stroke or nervous breakdown or something and I couldn't get to her in time to save her.

"Ms. Liquori! Are you all right? What happened? Ms. Liquori?"

I lean in close to see if she's okay. The car's still running, so I know it didn't stall. She had to have thrown it into park in the intersection on purpose and had better have a good reason.

"I don't know why I bother to care. Doesn't anyone care about artistic integrity anymore? Doesn't anyone love the craft or appreciate those who've dedicated their lives to their profession?" she cries, her head still hung low.

"Oh, hey, I'm sure they do. Why don't you pull over and we'll talk about it."

She pops her head up and leers at me. "Don't you dare patronize me! Do you know who I am?"

So much for my one attempt at "nice."

"Yeah, you're the lunatic holding up traffic and pissing off a lot of people right now. Not good for PR. And traffic citations are never good for someone on parole!" I shout at her.

I feel a warm pair of hands settle on my shoulders. Dante stands next to me and looks down at Jackleen.

"Excuse me, aren't you Jackleen Liquori? I loved you in *Diary of a First Lady*."

Her features soften as she takes in the sight of Dante. I can't blame her. He's a beautiful creature. She settles down.

"Why, thank you, sweet-baby. Playing the First Lady came easy to me. It was a gift role."

"You were perfect," he says, until a van behind us beeps.

Dante turns to the van and calls, "Hey! Don't you know who this is? It's Jackleen Liquori, the movie star! She's having car trouble! Hold on!"

The guy in the van nods his head. A moment later, he comes out to get Jackleen's autograph. He's followed by a few others. Jackleen's face lights up at the attention and is more than happy to oblige her fans. A small crowd ensues, until a patrol car with its lights on, but no siren, pulls into the traffic. The officer gets out.

Okay, this is it. This is the part where he's gonna realize she's on parole and is gonna haul her sorry butt back to jail.

Dante greets the officer and explains in a lie how Jackleen is having car trouble and flooded the engine. The officer then chats with the actress, who oozes her star-quality charm on the man in blue. She autographs his pad of traffic citations. I merely watch the entire scene in awe until Dante approaches me.

"Say, Nina, how 'bout you drive the convertible back to the set. I'm gonna take Jackleen for a little joy ride."

"What? But she has to go back to film another scene."

Dante nods knowingly. "Don't worry, we'll go for a little

spin down Winter Island and back. Ten minutes tops. I think she needs it, if you know what I mean."

"But are you okay with all this? I mean, can you handle her?"

He prizes me with a low chuckle and his eyes crinkle to crescents. I can still see slits of blue-gray in them and I'm immediately appeased.

"Oh, all right. If she needs this attention, then fine. But watch her hands. She likes 'em young." I spy him as I say this. He grabs me by the wrist and gruffly kisses the side of my head.

"I'm not done with you yet . . . I'll see you later," he promises.

"I'm in the book, under Robertson."

I reluctantly pull from his grip and approach the convertible.

"What do you want?" Jackleen asks as she signs the last autograph. The patrol officer is busy clearing away the crowd surrounding the car to get the traffic moving again.

"I'm driving, hop out."

"Like hell you are."

"You're going on the Harley with my friend, Dante."

"I'd be delighted."

She opens the door, dramatically steps out, her gossamer-like robe flapping in the breeze. She blows a kiss to the crowd and when they applaud, she takes her bow.

Dante holds out a helmet for her and helps her mount behind him on the bike. She's got her robe carefully bunched into a fist as she drapes her arms around my guy.

Yes, that's what I said. *My guy*. Can I actually be jealous of an aging Hollywood movie star hugging my hunk? Well, yeah.

I purse my lips and get in the damn convertible. After following the instructions of the police officer, I drive through the traffic and head back toward Turner Street.

Up ahead, I can see Dante riding off into the distance

with Jackleen, who's waving at cars and blowing kisses to passersby.

Hey, at least the woman didn't get arrested today—yet. I need to be thankful for that.

The rest of the day doesn't go much better. How could it with Jackleen arguing over every artistic detail of every scene she films? In between, she and I haggle over guest appearances, television interviews, and press time. Getting an "okay" out of her is like pulling teeth with mittens on.

That night, I trudge into my apartment building, up the stairs, and into my apartmentette. In the middle of the living room floor, Brooke is pacing, the cordless phone pressed to her ear. She's frantically whispering something into the mouthpiece.

"Hi." I close the door. "What's going on?"

But Brooke still speaks in a hushed shriek into the phone.

"Okay, never mind, she's here. Yeah, I'll call you back!"

She presses a button and ends the call. She turns to put the phone in the cradle. But whatever bad day she's had, I'm sure mine was worse. So, before she gets into her newest crisis about running out of cellophane wrappers for her gift basket's chocolate penis pops or whatever, I have to vent to her about my day; she made me promise to tell her the details about Jackleen Liquori the minute I got home.

"Before you say a word, I'll be brief. Today was the day from hell. But I'm alive and I survived that evil woman."

"Um, Nina?"

"And Dante showed up! Can you believe it? Just as he and I are talking, Jackleen creates all this chaos. Then the next thing I know, Dante's calming her down. He's got her eating out of the palm of his hand."

"Nina, I've been trying to call you." She looks down the hall to our bedrooms and then back at me. "Why haven't you picked up your cell?"

"We couldn't have cell phones turned on while on the set, a ringing phone could ruin a lot of footage, you know?"

"Shhh!" She mashes her fingers to my lips to shut me up, and again looks down the hall. When I simmer down, she removes her hand.

"Wait a minute. Don't tell me Guy-With-No-Name is still here. You need help getting rid of him? I'll help you." I have to laugh to myself at her so-called crisis. If only she knew what a real crisis was.

"I have something to tell you, I have to warn you, so keep your voice down," she says.

"Look, with the day I had, I'm still in high gear. I'll take care of it for you right now." I plunk down my briefcase and head for her bedroom.

"Nina, please, keep your voice down. And get out of here while you can!" she shrieks quietly.

Halfway down the hall, I stop and look at her. "What the hell happened? Did he hurt you?"

"What?" she asks, clearly confused. "Wait, no, but, come back out here, please," she begs.

"No, this is our apartment. We shouldn't have to leave, or whisper, or anything else!" Determined to clear this up, I throw open her bedroom door. No one's there.

Brooke lets out a high-pitched squeal and looks to my closed bedroom door.

"The bastard's in my room? Why?"

I hate the thought of some stranger in my bedroom, going through my stuff, and leaving my friend so fearful. I reach for the doorknob, fuming. I mean, after the day I had, I'm rearing for a fight. I turn the doorknob, open the door, and burst in, prepared for anything. After all, Jackleen Liquori has already made my life a living hell and nothing could possibly make it any worse.

Obviously, I was wrong.

SEVEN

I beg your hard-on?

"What's he doing here?" I whisper in a shrill.

"Sleeping obviously!" she shrills back.

I tiptoe over to the bed, to the body sleeping facedown, entangled in sheets. Only one person hogs the sheets and wraps them around himself like that. And I spent plenty of nights naked and freezing to know who that person is. But I have to be sure. I carefully pull the sheet back off his face. It's him.

"Jeremiah?" I ask softly.

He doesn't answer. He does grunt and nudge a little, but resumes sleeping. His breathing stays constant and heavy, threatening to break into a snore any minute. Without disturbing him more, Brooke and I escape back to the living room.

"I don't believe it. How'd he get in?" I ask aloud, but mostly to myself.

"Did you ever get your key back from him?"

"Shit. No. He's probably got no place to go after he gave up his apartment."

"That's right! On account he'd be traveling so much, just before you two broke—never mind. I didn't want to say anything, but I did see his photo the other day, in one of your magazines lying around. He was covered in sand, in the desert. He had a turban around his head."

"Yeah, I saw it."

"Where was he? Iraq? Israel?"

"*Utah*."

"What?"

See, that's the thing about Jeremiah. He's so hell-bent on making a name for himself, he tends to sensationalize everything he does. From his early beginnings when he reported on summer thundershowers for a local network's evening news, his TV histrionics of standing in the rain, in "gale force" and "hurricane-like" winds made him famous around here.

But after landing a gig in New York, he ended up in exotic places like the Amazon Jungle or Thailand. Reporting on Thailand is how he got addicted to their culture and led to the demise of our relationship. I never exactly explained to Brooke how Jeremiah and I used to fight over that country. I found it too embarrassing that an entire foreign land could come between my fiancé and me. But I get the feeling the time has come to confess why we really broke up.

"Yes, Brooke, he was wearing a turban while reporting in *Utah*, of all places. He did a feature on dying desert towns, and then on Native Americans while every other journalist got shipped to the Middle East. He had to make all his photos look, well, 'current' with world events."

"Really? So he made himself look like he was in Afghanistan or something?"

"Mr. Sensationalist at work."

"But he loves going overseas, why didn't they send him? You know, to the Orient, Japan, or Thailand like he always does?"

"Well, uh, he wasn't always going over there for business the way I thought. Especially Thailand. More often than not, he was there for pleasure. Which explains why he never had any money saved."

"He spends all his money on vacations? And he'd go without you? Did you know this?"

"Not at the time, but when I found out, it was the last straw in the relationship. I couldn't tell anyone, it seemed too bizarre."

"Taking vacations alone after getting engaged was selfish of him, for sure, but I wouldn't exactly call it bizarre."

"Oh, honey, you don't know the half."

I plunk down onto the sofa. I couldn't be standing up for this if I were gonna have to get into the sordid details of what really happened between Jeremiah and me . . . and of course, Thailand.

Brooke plunks down next to me. Her face twists funny, which means she is truly puzzled by what I'm saying.

"What seemed bizarre?" she presses.

"Haven't you ever noticed how Jeremiah always had a thing for Asian women? In magazines? Or wherever we went? If he saw a young Asian woman, his face would light up and he'd blatantly stare at her. He never once looked at me like that."

"I remember you telling me he had a 'thing' for exotic women. Why?"

"I found out why he had such a 'thing' for them. I-I found . . . pictures."

"Was he cheating on you overseas with an Asian girl?"

"You could say that. More like *many* Asian girls."

"What?"

"Have you ever heard of a Man Tour?"

"A Man Tour, huh?" She shakes her head.

"Yeah, a Man Tour. Kind of like a Club Med, or an overseas vacation package deal. See, American men can take these Man Tours together to places like Thailand. Over there, red light districts are no big deal. Neither are massage parlors or prostitutes. Over there, our American guys get treated like gods. They go partying with these girls at the clubs. The girls visit them at their hotel rooms and party with them, and, let's just say they get the whole enchilada."

"Like orgies and stuff? This actually exists?"

Sadly, I must nod.

"Oh, yeah. They get fawned over, taken care of, made to feel like big men on campus—everything we 'modern' gals here don't do. So, guys who can't get girlfriends in the U.S., or who can't get laid at home, take these Man Tours throughout the year and get it all. They get every whim and desire fulfilled."

"No way. I don't believe it."

Clearly, she's flabbergasted. I sigh. Like Brooke, I didn't exactly believe it either, even after I saw the picture of Jeremiah partying with topless foreign girls in his hotel room. Then, a little more searching on the Internet proved they do exist. They actually have web sites for these things.

"So, Jeremiah likes to go on these Man Tours?"

"All the time. He got hooked. We fought about it constantly.

He said it wasn't 'cheating.' He called it 'research,' and that he had to do it to gain the trust of the locals so he could 'get his story.' Only, he never produced any story. I finally told him to choose. The Man Tour or me."

"And he chose the Man Tour?"

"At first, he offered a compromise. He showed me brochures of Man Tours for couples looking to widen their sexual horizons."

"No!"

"Yeah, he wanted me to come with him. Of course I didn't. Then he said, in that case, we can just introduce an Asian woman into our bed here in America."

"You're kidding!"

"I wish I were. I told him my ultimatum still stands. He went off and thought about it. I thought for sure I'd win this one, but the next I know, I'm getting a call from him, breaking our engagement."

My memory quickly flares back to the day at the bridal boutique. The day he called me on my cell telling me he chose Thailand over me. I honestly didn't expect it. I still can't forget how the sales lady yanked the wedding gown from my grip just before I used it as a very expensive Kleenex.

I shudder. Gosh, I haven't thought about that fiasco in days. Guess my mind really has been on other things, like my job for a change. And, of course, Dante.

"Why didn't you ever tell me?" Brooke asks as she rubs me on the shoulder.

"I couldn't tell anyone. I was mortified. I felt like such a loser that I couldn't satisfy him emotionally or sexually. I couldn't give him what Thailand could. I guess over there, they make you feel like a 'man.' Why do you think I feel like I failed our relationship even though I was the one ready to give up my job and stay home with kids so I could support his career?"

She continues rubbing my shoulder. "I'm so sorry. I really wish you could have told me."

"I would have eventually, when I was ready."

"So these really, truly do exist, huh?"

"Go on-line and book yourself on one. Takes two seconds. They take MasterCard and Visa."

Right then, the shuffle of footsteps can be heard from down the hall. We both look up to see Jeremiah make his appearance.

"Going on a trip somewhere?" he asks us. He must have caught only the tail end of our conversation, thankfully.

"Ah, no," Brooke quickly answers. "We were just talking about, ah, a 'friend' of ours, who was, ah, looking into sperm banks recently on the Internet. It's just *amazing* the things you can buy on-line these days, absolutely *amazing*."

"Huh," he says, scratches the back of his head, and shakes off sleep.

I take in the sight of him. He's still pretty cute, with a baby face on him, and dirty blond hair that he keeps cropped short. He always hated having a baby face. Always said pretty boys don't make it as hard-core reporters. It's the reason he works so much to get to do the rough stuff.

If I weren't so distracted these past couple of days, I'd probably still be missing him. But if I know him (and I think I do), he's probably been to Thailand at least twice since the breakup. My throat cramps at the thought, so does my heart.

"Jer-Jeremiah, what are you doing here?"

"Needed a place to crash, hope you don't mind."

He hopes I don't mind? That's it? That's all he has to say? Of course I mind. I can't have this guy waltzing in here assuming he can drop in and use my bed, and merely hope it's okay. But I keep calm. I have to.

"You could have called to warn me. Or have you forgotten my cell phone number already?"

"I did try, but it was turned off or something. And I didn't want to leave a voice mail."

Damn.

"I forgot. I had it turned off, with the filming going on and all."

"Filming?"

"For work, never mind. But I don't think it's all right that you're here, not at all right. But to be honest, I'm so floored, I really can't think straight."

"Well, I've been doing a lot of thinking lately, and we need to talk."

I remain seated on the couch and rub my temples, something I've been doing a lot today. Brooke rises and slowly walks over to retrieve her purse. She then heads toward the door.

"Listen, guys, I'm meeting Unity for brick oven pizza. So, you two go ahead and talk. Jeremiah, always a pleasure. Nina, if you need me, you got my cell."

I offer up a meek smile and wave good-bye.

Traitor.

Jeremiah watches Brooke leave. The minute the door closes, he turns to me and smiles.

"So, how's my girl been?"

"I'm not your girl. I still can't believe this. You're actually here. In my apartment."

"It was supposed to become 'our' apartment, once you booted out Brooke, remember?"

"Oh, I remember. But I'm still floored and surprised." I hoist myself off the couch and stand up to him. I look him straight in the eye. "How can you think it's okay to show up here after what you did to me?"

"What I did to you? I wasn't the one who made the ultimatum, Nina."

"Well, excuse me, but I don't believe I made an outrageous demand. I simply asked that you stop having sex with other women! Is that too much to ask of the groom?"

Oh, I finally got to say it! It has been welling up inside me for months now. He didn't play fair the day he called me at the bridal shop and I wasn't prepared to lash back at him then. Instead, when he broke it off, I nodded mutely, and finally squeaked out the words, "You've made your decision," and hung up.

"Look, I didn't come here to fight. I just need a place to stay for a week or two."

"Oh, did you blow your entire salary on, oh, I don't know, let's see, an *overseas vacation*?

His shoulders drop and he actually has the nerve to look wounded. What did he expect? He begins to pace the floor, tears his finger pads through his hair, and refuses to look at me.

"You don't know what I've been through these past months," he begins to say.

"And you don't know what *I've* been through. I had to face all our family and friends and make up some lame excuse about what happened to us."

"What did you tell them?"

"Don't worry. I told them your career took all your time and we knew it would be a mistake to get married."

He looks at me, relieved.

"Thank you."

"Don't thank me! I had to save face, too! I did it for *me*— God, you don't know how embarrassing it's been. And it hurt."

"I never meant for it to go so far."

"You never meant for *what* to go so far? Your trip down the aisle or your trips to Thailand?"

"Damn it, Nina! I'm in deep shit right now and I need your help!"

Caught off guard by his outburst, my spine straightens and I'm taken aback. Heck, this wouldn't be the first time for the guy to find himself in deep shit, and usually Jeremiah thrives on this sort of thing. But today, he looks sort of tired, and worried, if I scrutinize him close enough. Like something's been eating away at him, getting under his skin. Probably a venereal disease. I don't worry about myself in that department. The minute I found out about his clandestine activities overseas, I got myself checked out and in the clear. But, honestly, he truly looks shaken.

"What is it? What kind of trouble are you in?"

"Aw, it's bad. I had no place else to turn. The last place I tried to crash at got burned to the ground."

"Burned to the ground?" But I don't need to hear how he might be bringing danger into where I live. I stab a finger into his face. "So help me, if anything happens to this apartment building, I'll kill you myself. Too many innocent people live here for you to show up putting all our lives at stake!"

"No, don't worry. It happened in Ghana."

I thrust my fists onto my hips. "Oh, so burning down a building never happens in the good ol' U.S. of A?"

"They don't want the building. They want me. At least, they *will* want me, once they realize what I've got in my possession."

"They? They who? What have you got?"

"It's a long story. The less you know, the better."

"Jeremiah, start talking."

"I got some footage of guerrilla activities. They want the tape. They're not getting it."

"Did you turn over the tape to anyone? *ABC? NBC? TNT? CBS? CNN? BBC? CNBC? MSNBC?*"

"No. Not yet. I just got back into the country. But I plan to meet with people in New York about the tape. The time isn't right to hand it in just yet. I've got to edit it first, before the meeting. These guerillas, they're ruthless. They're not sure if I'm the one holding the tape, but they're suspicious. And if they find out I have it before I get to New York . . ."

He makes a gesture as if to slit his own throat.

I listen hard to what he's saying. He's got a sincerity in his eyes that I can't ignore. It's the same look he gets when in the middle of a crisis on TV. But I also see a rare pleading in his expression, indicating his seriousness. He's really starting to scare me.

"Jeremiah, this is way too close to home. I mean, how did you ever get yourself into such a mess and drag it back home?"

"You know I always want to be in the middle of the action. But this time, I'm in way over my head."

"But how did it get so bad?"

"I've been working on these kinds of assignments for months. Haven't you seen me on TV?"

"Well, yes, of course, ah, no, actually. It would hurt too much to see you on TV."

"It's understandable."

"But I've come across your picture in some magazines. You looked good in *Time*."

"Thanks, I was proud of that one. Of course, that assignment featured in *Time* is what led me to this point. To right here, in your apartment."

"But why me? Why here?"

And why now of all times?

"Because I need you, Nina. I need you more than I ever needed anyone in my life."

The last time he said those words, he wanted to get me into bed. It worked like a charm, too. But something tells me he's not looking to have sex right now, then again . . .

"Really," I say, "I don't know how I could possibly help you. What can I do?"

"Go public with me. And let me spend a week here, two tops."

"Go public? You mean tell everyone what really broke us up?"

"No, quite the opposite. I need you to be seen out in public with me. If I'm out at different functions with you, it'll look like I know nothing about the taping of guerrilla activities. And with you on my arm all night at any gig, you can do your gracious thing by distracting any man who approaches me with questions about that tape. You've done that sort of thing for me before."

I sure have. When Jeremiah and I would attend some political dinner and conversation was about to get contentious, I'd just pull a "Jackie-O." I'd bat my eyelashes at some steamed politician and ask a sweet-but-intelligent question about a less controversial topic. I became an expert at diffusing any potential hostile situation by using a little feminine wile.

"I'm not buying it, Jeremiah. How will your public appearances make the bad guys not come after you?"

"Let's put it this way, would a guy with a tape risk his life by cavorting out in public? No. He'd be on the run. Or go into hiding. So, if I'm in the public eye, they'll probably assume I got nothing. Like reverse psychology."

"And you need to do this with me?"

"Right. Work your magical charm in PR to show I'm alive and well and in the spotlight without a care in the world. Make it look like we're getting back together. I know it's a lot to ask, but I need you. So, what do you say?"

"Sounds like you're looking for free PR to me."

"Does a guy who makes it in the pages of *Time* magazine sound like someone who needs free PR?"

Admittedly, he has a point. But I'm still not too clear on my role in all of this. He's coming on so strong, so fast and furious, I have to take time to digest the information. Kinda hard to do when I'm still so messed up about our past.

"So, Nina, what do you say? I got to get myself in the pages of some trades . . . the *Columbia Journalism Review*, the *American-Review*, anything with the ASJA. And get Roman Esco talking about me on Poynter's daily resource section of their web site. Date me publicly and I'll get to live."

"But if these guerrillas do find out you're the one with the tape, and we're together, won't they want to kill me, too?"

"Nah, doesn't work that way. They'll only want me. These guys are very focused. I know they're keeping an eye on me already. If they find out I've got the tape, it'll only be me they'll want to kill. So, how about it? I'm putting my life in your hands."

"No pressure there," I say and ruminate on his plea. "Let me get this straight, we're going to fake-date by going to a few functions and you'll be in the public view enough for the guerrillas not to think you're 'their guy.' To kinda throw off your stench—er—scent. This is what you're telling me."

"Actually, that's all I can tell you. I don't want to endanger your life any more than I have to."

"You've always been so considerate." I cross my arms and stare up at him. "I never thought I'd see you again. Yet, here you are, under the most bizarre of circumstances."

"Would you expect anything less?"

"Not exactly the way I fantasized about how you'd come crawling back to me."

"Seriously? You fantasized about that?"

"Maybe once or twice. But I really need to think about what you're asking. Things have changed around here. I've changed. I've taken charge of my life. Set goals. I put myself first now, deciding what I want, instead of always adapting to what others want."

"That's, um, great, good for you. I'm sure you'll do well in whatever you decide to do." He frowns and shakes his head.

"You don't sound too convinced."

"No, ah, sure, whatever you say. But my life's at stake here and I'm asking for your assistance. I'm a little surprised you actually need to *think* about it!"

"Hey, don't raise your voice to me, pal. You're talking to the New Nina, the post-engagement Nina, *sans* Jeremiah. Give me a minute, arrright?"

"Sure, I'll give you a minute. Take your time, sweetheart. Take all the time you need. In fact, all I've got to give is time. Borrowed time. Why not? Like I say, they already suspect me. The minute they find out I'm their guy, then I'm a dead man walking," he says slowly and lowers his head.

Oddly enough, I try not to relish in this situation, but it's awful tough. Despite the dire circumstances, it actually feels good for Jeremiah to need me. For once, someone else is relying on me and what I have to offer.

Yes, Jeremiah's life is on the line, but so was mine when he broke my heart six months ago. I also know whatever decision I come to will be a crucial one. After all, careers and lives are at stake. But I just started turning my life around. Do I really want to go down this path? I'm honestly not sure. But I do know this; whatever decision I come to tonight about Jeremiah's fate will probably mean nothing but trouble for me.

"Can I join you guys?" I ask Brooke and Unity who are seated in a booth at Bracci's Brick Oven Pizza.

"Hey! Yeah, come sit. The pizza'll be here any minute, good timing," Brooke answers.

I sit beside Unity and enjoy the Italian smells in the air, including oregano, tomato, and garlic. It feels good to be at an old stomping ground. I look to the worn Italian street signs adorning the brick interior walls and then to the small bar off to the side where a few people sit and chat. I let out an exaggerated groan, until the waitress comes by to take my drink order. I get the usual: a D.C.

"So, Brooke filled me in on your little visitor, Jeremiah. She also told me about his 'special' trips overseas. Pretty shocking stuff. I thought I heard it all."

"Well, you officially *have* heard it all."

"So where is he now?"

"Jeremiah? He went out for a few hours."

"For a few hours? You mean he's coming back? What the hell happened after I left?" Brooke asks.

"He asked to crash at the apartment for a week or two. I finally agreed. I hope that's all right," I say to Brooke.

Brooke shrugs. "Hey, it's your call. But I think you're crazy. I would have thrown him out on his ass. I don't know how you ever fell for him."

"I didn't *fall*. I was *pushed*. He just came across so charming."

"I guess. If you want him stay, it's no skin off my nose, I'll be in and out a lot anyway. So, was that all he wanted from you? A place to crash?"

The waitress reappears with my soda. I take advantage of the moment to sip heartily and hold off on my answer.

"Ah, not exactly. I can't get into it, but he's in trouble and asked me to be his escort during all his public appearances. Apparently, his life depends on it."

"You said no, right?" Brooke yelled.

"I did at first." I take another sip. "I told him I needed time to decide. I mean, it could be awkward, especially if I was seeing someone. How would that look to my dates if I have my ex-fiancé hanging around and I'm publicly fake-dating him? Nothing could kill a potential relationship faster."

"Good for you!" Brooke says. "Then what happened?"

"He didn't take me seriously. He couldn't imagine I'd be dating others only six months after our breakup."

"What? Sheesh, you've done a lot more than that," Unity blurts. She realizes what she's said. "Oh, right, Brooke also filled me in about your one-nighter with Dante."

"Speaking of Dante, he's the one you should be obsessing over, not Jeremiah," Brooke asserts.

"Oh, I don't know," Unity chimes in. "Could be karma at work with Jeremiah suddenly back in your life. These things happen for a reason. I mean, you two got together twice and broke up twice. Third time's a charm usually."

"Don't listen to her, Nina!" Brooke slaps a hand on the table. "*Chicka boom*, remember? Look how far you've come!"

"Relax. No one said we're getting back together. I'm doing him a favor. No biggie. He kept begging me, so I finally gave in. He already promised not to interfere in my private life."

The waitress appears and places an enormous cheese pizza on the table.

"We got an extra large," Unity says and pulls at a slice. "Brooke was planning to bring some home for you."

"So, you're really going to do this? And you really think he won't interfere with your new goals, hmm? Well, I'm not buying it," Brooke grouses.

"He got down on his knees and promised he wouldn't be too much trouble."

"'Too much' being the operative word."

As I think about Brooke's comment, something doesn't sit right with me over this whole thing. The last time he got down on his knees, he proposed. Look what happened then. But being exhausted from my all-nighter with Dante, followed by dealing with Jackleen had left me vulnerable, and I caved. What can I say?

Just as I tug at a slice of pizza, my cell phone rings. Caller ID reveals it's my mom.

"Hi, Ma, what's up?"

"I wanted to see how it went with the movie star today. Did she talk about the four husbands who defected on her? Did-did you get an autograph?"

"No, no husband-talk and no autograph. The day went as I expected. Lousy."

Unity taps me on the shoulder. "Nina, does your mom know about Jeremiah's staying with you?" she asks within earshot of the phone.

I quickly cover the mouthpiece and cast her a warning glare. I whisper, "No, and I want to keep it that way."

"What? Jeremiah's back?" I hear Mom say into the ear pierce. I roll my eyes. "When? Where? Are you two back together? What's going on?"

I lean over and pinch Unity.

She yelps and pinches me back. "How was I supposed to know you didn't want her to know?" she snaps at me.

"What?" Mom says again. "Why didn't you want me to know? Nina, what's going on?" she cries.

"It's a long story," I say into the phone.

"Jeremiah's back! That's wonderful news! I don't know why you ever let him go."

"I didn't let him go! He chewed off his own arm and ran!"

Mom scoffs. "So what's he doing here?"

"He's just crashing with me for a while. Nothing else. Did you need something?" I ask, exasperated.

"I need your opinion. I'm making a new hat for the Divas Club. I'm taking a big straw hat and layering it with silk rose petals. Should I use felt red ribbon or satin as a border?"

"Oh, um, I'd say felt ribbon."

"Satin it is."

"Okay, Ma, gotta go."

At that, I hang up and dig into the pizza. The rest of dinner goes smoothly. After the pizza-night-out with my co-whores, I head home. Brooke and Unity decide to grab cocktails (cocks and tails, as they refer to it) down at the Wharf.

I enter my apartmentette, and note Jeremiah isn't back yet.

He said something about meeting up with a colleague and swapping information about the controversial footage he's working on. He's got a key obviously, so I'm not worried. I open up the pullout sofa, and leave out sheets, blanket, and pillow for when he comes in. He'll have to make his own bed. I have to draw the line somewhere.

I stare down at the pile of linens. How weird, to be leaving out this stuff for a man I'd been so intimate with, who'll now sleep on the sofa. And here he is, back in my life at the strangest of all possible times. It still smarts, I must admit, to see how my life has turned out. I never realized until I lost Jeremiah twice that when it comes to heartache, I'm a bleeder.

Right now, I should be gearing up for a church wedding. Instead, I've had to pull myself up by the Prada boot straps, and pick up the pieces of my life. So, how did my plan suddenly include saving the hide of the very man who crushed my heart?

Too tired to think anymore, too tired to even care, I drag my sorry carcass into my bedroom. I change into something satiny and cool and slide under the covers. Normally, a big T-shirt would suffice, but something has awakened inside me, something womanly and sexy, and it's all thanks to Dante. With my thoughts giddily on him, I settle in comfortably against my pillow for a quiet night's sleep.

The sleep lasts several hours, until a rapping on my bedroom glass slider door wakes me. I look at the glowing green numbers on my alarm clock. Three o'clock in the morning. I whine. I have to get sleep if I'm to deal with Jackleen's mall appearance tomorrow.

The rapping starts again. But it sounds more like rocks being tossed against the glass slider in my room. I hobble out of bed, push aside the window sheers, and look out to the balcony.

I see nothing. I open the glass slider, step out to the balcony and from my second-story perch, I look around and then down.

I see him in the lamplight.

"Dante? What are you doing here?" Despite my sleepiness, I can't help but smile.

"I'm coming up."

"Sure," I say, not that he *asked*.

He starts climbing the pipe running up alongside the building and jumps to the fire escape, then to my balcony. He climbs over the wrought-iron railing, wraps his arms around my waist, and roughly hauls me into his embrace. Good thing, too, or I would have done the rough-hauling. We suck face like two hormone-swollen teenagers.

Good-golly, let me tell you about his mouth—his beautiful, beautiful mouth. Just warm and sweet and moist enough to make me want to kiss him all night. The heat of his mouth alone makes my tummy dip and my spine tingle. And I can't kiss him back hard enough. He must be reading my unchecked need, because he grips me harder and holds fast. As for me, I'm holding on for dear life, too. He's become my lifeline to a promise of sensual bliss. After endless minutes, he stops kissing my mouth, which is already puffed from kissing him so hard, and runs his lips along my neck, sending skitterish tingles down through my spine.

My nipples jut forward and my chest swells in response to his touch. I arch into him with a female heat crying out to be fulfilled. He presses his rock-hard torso against mine. Let me tell you, his torso ain't the only thing that's rock hard on his body. I want to rip his clothes off, but first, I need to catch my breath, both physically and mentally.

"You are just full of surprises," I say.

"I told you I'd deal with you later." He drops to his knees

and lifts my short satiny nightie waist-high. And hell, I let him. He kisses my belly, then runs his tongue just along my lower abdomen, along that sensitive area where my bikini panties meet my skin, leaving a tickly line of moist warmth. His stroking lips make me shudder and quake.

"Ahhh . . ." I have to stop to moan and it's all his fault. "What took you so long to deal with me, hmm?"

"Had some people to see."

"People? As in girlfriends?"

"No girlfriends," he rasps, which makes me smile in selfish delight. "But I wanted to see you before I disappear for a while. I just had to see you." He rises to his full height and stares down at me. The nearby streetlight catches his irises just so, making his mischievous eyes flare and dance. "I hope you don't mind that I came here."

"No. I don't mind at all. Where you headed?"

"Thataway." He looks out into the distance, but never once takes his hands off me. They keep stroking every inch of me. From the breasts to the buttocks. Of course, I'm doing the same thing. I crave to know every inch of this man. "I'm just taking off for a while on the bike," he tells me, and returns his hot gaze onto me. I know it's hot cuz I'm melting before him.

"You're taking off? Just like that?"

"Just like that."

He kisses me again and a white hot bolt of horniness zips through my insides. I can't help but groan. God, I missed him. Which is not good. Not good at all. He's only a boy-toy and I have to remind myself of that. And I will. Soon. Tomorrow, perhaps.

"I have to tell you, I'm psyched to see you, even if it is in the middle of the night. But you know, not everyone can take off on a whim. Some of us have responsibilities. I have to deal with Jackleen again tomorrow and I'll need sleep if I'm to put up with that woman," I scold. *Yeah, right*, as if I'm actually annoyed.

"This won't take much longer," he says and kisses along my shoulder. He eases me into the plastic lawn chair, pulls up my short satin nightie again, and lays his palms on my legs. He kneels down, tugs off my panties, and dips his head low between my thighs.

EIGHT

I'm here to give oral support.

"You have no idea what you do to me. You're crazy, you know that? Ahhh!" I choke on my words while his tongue plays me, sending me into orbit, until I shudder from instant orgasm.

How the hell did he do that? Never in my life has anyone worked magic on me like that before. If I wasn't totally addicted to Dante (and his tongue) before, I'm a full-blown addict now.

Gasping, I bring his head up and kiss him, his taste and mine mingle on his lips.

"What did I do to deserve such a treat?" I ask between breaths.

He chuckles. "You opened your . . . glass slider."

Somewhere deep in the apartmentette, I hear the door in the living room open, and then close. My stomach drops. What if it's Jeremiah?

"Someone's come home . . . um, my roommate, Brooke, I mean."

At least I pray it's Brooke. I really don't need Jeremiah sauntering into the bedroom, acting like he owns the place the way he did this afternoon. I want to stick to my guns about keeping my private affairs from him.

"It's okay," Dante whispers, "I just wanted to stop by to say hi."

"Hi," I murmur absently, dreamily.

"And to be sure you didn't forget me."

"Never."

"Have fun tomorrow with your movie star."

"I'll try. And thanks for helping me out today with her. I hope your bike ride went okay."

"She was harmless. Even kept her hands to herself most of the trip."

"Most of the trip?"

He cocks an eyebrow, then licks my thigh.

"I'll see you 'round."

Dante breaks from me, hops the railing, and shimmies down the drainpipe. After he mounts his bike and takes off out of the parking lot, I stand, but then collapse on the balcony. Following a curse, I rub my thigh muscles, which have turned to mush because of the effect of Dante's tongue.

Not that I'm complaining, good-golly no. And I shouldn't complain. I'm the one who wanted to make the dramatic transformation of my life all at once in the span of a day. Now, I need to learn to live with its delicious consequences.

I get on all fours and grope in the dark for my panties, until my abdomen starts cramping. Apparently, I've used lovemuscles lately in ways I haven't in quite some time. I work through the wonderful pain, and continue crawling on all fours looking for the lace underwear. My fingers finally land on them.

While on the floor, I stab my feet through the openings and tug them on before someone finds me bottomless and sprawled out on the balcony floor.

After a deep breath, I will my wobbly legs to support my weight, and force myself to stand. I stagger through the glass slider, cross the bedroom, and stub my toe on the footboard post. I let out a squeal and limp down the hall to see who came home.

"Brooke?" I ask down the hall. "Is that you?"

"Nah, it's me."

"Jeremiah?"

I enter the living room and sit on the sofa to inspect my throbbing toe. I look up at Jeremiah, who just stands there, looking tired. Lost.

"What are you still doing up?" he asks. "I thought you'd be dead to the world."

"I was, but, ah, something woke me from my sleep."

"I hope it wasn't me."

"You?" I smirk. "Let's just say I woke before you came in."

Jeremiah inspects my face closer. "Why are you that color?"

I bring my fingers to my cheek. "What? What color am I?"

"You're all . . . pink. Flushed. Like you've been out for a jog . . . and your mouth. It's all red."

"Oh, I got hot, really, really hot, under my covers. And, and then I stubbed my toe. Is it hot in here now?"

He gives a look of confusion. "No, not hot at all. You sure you're all right? Are you sick?"

"I'm fine. Just fine."

Translation:

I'm better than all right. I've just had the most intense orgasm of my life—hell I'm still shuddering—and I intend to wallow in the memory as long as humanly possible.

"So, um," I begin, "how did tonight go?"

"Tonight? What about tonight? I mean, yeah, the meeting went fine. Sorry, I'm still a little preoccupied."

"I guess I would be too if killers were after me and some videotape of mine."

We both remain in awkward silence, not discussing what we should be discussing. Things like, what the hell happened between us. Or why he's so obsessed with women from Thailand. Or where exactly did I go wrong? But I'm not really up for exploring those kinds of questions tonight. I'm still adjusting to Jeremiah's simply being here.

"I guess I'd better head back to bed. Got a big day tomorrow. I've been assisting Jackleen Liquori with her promotional appearances in the area. She's signing autographs at the mall."

"The movie star? Isn't she in prison?"

"She was. But she's out. It's old news."

"Wow. I guess you really are moving up in the world."

"Yep. I guess I am."

And I'm doing it without you.

Again with the awkward silence.

"Aw, Nina, I'm sorry things didn't work out. I don't know how things got so screwed up between us. I'm a selfish bastard." He slumps down on the sofa next to me. He rests his head in the palms of his hands. "I messed up your life. And now I messed up mine."

I rub him on the back. "Oh, hey, everything happens for a reason," I regurgitate Unity's karma-mumbo-jumbo. "Honestly, I'd rather be broken up *before* the wedding than after. It would have been much worse if we'd tied the knot. Talk about messy."

He lifts his head out of his hands and rests it against my shoulder.

"You're right. But it's been rough not having you around, especially when I'm on the road. I got so used to you being there whenever I picked up the phone to call you, hearing your voice, supporting my work. I've missed you, Nina."

I stiffen. Is he actually saying this to me? I sit there and rub his back some more, but sleep slowly consumes me. I realize I don't feel awake enough to have an all-night hash-out session over what might have been. I need to nip this in the bud.

"It's been a really long day for the both of us. What do you say we get some shut-eye before one of us says something in a sleep-deprived vulnerable moment? I'll see you in the morning."

I stop rubbing his back and ease his weight off me. I go to leave, but turn back one last time. He's watching me abandon him, and he looks miserable.

Good.

I trudge off to my bedroom and fall into bed, not bothering with the blankets. I forget about Jeremiah and allow myself to be lulled into sleep with lustful memories of the wet and wonderful things Dante did to me tonight.

As I drift in and out of consciousness, about to doze off again, the phone rings.

"What now?" I whine. "This better be Brooke telling me to lock up with the dead bolt 'cause she's not coming home," I grumble at the phone. "Hello?"

"Hello, dahling, it's me!"

"Jackleen? What are you doing? I gave you my home number only in case of an emergency."

"It is an emergency, dear. And I need your help."

"What could you possibly need from me at three in the morning that can't wait until a more reasonable hour?"

"I need you to get me out of jail, dear."

• • •

"Thank you for coming to my aid. You're a good girl, Nina," Jackleen says as we walk out the doors of the police station.

I don't say anything. Instead I stomp down the cement stairs of the police station. I'd be fuming even worse, but I've only gotten four hours of sleep and need to conserve my energy for the rest of the weekend. I really didn't expect to have to throw on an old pair of jeans and sweatshirt in the middle of the night to go save my client. Instead of chewing her out, I keep on saying nothing.

"Nina, I'm speaking to you. When someone thanks you for something, a gracious response is usually expected."

She's talking behind me, and is trying to keep up. I can hear her heels clicking against the stairs with every step.

"You want a response?" I say and spin around. I climb back up the stairs and face her head on. "I'll give you a response. What were you thinking? Do you want to go back to prison? Because that's where you're going to end up. You're still on probation."

"Am I in prison right now? Do you *see* me in prison?"

"No, because I got you out of jail. You must have done some sweet-talkin' in there for the cops not to extradite you back to California."

"But I *wasn't arrested*," Jackleen says in her own defense, her palms open wide, her body language indicating she believes in her innocence. "I was merely *detained*."

"Oh, that's right. They hauled you in there until you cooled off."

"Exactly!" Jackleen says. "It wasn't my fault when the officer pulled me over. I was simply driving along—"

"Without your license!"

"Yes, I left it in my other purse, which didn't go with this outfit." She points down at her long black silk dress with gold beading and embroidery swirled all over it. "Surely, they should understand these things happen."

"No, they shouldn't understand, not based on what they told me in there. They thought you were drunk-driving."

"That's ridiculous, I hadn't gotten that far yet. Why, I was barely able to juggle my flask with one hand on the wheel and the other making a call on my cell phone."

"Making a call? Carrying a flask? They actually caught you with the flask?"

"Goodness, no. It fell under the seat before I even had the chance to open it."

"So what were you doing weaving like a maniac all over the road?"

"Dahling, in L.A., we call it *driving*."

"Here on the East Coast, we call it attempted vehicular homicide and resisting arrest!"

The police officer had filled me in on the evening's events. Jackleen was driving recklessly in her Mercedes convertible, shouting uncontrollably into her cell phone when a patrol car spotted her swerving all over the road. Assuming she'd been drinking, he followed her and pulled her over.

Even after he approached her vehicle, she continued her ranting on her phone. When he told her to end the call and produce her driver's license, she held up her open palm and told him to basically "talk to the hand."

"Look, Jackleen, all you had to do was end your phone call. But instead, you yelled at the officer to pipe down, that you couldn't hear, and continued screaming into the phone."

"What did you expect me to do? I was on the phone with

my *agent*." She brushes past me, and floats down the stairs of the precinct. "That bastard-agent of mine is trying to squeeze more money out of me. Oh, the cruel things he said to me . . . he was completely out of line. He used to tell me he loved me. Now, I'm nothing but a commission check to him. Even if he is one of my ex-husbands, I simply couldn't have him speaking to me so negatively. What would you have done if you were in my shoes?"

"I don't know. I don't *have* an agent who happens to also be an ex-husband."

"Believe me, if your career was on the line, you, too, would be confronting the person making life difficult for you."

"My career *is* on the line!" I march after her. "And you're the one making life difficult for me!" I say. "I've known you less than twenty-four hours and already my budding career's in the toilet! I'm hosed!"

"Dear, what are you saying?"

"Forget it." I sigh and plop my butt down on the bottom step.

Two police officers appear on the street and pass us on the steps, until they stop to gush over Jackleen, telling her how much they love her. She signs autographs for these sweet-baby-dolls and flirts the entire time. When they're gone, she daintily bends to sit beside me on the step. She pulls a silver cigarette case out of her little black purse, selects a cancer stick, lights up, and takes a good long puff. She holds the case out in front of me.

I'm tempted, but I don't smoke. I shake my head no. She tucks the case back into her purse.

"Now, Nina, what's this all about? Talk to me, dahling. It's the least I can do after you helped me out tonight." The swirling plume of smoke snakes its way around her like a feather boa. I'm reminded of her older movies.

"It's my problem, Jackleen, not yours."

"I'm making it my problem, too. Now talk to me or I'll get on my phone and start screaming again, right here, in front of the big house."

I'm scared shitless she'll do it, too.

"Okay, okay. Please no more scenes tonight. Do you realize how lucky you are that they didn't press charges?"

"Even if they tried, not much would come of it. My bastard-agent told me I've been assigned a new parole officer. Says he's a real pushover, a big fan."

"But you can't afford more trouble. What about your career? Your big comeback movie, *Cacambo!*"

"Trouble only helps with ratings," she says with a large, glistening, lipsticky grin. She takes another drag.

"I just wish you'd take this a little more seriously. Your run-in with the law tonight goes beyond ratings. Your freedom's at stake, not to mention my job promotion."

"A job promotion? So that's what's upsetting you? Oh, baby-doll, no job is worth getting so upset over."

"This one is. It's very important. Since my fiancé broke our engagement, I'm trying to move on with my life. That includes handling your PR, or else I don't get promoted. I'll end up a total loser in all departments: life, love, and work."

"Oh, sweetheart, never put all your eggs in one basket. Just because you might fail in one area, doesn't mean you fail everything. Especially love. I've been married for sixteen years, granted not continuously, or to the same man, but I know what I'm talking about. Never give up on love. It's what we humans live for. I'm living to meet husband number five any day now."

She pats my hand in an endearing gesture before taking a final puff of her cigarette. I can't help but smile.

Wow. I'm actually sitting here sharing my problems with a movie star. Granted, she's got a demented view of life, but she's trying. She seems almost, well, normal and nice right now. Still, it's hard to take advice from a woman who takes wedding vows as often as she takes a breath.

"I'd better get you back to your hotel. You can't be caught driving your car without a license again. We'll have someone get the convertible tomorrow. And we certainly don't want to be cited for loitering. Come on."

As we quietly make our way to my Honda, I realize that Jackleen Liquori might not be so bad after all. Although she might represent everything I wouldn't want for myself, including needing a constant avalanche of love to feel validated, I'm still glad to see a softer side to her. If given the chance, perhaps Jackleen Liquori truly can be a sensitive, kind, and caring human being.

NINE

This job is giving me labor pains.

"Jackleen Liquori is the biggest, meanest, nastiest bitch-monster I've ever met in my entire life!"

I'm screaming this as I storm into Ray's office Monday morning, and bellow to my boss exactly what I've been going through with the woman.

Sure, on Saturday night, Jackleen was a pussycat, but by Sunday afternoon, she was back to her old lunatic ways. The mall appearance, which began on a positive note, turned out a disaster. Fans showed up. Lines were formed. Autographs got signed. Since Jackleen Liquori adores being adored, she was in her glory.

This lasted all of ten minutes, until some woman who'd found religion exchanged words with the actress. The lady showed up to lecture Jackleen on the evils of her many non-Christian movie roles, especially this new movie, *Cacambo!*, where she plays a witch. Jackleen tossed back a vile response. That's when the pious woman leaped the table to get to the actress's throat.

I rant and rave and relay all this information to Ray who sits at his desk, patiently listening to my tirade.

"Oh, and it gets worse." I cement my hands on my hips for emphasis. "After security broke up the raucous, Jackleen went all Jekyll-and-Hyde on me and berated me in front of hundreds of people. She starts screaming, throws a freakin' temper tantrum, blaming me for the lousy security, and then she throws a glass of water in my face!"

I then fill him in on her other antics, including calling me in the middle of the night to haul her out of jail. And the scene she created on the set and going off on the deep end in traffic.

"And if she calls me sweet-baby-doll-darling one more time, I swear, I'll tear her hair out! Augh!"

I end my tirade and wait for a response while I catch my breath. Being my mentor, Ray is good for calming me down in work-related snafus. He places his elbows on the desk, steeples his fingers, and rests his chin on the tips. He's deep in thought as he regards my horrific story.

"Have you found a date for the Spring Fling? You know, it's just a few weeks away," he says.

My jaw drops. Is that all he has to say to me? My dignity and reputation and job are all on the line and he asks me about having a date?

"Ray! Didn't you hear me?" I flail my arms, leap up and down, and mouth off again about "that horrid woman," and "I'm not doing this anymore," and "I want to die."

After I wear myself out completely from my verbal diatribe, I collapse into the guest chair. I take a deep breath and blow out for the count of three. I look at Ray, who's still waiting for an answer. I have no choice but to acquiesce.

"No. I haven't found a date—and how'd you know I lied in the meeting about having a date for the gala?"

"Because you would have said who it was by now."

"True."

Granted, this isn't the sort of conversation that would usually occur between two employees in a business setting, but I've known Ray for a few years now, so it's no wonder a comfy relationship has formed.

I'm still not going to tell him about Dante, though. No, I'm keeping my hot one-night stand to myself. But then, Jeremiah quickly comes to mind. I decide not to mention Jeremiah to Ray, either, since he's hiding out and fearing for his life. And I don't need the lecture.

"I don't know who I'll bring to the Spring Fling."

After I hear my own sobering proclamation, I hoist myself up from the guest chair and make my way out the door.

"Ah, Nina," Ray says before I beat a hasty retreat, "John Avalon wants to put together the final guest list this week for the Spring Fling. Security reasons. You'd better come up with a name."

"Will do," I say with a nod. "And I'll get the updated schedule and status report on Jackleen to you by this afternoon. Before her last temper tantrum, she and I hashed out some ideas for her new line of cruisewear and wigs she wants to peddle to the shopping channels."

"Good, because Chad's already got his report in to Harry,

who approved it before handing over the findings to John. Wouldn't want you to lag behind."

Chad's already got in his report? Son of a bitch. Why am I not surprised?

"But it's only eight-thirty on a Monday morning. No one is even in the office until nine-ish. We have until five o'clock tonight to turn it in."

"I'm just saying, around here, it's the early bird who usually gets the promotion."

"I hear you loud and clear."

I drag my exhausted ass down the hall toward my bay. As I'm walking, Chad is approaching me. He's coming from my office area. I paste on a bright smile as we come face-to-face.

He smiles back at me; it looks sincere, except for his exceptionally long incisors. It's a trademark feature of most of the Gorham family members. The political cartoonists in the Boston newspapers always have a field day when drawing any Gorham.

"Hey, I was just leaving a call report and production schedule with the account executives down this neck of the woods," he says.

"How'd your weekend go with the golf guy?" I ask.

"He's one party animal, for sure. But I can hold my own. And you?"

"Jackleen's a handful. Never a dull moment!" My tone drips with sicky-sweet cheer.

Chad slips his hands into his pants pockets and cocks his head to one side as he stares at me. "Nina, I have to ask. Aren't you happy with your current position? I've never heard you complain. What went wrong?"

"Nothing went wrong. I like what I do."

"Then why the sudden interest in hopping from job to job?"

"I hardly think going for one promotion is hopping."

"It looks like hopping. You're so good at what you do, why mess with a good thing? This new job means longer hours. Lots of weekend work. Travel."

"I guess I'm ready for something more gratifying."

I smile to myself at using his own so-called rationale for wanting this new job. How could he refute my explanation when it's the same one he's using?

"I just don't want to see you hurt when—" He pauses. "I mean, if you don't get the job."

"I wish the same for you, Chad. No hard feelings, either, no matter who gets it. You have to remember, I've been in account services for a few years now. I've got a bit of experience behind me. But you've got the connections. It's a toss-up who they'll choose. I'd say they've got a tough decision come the end of the month."

"Right. Tough."

For the first time, Chad actually looks worried that he might have real competition. He flashes me those incisors again in what looks to be a nervous smile.

"Hey, maybe we should do lunch. Swap notes, for the good of the company."

Translation:

Oh, hey, why don't you give me all your information now and spare us both the time and hassle of expending unnecessary energy. That way, I can pummel you now and connive my way into the job, leaving you in the dust. Then we can call it a day. Maybe you should even sleep with me, too.

"Rigggght. Lunch."

There's a vague response if I ever said one.

Once we finish the pleasantries and not-so-pleasantries, I return to my bay and turn on my computer. A glaringly bright blue screen appears with neon green letters. The message says something about a virus detection and attempting recovery now. But even the message window seems to be hung up. After ten minutes of this, I call Network Security. I've got to get cracking on the report.

"It's hosed," Ned, the network security guy, states after an hour of attempting to resuscitate my hard drive.

"So, there's no hope?" I squeak.

"I'm sorry. I did all I could."

He shakes his head solemnly as he rises from my office chair. He takes computer crashes to heart. And now that it's happened to my computer, so do I.

"But it can't be hosed. Surely, there's more you can do. Some antidote, like an antivirus software to bring it back. You have to bring it back."

"Sorry. Nothing more can be done."

After he sighs, he notes the time on his watch, pulls a pen from his pocket pal, and starts to write up a report like a coroner who just declared the time of a victim's death.

"Wait! I'm on the network; you back up the company computers every night, so it's okay, right? You can just call up my files and reinstate them in a new computer, right?"

"Yes and no. Look, it'll take a while to find out where this virus started from, but it wiped out everything from last week. We back up and replace only what you have on your computer to that point in time that day. The virus cleaned out all your recent directories before our backup."

"But you're my network security. 'Network' as in 'net.' You're my net, Ned. Don't you have a backup to the backup? Can't you look for those hidden 'cluster' files you're always talking about, whatever those are?"

"Look, I tried to get to any residual ghost files buried in your hard drive, but they were all corrupted. This is one nasty little bug you picked up. What did you download off the Internet anyway? You know the policy against downloads and this is why."

"I downloaded nothing."

"Man, Nina, you can get fired for this sort of thing if it ever compromises network security. What were you thinking?"

"I told you, honest, I didn't download anything."

"You had to, with this kind of damage; I'm going to have to fill out another report form. I'm sorry, Nina, the evidence speaks for itself."

"What evidence?" I shriek.

Ned rolls his eyes and points to the inert computer. "Any more dead and the monitor would have a flat line running across its screen."

"So you assume that I did something wrong? I'm telling you the truth! We're buds, you know, like 'pocket-pals.' I wouldn't lie to you."

"I'm just doing my job, Nina. I'm sorry."

"I can't believe this is happening. My entire itinerary for Jackleen Liquori was on that machine and now it's gone. My notes and ideas for her lines of clothing and wigs. All wiped out, which means endless retyping, eating up precious time that I don't have. And now I'm getting accused of doing something I didn't do and might get fired for it. I'm supposed to be going for a promotion, dammit."

"Going for the special projects job, huh? Yeah, I heard that. You'll be great, just don't trash any more equipment. This isn't the first time you've wrecked equipment around here. I swear you're cursed. But good luck anyway."

He smiles a genuine good-luck smile, revealing his bottom-only braces, then crams his pen into his pocket pal before waddling off with his damn report wedged under his arm.

"Good luck, my lily-white ass," I grumble. "This is just another reason why I should be given a laptop."

"You had a laptop. You broke that, too. I'll get any old files of yours to you by tomorrow," he calls from down the hall.

"Tomorrow?" I ask back. "Why so long?"

"These things take time."

"And what about my *recent* files?" I whine at him.

"Didn't you make printouts of your recent work?"

"We're supposed to be a paperless society by now! Anyway, yeah, I've got printouts, at least most of the stuff, but now I have to retype everything in. In *what*, I don't know, since my computer is dead but I'll find one around here somewhere. And I've got a deadline today. Plus I gotta type in all my mounds of notes from meetings with my client from over the weekend. I have to redo graphics, spreadsheets, and schedules. What a mess." I let out a groan of defeat.

"Geez, I'm sorry, Nina," he calls from down the hall.

"Yeah, me, too. Very sorry."

The reality of my plight sinks in; not only is my computer hosed, but so am I.

How do people do it?
For the rest of the day, the question plays over and over

in my mind. How do people balance their lives? Hell, I can barely balance a checkbook. And when I do try to make strides toward my destination to fulfillment, why does disaster have to strike?

After hours of piecing together bits of scrap information tossed into a manila folder labeled, "Liquori, Jackleen," I manage to pull together a small report. Of course all this occurs between dousing fires in other clients' accounts, including one print ad sent into a law publication with the word *penis* instead of *penal* in the body copy.

Occasionally, though, I get to drift into the sweet memory of Dante's tongue, which usually gets blasted into oblivion with thoughts on what to do with Jeremiah. Not to mention my ringing phone, or getting paged, or fetching costs for a particular four-color print ad about sanitary napkins. I'm not sure why today has become the day from hell when I have to recreate an entire preliminary marketing report on Jackleen's potential advertising strategy, as well as her promotional schedule.

"Five o'clock on the nose," I announce proudly, and a little out of breath, as I stand before John Avalon in his office and present him with my report. "Ray's already approved it."

The agency owner glimpses down at the thin report with a simply typed title on the front. I watch his eyes dart to Chad's report with the full-color cover of the golf pro swinging a club on a golf course at sunset. He grimaces back at my flimsy-looking handiwork.

"I had more graphics, but my computer crashed this morning. I lost all my data from last week and had to redo it. The report may not look pretty, but the content is substantial."

He grumbles an "um-hum" while he thumbs through the meager number of pages. "I understand you downloaded a virus from the Internet and trashed your entire system."

"You've got to believe me, I didn't download a thing. I wasn't even on the Internet before I left work on Friday."

He looks up at me and squints. Not an angry narrowing of the eyes in disbelief, more like a squint of confusion. "And you also didn't play four games of solitaire late in the afternoon on Friday, either?"

I swallow a wad of guilt and couldn't stop the creeping heat spreading up my neck and into my cheeks. "Oh, right. Yeah, um, solitaire. I did play a little while I waited for something to come out of the printer."

I lower my head in shame. Ashamed of what, I couldn't be sure. A game of solitaire at four o'clock on a Friday didn't seem as detrimental as breaking company rules by harboring a deadly computer virus. But I didn't harbor anything. I'm sure of it.

"Network Security records show you playing a few computer games, then signing onto the Internet. Ned's attempting to find another explanation for this, but it's all in their mainframe. Hardware doesn't lie about stats, Nina."

"I realize that, but I have to stick to my guns here. I don't have an answer. I can only tell you I'm still sleep-deprived and have bent over backwards to baby-sit a brat of a star to get a fabulous report to you only to have it disappear into thin air!"

Okay, yeah, the tone and the 'tude could be a little less sarcastic when speaking to the owner of Avalon Advertising, the one man responsible for my paychecks and entire future, but honestly, it's been a long day. After saying what I said, I step back and wait for the reaming to begin.

He rolls my report into a tube, then grips it like a mini baseball bat, as if gearing up to swat a ball (or beat me on the head, I'm not sure). With every squeeze of the rolled up report in his palm, I feel my diaphragm constrict, squeezing the life out of me. I did it to myself; I didn't have to bark at the man.

"Chad got his work into me this morning."

"Chad didn't have his computer keel," I answer, shocked to hell I haven't gotten the boot yet. "Five o'clock is five o'clock. I know we aim to exceed expectations around here, not just meet them. I made every attempt."

I left it at that.

So did he.

Without further *fondue*, he glances in the direction of his door and returns to his paperwork on the desk. I read his disregard as a cue to get the hell out of there and slink out the door. Once in the foyer shared by the Trinity offices, I slump my shoulders and take a heavy breath. When I look over at John's secretary, Marilyn, she smiles sympathetically before returning to her reading.

I start to drag myself toward my desk when Ray comes strolling down the hall.

"You saw John? Did you give him your report?"

"Uh-huh."

"What happened in there? You look a wreck."

"I mouthed off at him that I didn't go on the Internet last Friday."

"And?"

"He dismissed me out of the office."

"Ah, the ceremonial out-of-the-office dismissal. I've had my share over the years. Don't worry about it. It means he considers you innocent until proven guilty."

"But I already look guilty big-time."

"You're not guilty, right?"

"Absolutely not."

But as I head back to my bay I'm not so sure about my innocence. Sure, I may not be guilty of giving my computer a viral infection, but I'm sure guilty of a whole slew of other offenses. Guilty of always needing immediate gratification. Guilty of trying to jump-start my way to happiness. Guilty of attempting to get to all my destinations faster by taking two steps at a time. Guilty of thinking I could simply pole-vault up the corporate ladder and force all the pieces of the puzzle together on my own terms.

I'm also guilty of the worst possible offense: believing that hard work would undeniably result in a big payoff.

Yeah, just the way good little girls always think.

Okay, so maybe I slipped into my old mode of thinking. Everyone's entitled to a mistake. I have to remember I'm playing with the big boys now. And dealing in real-world dilemmas that only I can resolve. As it stands, the weight of my world has heaved itself onto my shoulders, leaving me lopsided and hunched Quasi Moto style. Drastic times call for drastic measures. Getting my life in order takes hard work—harder than anything I've ever attempted before, but I have to remain determined to accomplish my goals. The newfangled go-getter-girl in me will see to that.

So why is a little teeny good-girl part of me trying to claw her way out and cry the words, "Way too hard, people!" to anyone who will listen? She wants to whine out a confession that the old way of thinking, which includes conserving a girl's energy for the big wedding day and ultimately developing birthing hips, is still an eensy-weensy bit appealing. If things get any harder, if I'm not careful and she keeps clawing to be free, I just might let her out.

TEN

Lead me not into temptation, I can find it myself.

∝

The ol' feet are screaming to be freed from the clutches of Prada. I appease them the moment I walk through the apartmentette door at six o'clock that night. I pull at the strappies and kick them across the room. My flying blue blazer comes next. This is followed by a wad of balled up sensible-blue hosiery, which is caught midair by Jeremiah who just stepped out of the kitchenette. He holds the wad of hosiery like a football and assumes a player's stance.

"And it's blocked by an amazing defense, who makes it to the goal line! The crowd goes wild. Ahhhh!" Jeremiah starts doing his own rendition of a white-boy touchdown dance on his toes.

It's the first lighthearted moment I encounter all day. I can't help but laugh. Gawd, he's such a goof. I almost forgot how much I missed him.

"Gimme a J! Goooo Jeremiah!" I say and clap my hands like

a stiff cheerleader. But I don't get much farther. Some seafoody aroma wafts toward me and seduces my olfactories. I grow weak in the knees.

"You didn't!" I cry out in ecstasy.

"I did."

"Pan-seared and everything?"

"*Haute-couture* cooking at its finest. Nothing but the best for my girl."

I don't know what he's trying to pull, but I don't care. Pan-seared salmon, here I come. In a food trance that takes me back to happier times with Jeremiah, I glide past the little dinette table set with candles and place settings for two and drift into the kitchen. I admire the pan full of sizzling, golden, flaky fish that I haven't had since Jeremiah walked out of my life.

Don't think. Just enjoy.

He called me "his girl." He pan-seared my favorite food. He danced his goofy white-boy-can't-dance dance. What the hell is going on?

Thinking again. Supposed to enjoy.

I still want to ask what he's doing and why, but he holds an enormous raw oyster in its shell up to my mouth and is tipping it toward me. Before I can say anything, my lips reflexively part and the oyster slides down my throat. I barely have time to appreciate the rare aphrodisiacal treat when he slips a large wineglass of white Zinfandel into my hand.

I'm standing non-shoed, non-blazered, and non-hosieried in my kitchenette, all-pampered and doted-on by the man I was supposed to marry. The smell of salmon, the slippery sensation of the oyster, and the sipping of spirits send me into an indulgent tailspin and I forget all my troubles *du jour*.

Still, I have to take a minute to register every surrounding detail. On the stove sit pans of cooked white rice and green beans; on the counter, a plate of chocolate-dipped strawberries obviously meant for later.

I don't want to analyze dinner. I don't want to read into it at all. I know Jeremiah well enough to understand when he gets a wild hair across his glutes, there's just no stopping him. If he wants to create a tantalizing dish, then who am I to stop him?

But I have to ask one little question.

"Why?"

Jeremiah fluffs the rice with a fork before turning to me and smiling. "There's got to be a reason?"

"For you, no. For the rest of us, yes. So, I'm asking . . . why?"

He drops the fork and regards me seriously. He holds my hand and kisses it, before releasing it.

"I want to thank you for all you've done for me, for taking me in. Most women would have put out a restraining order if they found their ex-fiancé squatting in their apartment with killers after him. But not you. That's why I've always loved you. You've always been special in the craziest of ways."

"Jeremiah, please," I begin to say, but it's hard to stop his niceties when a longing the strength of a boa constrictor keeps squeezing my heart. "Why are you saying all this to me? We broke up."

"Yeah, we broke up. But it was your ultimatum that ended our engagement. Not a lack of love."

"Wasn't there a lack of love? At least there wasn't enough of it to overcome our one obstacle."

He winces at my words, but they have to be said.

So there you have it. We're finally discussing what we should have discussed so many months ago if we are to have any emotional closure. And at least we're having our long overdue discussion at a reasonable hour in the day, too.

"I understand what you're saying," he admits. "I know I'm obsessed with Thailand; I prefer to call it a weakness of character. It's something I been working on." He turns to the pans and transfers the food to plates.

"You been working on it?" I need clarification.

"I haven't been to Thailand since our breakup. How's that for irony?"

He knows how I feel about irony in my life; I hate it. It stalks me like a wolf. So I'm sure Jeremiah knows I'm appreciating the irony infiltrating his life instead of mine for a change. Murphy and his Law can go to hell for all I care.

He brings the plates of food to the table and we sit down. "Anyway, think of dinner as a thank-you for helping me and agreeing to publicly save my life."

We raise our wineglasses in a toast to our new agreement and heartily dig in. I decide not to ruin dinner by digging for more information about Thailand. What's to dig for? He's admitted his Asian sex-obsession and hasn't gone there since. I'm more than happy to leave the topic alone.

So, we talk about everything else. We talk about where he's been the past several months, including Utah. We talk about my recent decision to climb the corporate ladder and become a more self-evolved human being. Of course, I leave out the humiliating details leading up to my life-altering decisions like the shopping spree for sperm, the wedding gown incident, and the recent quest for heart-stopping sex.

I also fill him in on my mother missing him terribly and any recent antics pulled by my co-whores, Unity and Brooke.

"Oh, yeah, Brooke left you a note on the fridge," Jeremiah informs me as we head toward the conclusion of our meal. "She's got to deliver some sex-gift-baskets and then she's stopping by Unity's place to sit and watch her new yoga video. She'll be home around eleven."

"She warned me she wouldn't be around much lately."

"I hope it's not because I'm intruding."

"I don't think so. She's okay enough with you here. Springtime is really busy for her with her catering job and gift baskets," I say and let the final bite of salmon melt into the back of my throat. I wash it down with another swallow of wine.

"I guess that leaves you and me tonight," he says.

"I guess."

"What are you doing tomorrow?"

"Tomorrow? Um, I'm taking Jackleen Liquori into Boston. She's the guest speaker at the Gardner Museum to a ladies garden society dedicated to historically accurate plantings. They replant appropriate botanicals in historical landmarks and cemeteries all around New England."

"Really? Why'd they pick her?"

"Apparently, she played a gardener in a movie a while back. The society thought it would be fun to honor her for her accurate portrayal."

"How'd they know she was in town?"

I look at him funny.

"Hello!" I then say with a laugh. "It's what I do for a living, remember? It's my job to make sure the entire world knows what they need to know about my clients and their products, even on short notice."

"Sorry, dumb question. I guess it'll be good for her to promote her new movie while she's there."

"Yeah, but it's also a great moneymaker for the society so they can raise funds for a floral pilgrimage to England. So everybody wins. Great cross-promotion."

"Wow, how do these people think of these things?"

I look at him funny again.

"Oh, right!" He smacks his head. "Hello! You're the mastermind behind all this. I get it now."

"What can I say? It's a gift." I laugh. "It truly is. I can take two totally unrelated things and find a connection between them. And voilà! Cross-promotion is born. Or as I like to call it, cross-pollination. You know, spread the wealth."

"Speaking of which, I'll bet you'll get that promotion. You deserve it."

I don't answer. In fact, I stop any more chatter right then and there and cram my mouth with a last bite of green beans. To use a favorite expression of my mom's, "I'm in astoundishment" right now. Jeremiah never actually spent more than mere seconds inquiring about the events of my life the entire time we were together, let alone compliment any achievement. He always found listening to his own exploits much more interesting than listening to mine. Admittedly, they usually were more interesting than mine.

And now, I find myself enjoying conversation with Jeremiah. And he's actually interested in what I'm doing with my life. I'm really, really relishing this. But there's a little more going on inside me.

Remember the little girlie-girl part of me who's still wanting to cling to the old way of life? And tempting me to go back to my antiquated mode of aspiring only toward marriage, two-point-five kids, and a drop-dead gorgeous, wealthy husband? She's clawing and mewling again to be set free, to get to Jeremiah, and fully explore what's happening here. And she's winning, too. I'm at a vulnerable moment right now after the kind of day I've had.

The mewling is deafening. I really ought to squash it ASAP.

"So, you asked what I was doing tomorrow and now you know. How come?"

"I just thought we'd do something like go to lunch and talk about the different events this week. Make a game plan about appearances, while I work on this segment to show the footage soon. Get my name tossed around the ASJA, get into some trade pubs and on some web sites."

"Why not talk tonight?"

"I haven't got much nailed down for the next few nights, but the really big night to go public is this coming Saturday. There's an awards ceremony for some top public officials at Faneuil Hall with a reception after. Media'll be crawling all over the place. We should definitely go."

"Who are the top officials?"

"No idea, but it would be a chance to get me and you out there in the public eye. I'll know the journalists from the *Herald* and *Globe* covering the ceremony. All the major networks will be there. We'll go to the reception after. The officials are announcing some foundation for underprivileged kids, too. It would be good to get some face time in there."

Face time.

I remember the first time he used that expression when he was trying to land a job with a local morning news show. I recall how we'd just started dating when he'd gotten his first break. He celebrated by making the exact same dinner as tonight.

I also remember when he got his first really big assignment; he'd been sent to Georgia to cover a murder. After that, he landed assignment after assignment. I can still feel how the excitement zipped through me to hear him speak of all his adventures whenever he got home: dodging street gangs' bullets in New York, hovering in a ditch to avoid a tornado in Oklahoma, and even meeting the president of the United States while in Washington, D.C.

Right now, my heart is thumping hard the same way it did back then. He's come so far since those early days, and his sense of danger turns me on now as much as it did back then. Jeremiah is right in one respect. It certainly wasn't lack of love—at least on my part—that broke us up.

"I'll go to the awards ceremony on Saturday," I say, "as long as you think it's safe."

"I'd never let you go if it would endanger your life."

He leans over and kisses me on the cheek. We chat about smaller social occasions we could attend this week, and I can tell he's surprised how booked my schedule is. Once business gets done, he clears the dinner plates, insists I don't get up, and disappears into the kitchenette. He returns with the plate of chocolate-dipped strawberries.

I watch in quiet surprise while he sits and selects a piece of sweet, bite-sized fruit. He leans in close, staring at my mouth, and raises the strawberry to my lips. The sweetness mixed with the dark chocolate becomes more than I can bear.

I look at him; he at me. Silently, we both finally acknowledge the massive sexual elephant in the room that's been dining with us. He leans in for a full kiss on the lips.

God help me, but I let him. The familiarity, the comfort, and the sexual heat of him weakens any resolve I might have had not to give into this temptation. Oh hell, why not let the girlie-girl part of me indulge in her little Cinderella Complex just this once? Why not get swept away on how it might have been had our engagement continued and had I innocently believed I would one day be Mrs. Jeremiah Stone?

The next thing I know, Jeremiah sweeps away the plate of strawberries, the glasses, and bowls. He hoists me up on the dinette (I'm already certain it can support us based on previous encounters), and kisses me more passionately than I ever remember. I miss his pressing weight. I miss the way his fingers grapple with my buttons and bra because he's so impatient to touch me. I miss how he unzips my skirt and takes care not to rip it, like he's truly concerned. What can I say? I feel good. I feel wanted. I feel sought after.

I'm just as impatient. His pants are barely unzipped and I'm pulling his hips against mine. I feel his hard, hot bulge push against me and I'm already writhing in anticipation. I'm holding on to him, yet I'm also holding on to the way things used to be between us. And it feels good. I let my daily worries melt away. I let myself be taken care of for a little while longer.

Just as I feel full of him inside me—just as I excite in the thought I might come in a little while since he's familiar with pressing all my right buttons—Jeremiah tenses with a final thrust and releases.

A moment later, he relaxes and pulls out. He then gratefully clings to me as if he can't let go.

And I can't let go of the fact that I somehow got short-changed.

"Sorry." He breathes the word; it feels hot against my skin. "You turned me on so bad, I couldn't help myself. This is all your fault, really, you're just too hot for your own good." He plants a kiss onto my neck.

"Is this where I'm supposed to apologize?" I ask, still

throbbing for release so bad I fear I may become the first woman in history to develop instant blue balls.

He kisses my neck again. "I'll make it up to you next time. I promise. I couldn't take it anymore. I just had to have you."

With a compliment like that, how can I be mad at him? Oddly enough, the thought of the salmon, the wine, the attentive dinner conversation, and the chocolate-dipped strawberries is enough right now.

I nod and with a stiff upper lip, I say okay.

Besides, I think to myself, I can always turn to "Bob" who waits for me in the bedroom whenever I may need him. He's my "battery-operated boyfriend." He can always finish later what Jeremiah had started.

Thank God it's Friday is all I have to say and a little retail therapy is the perfect antidote to a wild workweek filled with more problems than you can shake a schtick at. With work through, I'm now mindlessly wandering amid the sale racks of formal gowns at Filene's Basement—or as my friends and I call it, *Feeleen's*.

Speaking of friends, Brooke and Unity tagged along with me and are somewhere amid the nearby racks. They refused to let me wear any old thing from my closet and insisted that the new me requires a new gown for the Spring Fling. So they're doing their best to help me in the pursuit of finding the perfect evening wear for the event just over one week away. But as with most women, they're already distracted by the pretty glittery gowns in their own sizes. So, I can't find them now that they're lost deep in the trenches of the sale war zone.

Being payday and all, Filene's Basement is busier than the average workday, despite being the height of cocktail hour (which we are missing) and the fact that it is quickly closing in on dinnertime (which we are also missing).

I'm impressed with the sale prices on the designer gowns; they rival those of the department store's own annual bridal blowout sale. With prom season over and brides-to-be already stocked up on bridesmaids' dresses, the store looks to unload all the taffeta and silk it can in order to gear up for the incoming summer fashions. The timing is incredible as I have absolutely no dress to wear to the Spring Fling, which is appropriate as I have absolutely no real date to speak of.

Oh, I could ask Jeremiah, but something is stopping me. Or should I say *someone*. Who could that someone be? In a word . . . Dante. Yes, oddly enough, Dante is the one holding me back from doing the logical thing. Only he isn't actually *holding* me.

The image of Dante actually holding me warrants a contemplative, indulgent moment. And so I stop to fantasize about such a treat. My thoughts drift and float along the contours of his pecs and sharp planes of his six-pack abs. My mind's eye traces the black hairs on his chest as they dovetail their way into a thin line down his abdomen. This black line of hair then sinks low and disappears underneath the metal button of his Levi's. I can actually feel myself reaching for the little metal button, popping it open and unzipping his fly, the same way I'd open a precious gift. I'm reaching for him. I'm reaching for it.

I feel a tug on my arm. I look to see Brooke standing before me. I also notice my arm actually extended out to a sale rack and clutching the crotch of a lime-green sequin jumpsuit on a hanger.

"Hah-low?" Brooke sings out to me. "Anybody home?"

"Huh?" I mentally spiral back to the here-and-now and re-focus on my friend. She's staring at me and looks all worried, which in turn gets *me* all worried. "What's wrong?" I ask.

"Nothing's wrong. Unless you decide to try on that butt-ugly jumpsuit 'cause then I'd have to kill yah for harboring such bad taste. Anyone willing to wear that deserves to be put to death."

I pry my grip from the sequined crotch and my arm drops, along with my spirits. I leer at the few gowns hanging limp in my arm. Not one sings to me. Did I have to wait till the last minute to go gown hunting? Yes, I guess I did, seeing as I was going to just pull something from my closet, or borrow something from Brooke. But they're right, I do need a new dress, and I need one almost right this very minute.

"Aw, who am I kidding? I'm never gonna find a gown that says smart, thin, and fabulous within the next week. And who cares? The bigwigs at the agency are gonna know I lied about having a date for the Spring Fling when I show up without one."

"What's the worst that could happen if you go alone? Could it really end your so-called career?"

"Are you kidding? Of course it could cost me the promotion! They'll know I fudged my way out of going with Chad to the shindig. They'll think I'm some female maverick; a man-hating employee willing to sacrifice the good of the agency for my own advancement. And that I'm only looking out for myself."

"How do you get all that out of turning down Chad?" Brooke crosses her arms over her chest, which doesn't look too easy to do with her purse and the four gowns on her arm.

"You don't know how the Trinity operates. They want em-ployees who'll sacrifice themselves to get the job done, like the baseball player who makes the 'sacrifice-fly' for the sake of the team. I'd look like I'm only worried about my own 'numbers.' They read into this sort of thing real bad. It's the old-boy mentality at its worst."

"Isn't that what Chad does? Worry about his own numbers?"

"Well, yeah, but they love him. They think his shit is dipped in gold. They see him as a go-getter. But not so for the girl. We're talking total double standard."

"Man, that rips."

"And I've had troubles these past couple weeks. Accounts messed up. Computers breaking. The timing couldn't be worse. It's hopeless."

Unity makes her appearance between us. "Hopeless shouldn't even be in your vocabulary. Never say hopeless." She pulls a gown from the three in her grip and drapes one on top of the others I'm holding, adding to their heaviness. "Try that one on first. The blue will bring out the lightness in your eyes. Think water and sky. Serenity. You'll be calm, cool, and collected when you show up at the Spring Fling in blue."

I regard the gown she imposed on me. It's not quite my style; it has no back to speak of. Then again, it has no front to speak of either.

"Ah, Unity, the two pieces of thread holding the front of this thing together will barely cover my nipples."

She looks at me wide-eyed and tilts her head the way a confused puppy-dog does when you try and tell it to "come" for the first time. She really doesn't see the apparent lack of nippular coverage as a problem with the dress. I'm not in the mood to remind her that some of us aren't the width of a stiletto heel the way she is.

Instead of arguing, I simply say, "It's a lovely shade of blue."

She smiles with pride.

"Now if only I could find a life-mate willing to wear a white tux with a baby blue cummerbund, ruffles, and bow tie to match me." I say this brightly, and yes, sarcastically, but the grain of truth embedded in my comment is big enough to choke on.

"Oh, now, enough with the dramarama," Unity says as she readjusts the weight of her own chosen gowns on her arm. "Just ask Jeremiah to go to the Spring Fling. He'll be around until then, right? It's one night. And you're supposed to be seen out in public with him anyway."

"Yeah. I know, but . . ."

Brooke pushes her way in front of Unity and points a threatening forefinger at me.

"You listen to me, Nina. You said you wanted to keep Jeremiah separate from your personal life. It's bad enough you agreed to be his call girl to save his ass, but don't start relying on him to save yours. Tell me you're not falling for him again."

"Wow, Brooke, you really don't like him."

"Neither do you, remember?" She squints at me and inspects my expression. I hate it when she does that because the bitch reads me like a book and can be so damn irritating. "Come on, I'm waiting for an answer. Tell me you're not falling for him again." She levels me with her typical, knowing glare.

"Quit looking at me like that!" I whine.

That's when her jaw drops and she belts out this dramatic gasp. I hold up a gown to my face so she can't read me anymore.

"Nina Robertson! You slept with him! Admit it!"

Unable to face her, I do a one-eighty and scurry toward the ladies' dressing rooms. I hear her yelling my name amid calling me every other name in the book.

I seek shelter in the dressing room, but really, it's one big room with one big mirror so all the women can be lumped together to feel inadequate next to the one tanned twenty-year-old with the perfect proportions. Today, fortunately, no one is in the dressing room, but I know my relief is short-lived because Brooke's shouts are getting louder by the moment. I also hear Unity shouting over her, yelling things like, "karma," "soul mates," "cosmos," and "root chakra" and something about this being bigger than all of us.

I hang up the gowns and in the reflection of the mirror, I see Brooke make her entrance. Unity is fast on her heels.

"You do what's right in your heart!" Unity shouts in my direction before Brooke can lay into me again. "You're only going to wind up with Jeremiah in your *next* life unless you two come to terms with the issues between you. I'm telling you, if you don't, you may even end up reincarnated as a little Asian girl dancing to make a living in Thailand—"

"Hold on," Brooke stops in the middle of the dressing room and holds up a hand. "Before we all get out of control, just answer me one thing, Nina. When were you going to tell us?"

I stare at the reflection of my two dearest friends with arms chock full of gowns with sale tags. Brooke appears hurt that I didn't confess sooner about my clandestine sexual encounter with my ex-fiancé. Unity looks anxious and truly worried I might ruin my chances for future happiness in my next life. She really believes I might end up eating dog in Thailand.

I lower my head in shame. I turn to face them both. "I'm sorry. I didn't know how to tell you. I had a weak moment. Jeremiah wooed me. Relentlessly. He . . . he made me salmon."

"Pan-seared?" Brooke asks sadly.

"With a side of rice and fresh cooked green beans. I won't get into the raw oysters. Or the chocolate-dipped strawberries. He pulled out all the stops."

"Oh, man, he worked you over good." Brooke shakes her head. "You didn't stand a chance."

"Did I mention the white Zinfandel?"

"The bastard. Does the man have no scruples?" she asks.

"Now do you understand? I had such a bad day on Monday and he made the world right, at least for that night."

"Nina, this happened on Monday? Like, four days ago?" Unity pipes up. "Have you two been doing it all week?"

"No! I swear! It happened only once. And barely," I admit. "In fact, I've hardly seen the guy. We've gone to a few public 'things' here and there, and he's sweet when we're together. He's even cooked for me a few times and has left dinners for me in the fridge if I'm working late. But nothing's happened between us since Monday. He's gone a lot. He's working on some really intense project right now."

"Are you okay with this? You know, not seeing him much except for public dates after what happened between you two?" Unity asks.

I offer them a genuine smile and nod.

"Yeah, I'm okay, I really am. I'm not kidding myself that we might have any more than a slim chance together. I really believe that since I've been holding myself accountable for my own life, I've been seeing things in a different perspective. Honestly, I'm just too busy to obsess about anything nowadays."

"Wow, you know, I believe you've come around," Brooke says.

"Let's not rush things. This is still all new to me. And I need you guys. So, tell you what, I'll do my best not to withhold information anymore," I promise. "From now on, I'll tell you everything."

"Wait a minute, I don't have time for you to be unloading *everything*," Brooke says, shaking her head. "I have a life, you know. Just don't hold back on the crucial stuff, is all I ask."

"Deal. Now can we get down to business here?"

I point to all the gowns they're holding. Gratefully, they agree. I cross the large dressing room and help them hang their selections on hooks. As they start to try on their various choices and I zip them up, I fill them in on the gory details of the sexcapade with Jeremiah.

"So, where does this leave you two?" Brooke inquires while adjusting her cleavage in a plunging pink beaded gown.

"Nowhere. Honest. He's only in town for a while. Our one-nighter just sort of happened, you know?"

I have nothing more to offer them because I truly don't know where we left things. I don't know where we stand, because I don't know where he is most of the time.

Okay, so maybe it smarts a little that nothing will probably come of Jeremiah and me. But even worse, and what really hurts right now, is that I know deep down that I have no real future with, well, *anyone*.

I go over to my stash of dresses and rummage through them to get the Zen-blue gown. I inspect the strips of fabric meant for the top. For God's sake, I've had hairline fractures wider than these. Brooke interrupts my thoughts with self-criticism about her butt size. But between her complaints, she slips in a suggestion about asking Dante to go to the Spring Fling.

Upon hearing his name, I realize if missing Jeremiah is a

sting, then missing Dante is a flown-blown ache, in more regions than one. Because, of that, I don't respond to Brooke's comment. Maybe she'll just let it go.

"So? What about it? Why not take Dante to the gala?" she asks.

So much for letting it go. I try to find my voice.

"Why don't I take Dante? Let's see . . . I haven't heard from him for starters. It's like he disappeared into thin air. I don't even know how to get in touch with him even if I wanted to."

"Oh, right. I'm wicked sorry, Nina."

"What? Sorry?" I ask through a nervous laugh. "No, no, don't be. So we had a short-lived thing. It was fun. But it's over now. I'm okay with it. Honest."

Okay, so maybe I do feel a searing longing over not getting my Dante-fix since the night of the tongue incident. I have to accept that what we had was good-but-ephemeral. I tamp down the regret at not having a little more time with him. Okay, a *lot* more time with him. I probably would've had a blast with the guy at the Spring Fling, if I could have gotten up the courage to ask him. But would a guy like that ever agree to a formal engagement hosted by "the establishment?" I don't know, but I do miss him. If my mother were here right now, she'd tell me, "that's two-for-two in the 'defector' department."

Before I have to get into the touchy-feely issue of Dante defecting on me, I refocus my energies on the gowns. Brooke, too, is distracted by the task of trying on another dress. I'm grateful she's let this sleeping snog lie and I don't have to let on that I'm a tad bit hurt that I haven't heard from him.

I squeeze into the blue gown with the two pieces of thread that some designer had the audacity to call "top coverage." The rest of the gown doesn't quite fall right against my hips. Cripes, the whole thing fits me even worse than I expected.

"Unity, I appreciate the faith you have in me and my measurements but what the hell size is this? A negative-four?"

I'd look for myself but since I already broke into a sweat to squeeze into the thing, I'm not about to sweat another drop just to peel out of it to see the tag. Besides, I'd pull a muscle. Then again, it's hotter than a French whore in this dressing room, so no wonder I've got the sweats.

"The dress said a size six, but gowns usually run big."

"I know they usually run big. If anyone knows that, I know that. But maybe this designer is different. Because this gown definitely does not run big. Maybe it's an irregular. This is so bizarre. I mean, I know I've been eating like a pig from all the stress, but this is crazy."

I futz with the thin straps and yank on the fabric in all sorts of directions to force it to fall right. But bumps and bulges are popping through the stretchy fabric and it's clinging in all the wrong places.

Breathing is also tough. Before I have to take a deep breath, I suck in my gut in an attempt to look fabulous. I peer into the mirror. But my gut isn't sucking in the way it ought to. What the hell?

Brooke and Unity pause, too. They look into the mirror and gape at what they see.

"Ah, Nina, what's up with the boobs?" Brooke points to my chest.

"What are you talking about?"

I'm still fretting over my midriff (mid-*shift* is more like it), so I haven't even gotten a visual on the boobs yet.

"They're ballooned up . . . like buoys."

"Well, I can't be bloated, can I? I was up all night peeing like a racehorse."

"Boy, when you said the dress wouldn't cover you on top, you weren't kidding." Unity tries to sound lighthearted, but no one could mistake the surprise in her tone.

I pull my gaze from my midsection up to the rounded flesh busting out of the wide-as-twine top. I point to my reflection—more specifically, to the *bazoombas* in the mirror.

"Whose tits are those? Where'd they come from? I don't remember ordering these in an extra large."

"What's going on with you?" Brooke hikes up a corner of the lavender gown she's put on and comes closer to get a better look. "Honey, I've seen you naked plenty of times, but never in my life . . ." She pokes at the milky mounds, which sends undulating ripples across the tops of rounded flesh. "Is it that time of the month? Are you PMSing? Maybe you're bloated?" She watches my rippling chest in sheer fascination.

But I see nothing fascinating about the rounded globes, nor the protruding pouch of my belly. Brooke's question forces me to do a mental scan of the past month. She's right. "That time of the month" would be approaching, which would also explain the sweaty little hot flash I had while getting into the gown. But lucky for me, I just went back on the birth control pill. After losing Jeremiah, I went off the damn thing. I saw no sense in it. Big mistake. I have moody periods that come and go when they feel like it and I'm telling you, my ovaries have a life of their own. I only recently went back to the doctor to straighten me out with a different, low-dose pill to keep me regular.

"I started on a new low-dose pill a week or so ago."

"You didn't tell me that," Brooke says.

"You haven't been around so much, with your catering job. Besides, I've been so busy, I forgot to mention it. Anyway, if I were to have had my period, I would've had it . . ."

I start counting on my fingers . . .

"Umm . . ." I keep counting. . . . "Yep. I would have had it by now. Huh."

ELEVEN

The plot thickens . . . so does my waistline.

"Yes, that's right. I would have had my period by now if I weren't on this new pill. But I am on the pill. So, it's impossible for me to be pregnant," I blurt confidently, but still gawk slack-jawed at the straining, swollen breasts in the mirror. Baffling.

"You *would have* had your period?" My two friends squeal in unison.

"But, you don't? And this doesn't trouble you?" Brooke asks.

"Don't panic. I said I started a new low-dose pill. Therefore, impossible."

"Of course it's impossible," Brooke remarks sarcastically and slams her hands on her hips. "I mean, you only slept around with two guys while you might have been in heat."

"Hello? Did you not hear me?"

"Hello, yourself. A messed up ovulation cycle plus low-dose for the first time? Not a good combo. Augh! What if you are pregnant? If you think your boobs are big, just wait and see what pregnancy does to your ass!"

"Hey, you leave her alone!" Unity cuts in. "And before you start on her about the size of her ass, maybe you should take a good look in the mirror at the caboose you've been dragging behind you, Brooke."

"Excuse me, was I not just complaining about my ass size? And at least I got one! What would you call yours . . . besides flat as pancakes," Brooke retorts and turns her attention back onto me. "Shoot, what did your doctor tell you?"

"He told me to wait a whole cycle before having sex, if I could. Sometimes my cycle is only, like, two weeks long. And the package says waiting only two weeks is okay."

"Okay for a person with normal monthly periods. How long were you on this new pill before you were with Dante?"

"About a week."

"Oh, God, Nina! That's not long enough! What did you try to do, 'think' your way out of ovulating for added protection while you were with Dante? Like mind-over-matter or what?"

"No. I'm not dumb." I roll my eyes. "I used extra protection with Dante just in case, so there. I still had the 'celebratory' condom hidden in my purse, so I used that."

"You mean the one from a thousand years ago? Oh, no! I'm surprised it didn't disintegrate in your hand. Or break while you were using it, it was so old. Did you check it? Was it in okay condition? What about expiration date?"

"So they do have expiration dates after all? And did I check it? No! How could I? It was dark!"

"So I guess you didn't check it *after* you used it, either."

"Check it *after*? Who checks it after? Nobody tells me these things! I was on the pill all those years with Jeremiah so I don't exactly have a black belt in condomology and, no, I didn't check it. In fact, I don't know what happened to it!"

"Sheesh, Nina, for all you know, it could still be inside you!" Unity chimes in, panic-stricken

"You gotta be kidding," I say with a gasp.

"Give me a break, Unity. Now, please, let's not get carried away," Brooke says. "I can't believe you were still carrying around that old condom. I make sex-baskets. I've got hundreds of condoms lying around my bedroom. You could have helped yourself anytime. Textured. Flavored. Multi-stimulation. Glow-in-the-dark. Sheesh. How do you not know about these things?"

"I-I never had to. Jeremiah used a few for a while years ago; he took care of it, but then I went on the pill."

"Speaking of Jeremiah . . ."

"What about him?"

"Did you use a condom with him?"

"Well, no. He hadn't been with anyone since we broke up. And I was *almost* at the two-week mark with the new pill. I figured I was in the clear," I tell her.

"Why'd you go off the pill in the first place?" Unity asks.

"Oh, you mean due to all the oodles of sex I was having on a daily basis once Jeremiah dumped me?"

"Okay, okay, point taken." Unity backs off, hurt.

"I'm sorry," I tell her. "I went off when Jeremiah and I broke up. But my cycles were still so messed up, I decided to go back on something to regulate it. That's all. No big deal. Let's not panic. My doctor always prepared me that it might be harder for someone like me to conceive, not easier, due to my wacko system. So, if I'm not worried, then you shouldn't be." I never did like hearing that I might have trouble conceiving one day, but couldn't think about that now. "And don't forget about the weight gain and bloating from going on the pill. It all makes sense."

"You're right. I shouldn't have panicked," Brooke says. "Besides, I'm sure it's too early for you to have ballooned-up boobs from a recent conception. It's like you said, probably the new pill you're on. Even if you were only a few days along, you wouldn't be showing already," Brooke says lightly.

"Don't be so sure," Unity counters. "The very day that one of my yoga students conceived, she swelled up like a beach ball. I'd never seen anything like it." She turns to me. "Let's say you were gonna have a baby, who do you think the father would be? Who do you 'feel' is the father? Go with your gut instinct," Unity coaches.

"I don't feel anything either way. Because there's no baby."

But that damn girlie-girl part of me does wonder. What if I am pregnant and can't "feel" who the father is? What kind of person does that make me? Then again, is it possible that they could both be the father? I mean, cats can have the same egg fertilized by two different sperm, why should humans be any different? I could see it now. The conversations people would be having.

Oh, he has Dante's smile . . . and Jeremiah's feet.

I shake off the bizarre thought. I really can't be entertaining such notions. Even though it would be nice to have a family one day. Today is not that day.

"But I'll tell you one thing I'm feeling. I have to pee. Again. I've been going like crazy since yesterday. Somebody help me out of this stupid dress."

Brooke and Unity both come to my rescue. I bend at the

waist, bring my arms forward, and brace myself to be stripped out of the gown. I feel their hands on the fabric and they pull.

"It's a good thing I can't be pregnant now. I've just decided to get my life in order," I say through the fabric slipping over my face as they pull the thing over my head.

"Just think, several weeks ago you were trying to buy cybersperm on the Internet so you could get pregnant, and now that you don't want to be pregnant, you thought for a minute that you might be," Unity says.

"No, *you* guys thought I might be. Besides, do you have to remind me of the irony that follows me around?" I snap. "Sure, back then, I couldn't get knocked up if my life depended on it. This week, it's the last thing I need and it's an actual possibility!"

While I grouse, I look around for my bra. By now a small pile of gowns has grown at our feet. I rummage through them in search of my bra that must be somewhere on the bottom. I tear into the dresses and cast them aside one by one, taking out my aggression on the innocent clothing. What if I were pregnant? Which I'm not. But what if? Wouldn't that be a kick in the teeth? Now that my rampage about having an ironic life has started, I really can't stop.

"Augh! I hate irony! You guys know how much I hate ironic situations, which is ironic since my whole life is full of, well, *irony*! Just once, I'd like to be irony-deficient! I shouldn't even have to be thinking about this."

During my tirade, I find my bra and stab my arms through the straps. Unity lopes behind me to hook up the backside.

I stuff my bloated globes into the cups of my bra, squeeze them together to put them where they belong, and fit them just so. Full of indignation and denial, I huff while I do this.

Unity stands before me and looks me square in the eye. "You're upset."

"Yah think?" I quip. "Yeah, I'm upset."

I tug on my jersey and only now do I notice how clingy it is. Guess I've been a little distracted lately. And now I'm upset over everything, not just about today. Why wouldn't I be? I'm jumping through hoops to pursue a promotion, having a fling with a bad-boy so hot he makes ice burst into flames, and I'm stuck with a movie star as psycho as Norma Desmond from the old film, *Sunset Boulevard*. Oh yeah, let's not forget the sexcapade with my ex. But as distracted as I've been, I still should have been more careful, whether I was on the pill or not.

"Your system will settle down soon enough, I'm sure," Brooke offers. "As long as you're on the right dose of hormone with the pill. Give it another week. If you have to, you could always take a pregnancy test later. It would be too early now anyway. But you won't need one."

"I know I won't need one. But could you imagine if I were pregnant? I would not only be a graduate of the school of hard cocks, I'd be valedictorian."

"Well, don't you worry. You're fine," says Brooke. "Sorry I got you so riled back there. Your symptoms are a mere manifestation of going on a new kind of pill and your body adjusting to it. I can see that now. You're not pregnant."

Brooke makes me feel better.

"Or she could be carrying twins," Unity offers.

Unity makes me feel lousier.

"What makes you say that?" Brooke glares at her.

"Well, she slept with two guys!" Unity glares back. "Hence, two pregnancies!"

My stomach roils at the thought.

"I'm gonna be sick."

"Ah-ha. See? Morning sickness!" Unity yells.

"It's too early for any pregnant woman to have morning sickness!" Brooke yells back.

"Unless it's *twins*!"

TWELVE

*If you sleep with your ex-fiancé behind your boy-toy's back,
then sleep with your boy-toy behind your ex-fiancé's back, does it
constitute cheating? And if so, which party exactly is being
cheated on?*

Tonight is Saturday night and I'm alone in the apartmentette, getting ready for the political award ceremony thingy, which Jeremiah insists we go to. I have the place to myself since Brooke's long gone out on a date with a stockbroker. And yes, he's a few years younger than she is, but she's come to accept this sort of thing. Besides, she and this guy have known each other for a long time and have been trying to hook up for years.

I'm sitting at my little shabby chic, white-painted vanity in my bedroom, rifling through my makeup drawer to find the best colors for the evening. I have about an hour before Jeremiah arrives in a limousine to pick me up.

I'm not sure where he is at this very moment, but he vaguely mentioned a secret meeting with a production person who's "laying down track" for his controversial footage shot overseas. I wish he'd hurry up with his cloak-and-dagger activities so he can be out of this mess. The sooner he gets this project done and in public view, the sooner his life will be out of danger.

This past week, he and I have done pretty well attending various news events and getting our photos into the papers. So, tonight's date will probably be our last public appearance together acting as "fabulous fakes."

I apply some warm-toned foundation (Urban Rampage's Blistering Beige #69) to my face since I've been on the pale side lately. Speaking of faces, Jeremiah hasn't lost his keen ability to always show his best side to the camera while attracting media attention. During all this showmanship, however, he's been very attentive to me, both on and off camera.

No, we haven't done the "sexy" since that one time, but it's for the best. Kind of hard to focus on great sex when your mind wanders onto other things, like the best way for him to stay out of the morgue, or how to hide my thickened waistline. I forgot how bad the pill can make you bloat, not to mention my gastronomical feats of overeating from all the stress.

I brush on bronzer to fake a sun-kissed sheen. I follow up with an earth-tone eye shadow, earthier eyeliner, and very black mascara.

Tonight being a Saturday also signifies I have precisely one week left until the Spring Fling Gala. This year's summer solstice actually falls on a Saturday . . . *next* Saturday. Still, I have nothing to wear, and at this rate, how can I predict what will fit me in a week?

Like an Etch A Sketch, I violently shake my head and erase the thoughts of galas and increased dress sizes. Too much thinking! With renewed bravado, I apply a bronze-colored lipstick. I then rise and shrug into a simple black dress with plenty of elbow-room. I forego any strappy stilettos and opt for a simple elegant heel.

As I gaze at my put-together self in the full-length cheval mirror, I notice in the reflection, the small pillows piled on my bed behind me. Just for fun—just for the hell of it—I seize a pillow from the bed, ball it up, and stuff it under the dress. I reinspect my newly rotund form in the mirror.

The thought of actually having a baby slams me harder than a wrecking ball. *Oh, God, what if?*

I pant for breath and hate how my life has fallen into limbo. I rip out the pillow and toss it back onto the bed. The breathing eases.

That's it. I'm going to buy a pregnancy test once and for all tomorrow. Even if it may still be too soon to know for sure. And if, by golly, the damn test turns out positive, then I'll tell both fathers. From there, I'll go on *Maury Povich* or *Jerry Springer* to find out who the real father is. They'll foot the bill for the DNA test, I'm sure.

Telling Jeremiah is one thing; we have a history together. But what about Dante? And how am I even gonna find him to tell him of my current—*ahem*—situation? Should I even bother?

After all, he wouldn't want to be tied down to a woman he barely knows, with a kid he didn't mean to create. He doesn't stay in one place long enough to ever know if conception took place. He's too busy always taking off on his motorcycle with every whim. How could I expect that sort of man to be a permanent fixture in this little world I've just erected for myself?

Speaking of erect, I must admit, whenever I do see Dante, I swear my blood gets intoxicated with eighty-proof carnal lust. And when I see him straddling his motorcycle, I want him straddling *me*. It doesn't matter he behaves in a way indicative of a rudderless, rebel lifestyle; I simply turn a blind thigh to it.

Why does my brain, the body's sexiest organ, remain so fixated on *Dante's* organ? Okay, so maybe the guy leaves scorch marks on my skin as thick and deep as the skid marks he leaves on the streets. Oh, gosh, he's so damn hot, what if he really did melt the condom that night? Could he be responsible for the dilemma I'm in?

Falling for Dante is as smart as running with scissors, in the dark, drunk, and naked. Our lifestyles oppose each other, both diametrically and diabolically. This bad boy is the epitome of what I don't want, not with all I need to accomplish. He was supposed to be only one teeny part of my marketing strategy to successfully move on with my new life. I didn't leave room to get emotionally tangled with a perfect, handsome stranger who keeps me from diving headlong into the other parts of my grand plan.

But I simply can't help myself each time I get sidetracked by him. At times, I wonder if he's hell-bent on showing me I'm wrong in attempting to lead such a structured, goal-oriented life. Maybe he's got a point. Let's face it, every time things start coming my way, it's only because I'm in the wrong lane.

Maybe I do need to loosen my grip on this grand marketing plan.

Maybe I need to fly by the seat of my panties, the way Dante would want me to.

As for Dante, unfortunately, I may never see him again, despite my unfounded, unexpected, and overwhelmingly undeniable feelings for him. *Feelings?* Oh, hell, why does being so bad have to feel so good?

●　●　●

The moment Jeremiah and I step out of the black stretch limousine and onto the sidewalk nearest the Faneuil Hall entrance, paparazzi flashbulbs start exploding into my pupils. Through the red spots, I look up at the sky still lightened by a bluish twilight. The evenings are starting to stay a little brighter a little longer, just one more reminder that summer solstice is fast approaching, not to mention the Spring Fling.

But I can't think about that now. For tonight, I'm in Jeremiah's world and I've got to get through the evening. I try to concentrate on the here and now. Jeremiah makes it easy. He gently ushers me through the clusters of people and poses in just the right light to get into the best photos with the political heavy-hitters guaranteed to make the social and political pages of the *Globe* and the *Herald*.

He's also talking with reporters who came up through the ranks with him over the years and other journalists who recognize him from the networks. Oddly enough, these folks are keenly interested in me and my relationship to Jeremiah.

As smoothly as ever, Jeremiah dominates the interviews, feeding them just enough information to sate their voracious appetites for the lives of those in the spotlight. I'm grateful for his take-charge demeanor. I've got so much on my mind, and on my uterus, that I can barely think straight.

Jeremiah's statements to the press however, soon capture my attention. He's saying things like, "We're getting back together," "We couldn't be happier," and "We simply took some time apart." The journalists gape at him in surprise, pleasure, and astonishment. *So do I.*

Like my mother's favorite expression, "I'm in astoundishment," to say the least. Each time he says something wonderful, he gives me a tight, reassuring squeeze.

Could he actually have seen the error of his ways when he dumped me? Could he realize what he's lost?

Oh, I understand for the sake of the media, a person needs to watch his words and can't divulge dirty details, but honestly, his private behavior has indeed coincided with his public persona. I never thought I'd see the day. 'Course, I never thought I'd see Jeremiah Stone working his way back into my life, and apparently into my heart.

After demurely posing for the cameras till my spine aches, I follow Jeremiah into the great hall flanked with grand columns and quickly filling with local celebrities and political types. We take a seat as close as we can to the city's elite, but more importantly, in direct view of any noted cameras.

"Hey, isn't that Ted Kennedy?" I point to a white-haired gentleman shaking hands with the governor in the front row.

"No, that's Norman Mailer, the novelist. He lives down the Cape now. Ted Kennedy's over there." He points out the senator speaking with others in the great hall. Jeremiah then looks at me with his head tilted in a peculiar way. "Hey, you feeling okay?"

"Good enough, I guess. Why?"

"I don't know. You look a little pale tonight. Your skin's all translucent and veiny or something."

Even with all the naturally-falsified, sun-kissed makeup slathered on my face, there's no hiding the fact that my physical condition makes me look wan. So much for that crap about "glowing."

"I guess I'm a little tired, is all. Sorry."

"No, don't be sorry. You look . . . I don't know . . . frail and sweet." Then he smiles adoringly at me while a camera crew scans the crowd and films us. He doesn't seem to notice them.

He only notices me. "When you look like that, you make me want to take care of you forever."

Confused as hell, I smile back at him. But my smile is genuine. He's showing me a side of him I haven't seen in a long time. Boy, what a great side; an even better side than he could ever reveal to any camera.

The awards ceremony serves as a "who's-who" in Boston. Admittedly, I have more fun "star-gazing" at the crowd than listening to whoever is monopolizing the podium.

Shortly after, the limousine whisks us off to the reception for a round of shmoozing. Jeremiah shows me off to everyone I never got to meet while we were together. Never once does he let me go.

Following the guest appearance at the reception, we're driven to the Harp and Barb on Comm Ave. where the real partying begins. It's a good place for cigar-smoking Irishmen who appreciate real food and a publike atmosphere, not to mention all the journalists who happen to live in the JP area.

While at the pub, Jeremiah stays super-glued to my side, holding me protectively and proudly. Oh, how I'm enjoying the devoted attention. I could really get used to being put on a pedestal; this kind of treatment tempts me back into longing for the kind of life with Jeremiah I originally dreamed of.

Remember the little mewly girl deep inside me always wanting to scratch her way out? Well, her claws are unsheathed, ready to do battle, and confess just how much she wants this life to be real.

I'm falling victim to the Cinderella Complex again. I can't believe how much I'm capable of validating such a feminine phenomenon, which is up there with the Loche Ness Monster and

Sasquatch—you believe it exists only when you experience it firsthand.

Amid our weaving in and out of the boisterous crowd, Jeremiah pauses by a small, quieter alcove in the corner of the pub. He pulls me aside and kisses me.

"Thank you for everything you've done tonight." He kisses my hand and holds it. "You know, things are going so well . . . I hope you realize you're not getting rid of me in the next day or two, if you know what I mean. Do you understand what I'm trying to say?"

I nod. Not only do I understand it, I sense it. I see it. I taste it. I hear it. I feel it.

Maybe it's the hormones churning inside me. Maybe I've been so anxious, excited, antsy, and nervous because my secret "dream" has been handed to me on a silver-electroplated platter—to be back on the arm of the famous Jeremiah Stone. All I know is that I'm overcome with joy and relief. A rush of words rise up and fill me, ready to spill like a geyser. I can't wait to tell him I feel the same way.

"Yes, I know what you're trying to say. I understand. I'm so glad you've come around. Oh, Jeremiah, even if I am pregnant, at least I know everything will turn out all right. You're a good man." My stream of words pour forth and I let them come cascading from my tongue. I tell him how happy I am that we're back together, for good, this time.

I kick back my head to fight any tears of emotion I might have. Of course, I know I'm definitely leaving out parts of the whole story, things like, I slept with another man, but right now, the evening is going so perfectly.

His eyes widen and he's mouthing something—words, I assume—but only a gurgling comes out.

"Whoa, back up. Pregnant?" he finally croaks out.

"I know! I know!" I gasp, then laugh with delight. "I had the same reaction, sort of. I was shocked, too. Can you believe it? But don't worry, I'm not."

"Are you sure about this?" he manages to say.

"Oh, sure, I'm sure," I tell him lightly.

"So, you took a test and it came out negative?" He grips each side of my shoulders and his shocked gaze bores into mine.

"No, but I will tomorrow. I wasn't even going to say anything. It just kinda slipped out."

He drops his hold on me and lets his arms fall to his side.

"So you tell me this and you're not sure? You trying to give me chest pains? How am I supposed to go out there now and face all those people?"

"The same way you have been all night."

"You drop a bomb like that on me, and then expect me to act cool out there? And you don't know for sure if you're pregnant or not? How can that be? We only did it once. Just a little while ago. It shouldn't have even happened. Damn it, Nina, you're supposed to be the responsible one, to stop a guy like me when I get out of hand. Weren't you on the pill?"

"Kinda."

"Kinda?"

"I went off the pill for a while because I had no fiancé to be on the pill for anymore, remember?" I snap back. "But recently I went back on it, so I'm sure everything's okay!" This chat wasn't exactly going as planned.

"How could you let this happen? You were never this irresponsible. What happened to you while I was gone? You've changed big-time. I saw it the day I came back. What if you are pregnant? Hell, is the baby even mine?"

Oh, God, what a question to ask!

I stand flummoxed, unsure what to tell him or how to break the news about the little glitch in my story. You know, the whole part about the one-nighter with a really hot guy. What do you say to a man when you're not exactly one-hundred-percent sure about him being the actual father of your unborn child? If there is indeed an unborn child?

He must have read my stare dead-on and interpreted my hesitation, because he gives me a look of contempt. An ugly-icky-awful look. If he wants to assume there might be a baby involved, then so be it. He's certainly showing his true colors, that's for sure.

"Are you implying it might not even be mine?" He finally asks when I don't answer. "My original question was meant to get back at you for doing this to me tonight. And now it turns out to be a valid question? It really may not be mine? I don't know if I'm relieved or pissed as hell!"

"Well, it *might* be yours!"

"Christ, Nina, how many guys are you doing at the same time these days?"

"I'm not 'doing' any guy . . . right at the moment."

"I don't believe this." He digs his hands through his hair and begins to pace, always a precursor to the ranting and raving that's sure to follow. "You disgust me! No. No way! Not the woman I was engaged to. I've only been gone six months and you had some other guy's tongue down your throat?"

"That's not the only place his tongue has been!"

The look on his face grows really ugly. His disdainful demeanor repulses me the way I repulse him. I can't let him get away with a double standard just because I'm a woman.

The more I watch his reproachful reaction, the more furious I grow.

"Are you forgetting something? A little country we like to call Thailand?"

"Those women mean nothing to me!"

"So that makes it okay?"

"It's . . . it's . . . it's part of their culture."

"Well, it's not part of ours!"

"You can't throw Thailand in my face anymore. You're hardly a candidate for immaculate conception right about now." Droplets of saliva catapult between his teeth and I sidestep the spray of indignation.

"I didn't do anything wrong! I'm single! As in not *engaged*, betrothed, promised, or committed to anyone or any*thing*! You have no right to be upset!"

"No right? I'll have a fuckin' eruption if I want! This could be my kid; I was one of the guys you had sex with, remember?"

"If you call what we had 'sex.'"

"Hey! It's been a long time for me! But you wouldn't know what holding out means, would you?"

"Oh, please, you're not fooling me. To you, holding out just means you couldn't cough up enough cash to see '*sweee-Asian girl who a goo-fug*,'" I remark in my worst East-Orient accent.

I'm in his face and wait for a response. Before he can refute me, he looks over my shoulder at the crowd of media people pouring in and looking to party. He nods a fake pleasant hello to them, then returns his scornful gaze to me.

"Look, let's not fight about this until you take the damn test. Let me go in there for five minutes and then I'll get you home."

"Fine by me."

"You shouldn't have told me until you were absolutely sure," he mumbles as he gruffly brushes past.

"I told you, it slipped out, which is what I wish you did that night on the kitchen table."

"Damn you, Nina, you shouldn't have told me."

THIRTEEN

Instant slut—just add penis.

❧

The hot water pelts hard against my skin. I don't know how long I've been standing under the showerhead in my bathroomette, but judging by my pruned skin, it's been a while. Of course, some areas of my body are permanently "pruned," a nice term I use for cellulite, but that's not what I'm talking about. If I'm lucky, maybe I'll never have to leave the comfortable, wet sanctity of this shower. But if I loofah my skin a minute longer, I'm going to scour down to the bone.

Although I've washed Jeremiah right out of my hair, I'm still having a heckuva time scrubbing away the terrible memory of last night's contentious discussion with him. Had I known he was going to freak so much about the pregnancy, I definitely would have waited to tell him. It was bad enough to scare him off with my blurting out about the baby, but then he made me feel lower than sludge in a cesspool. His reception to the news went beyond chilly; I'm talking dipped in liquid nitrogen.

But I can't let him get to me. I simply have to remind myself that I'm not the one who cheated during our engagement, with the aid of a foreign country, and sent my life spinning in a different direction.

After I turn off the shower, I reach for a towel and damp-dry my skin. As if on automatic pilot, I perform minimal preening: comb out hair, slather on face lotion, apply toilet paper pieces to the nicks and cuts on my just-shaven legs.

All the while, last night's events unfold within the foggy chambers of my memory. Following our fight, I stormed out of the pub and into the limousine to pout while I waited for Jeremiah to wrap up schmoozing at the bar.

During the ride home, we sat in silence, until Jeremiah announced he would not be staying at my place that evening. The limousine pulled up to my building and the driver walked around the car to open the door to help me out. Jeremiah didn't budge. He merely sat there in the leather seat of the limousine and sulked. I expected nothing less from him, so I turned and entered my apartmentette alone and miserable.

How did the night, which began so well, end up so lousy?

But as far as Sunday mornings go, this particular one starts out nicely. Quietly. Uneventfully. I still have the place to myself. Brooke's date must have been a success, as she's apparently still on it this morning. Good for her. But one thought comes to mind. After last night's calamity, I definitely need to get to a pharmacy today. I'm gonna buy that damn pregnancy test and find out once and for all exactly what's going on with my body.

But then, as I finish preening, I hear a knock on the bathroom door, a usual announcement of Brooke to say she's come home safe and sound from her night. Wrapped in a pink terry towel, I open the door to inquire how her big date went.

But as I look at the person before me, I grip the towel knotted at my chest and stand there momentarily shocked.

"Dante!"

All at once, I'm thrilled and terrified to see him. I want to yap a mile-a-minute to tell him all that's gone on, but based on Jeremiah's reaction to my blurting out the baby news, God only knows how Dante would take it. So, instead, I soak up the sight of him, from his disheveled hair down to his steel-tipped black leather biker boots, and all the leather and denim-sheathed hot stuff in between.

"What are you doing here?" I ask three octaves higher than my usual tone. I'm actually so happy and so relieved to see him, it's truly frightening.

"I came to see you."

"Is Brooke here?" I ask and look around him out to the hall.

"No."

"Then how'd you get in?"

"I picked the lock. How do you think I got in?" His mischievous smile turns me all goofy inside.

"Why am I not surprised?"

I treat him to a dewy kiss. I can't help myself, remember?

He grips me around the waist and kisses me back hard.

"Hungry?" he asks.

I nod. "Mmm-hmm."

"Got any eggs and cheese in this joint?"

Again, I nod. "And toast and sausage. But you better hurry before the kitchen closes."

He brushes back a damp lock of hair clinging to my neck and looks at me head-to-toe the way he always does, which is amazing considering my non-made-up face and nicked-up, blood-dappled shins. But with everything I've been through lately, I really don't care if he sees me like this; it's good for him to witness all this unadorned glory. Since he doesn't stumble back in horror, I guess he's okay with it and is sticking around to make us some breakfast.

"You know what's driving me crazy most about you right now?" he finally says to me.

"What's that?"

"The fact that underneath this towel, you're all naked and wet."

"More naked and more wet than you can imagine."

Dante growls in restraint and sets his cougar-shaped gray eyes on me possessively.

"Don't tease me, darlin', or I'll take you right here."

"Oh, no you won't. You'll have to give me a minute so I can finish primping."

I hope I sound playful on the outside, on account of I'm a nervous wreck on the inside. Teeter-tottering between two men is a helluva lot more than I ever bargained for. And a helluva lot more exhausting than I ever imagined.

"Don't take too long primping. I don't know how long I can hold out. God, did I mention how hungry I am? And I'm not talking about breakfast."

The cadence of his voice is enough to make me drop my towel right there, but I need a moment to gather my wits about what the hell I'm doing. I've been physically and emotionally messing around with two men here, which makes me not-so-nice. If I keep this up, I'll have to start wearing a stamp across my forehead, "Have Vagina. Will Copulate."

"Tell you what," I counter, "how about you start the coffee and get the Sunday paper just outside the door while I get dressed?"

"The hell you will. Clothing is not an option."

"At least let me get on a robe."

"At least make sure it's see-through."

"I'll see what I can come up with."

I gently pull away with the promise I'll only be a minute and sashay into my bedroom. I close the door behind me and fall against it. Without warning, my heart starts pulsing wildly and throbbing against my rib cage. But my heart's not the only thing throbbing in my body. I can't believe how bad I need to jump this guy . . . despite my need to pull myself together.

I mean, did I not learn anything in the past few weeks?

Okay, there have got to be a few lessons to be learned here, right? I have to pause long enough to think straight so I can figure out exactly what those lessons might be.

Frantically, I formulate a mental list.

Okay, lesson one. I can't help the way Dante makes me feel. When he touches me, my brain says no, but my clitoris wails yes. And by now, we all know which organ is gonna win out.

Gawd help me, just when Dante disappears long enough to make me think our preciously short-lived time together has come to a bittersweet end, he returns and stirs the pot, or at least stirs the pot of hormones brewing inside me. The moment he appears, my insides crumble, along with any resolve not to get all mushy-lovey-dovey with a man whose idea of commitment is sticking around just long enough to make a girl come.

But how can I be feeling this way about Dante with everything I felt for Jeremiah last night? Or what I thought I felt? Or might still feel? Or what Jeremiah tried to convince me that I thought I felt?

Okay. I got lesson one covered.

It goes like this:

Lesson one clearly indicates that my feelings for these men are . . . not clear at all.

Which brings me to lesson two: I'm living proof a gal can indeed be crazy about two different guys at the same time. Just not simultaneously, as I'm quickly discovering. There is a difference. For me, the emotions pendulously swing back and forth between the two men.

When I'm with Dante, all reason and logic fly the coop and pure sexual energy takes over. But even more, my heart twists inside and out, and I can't figure out what it means. But I do know that when I'm with him, every problem, dilemma, and issue veiling my life seems to float away; they no longer exist. It's like I get socio-sexual-emotional amnesia the minute he comes into view. Believe me when I say, everything fades to black when I see this guy.

I never recall such heightened emotions with Jeremiah, even during our best of times, which makes me all the more confused. Jeremiah represents everything I ever wanted. And I loved him at one time, remember? Still do, I fear. Don't I? Yeah, okay, so he was lousy to me last night. Awful lousy. But I deserved it, dropping such a baby bomb on him like that, especially when his life is on the line.

I won't make such a mistake with Dante.

I may be crazy about two different men right now, but only one of those men is crazy about me. It doesn't matter how torn I feel because I won't need to decide between the two men after all. Jeremiah made the decision for me last night when he turned on me all because of one teeny little comment about one teeny little pregnancy. A pregnancy I'll have to confirm today after a trip to the pharmacy.

But as of this minute, I have a man with a body so hot, he's probably frying the eggs on his abs right this minute. And I can't let this perfectly good male specimen go to waste now can I? And why should the eggs be having all the fun sliding along the slippery slopes of Dante's torso?

Determined (and horny as hell . . . must be all the hormones), I stand up, and quietly scurry into Brooke's room, without Dante's knowing it. The other mistake I don't intend on repeating, is messing up the condom situation again. I'm sure he's got one in his wallet by now, if he's come here prepared, but I'm not taking any chances.

I rummage through her adult-basket stuff and find a pile of silver-foiled packs. I sift through them. Oh, hell, let's go with the textured one. The expiration date is good. I sigh with relief. Armed with the condom and a hell-bent need to grope this guy, I lose the towel, and scoot back into the bathroom. I start the shower. What's another round with the loofah gonna hurt?

I call out to Dante, "Oh, darn! It looks like I missed a spot on my back and I can't reach! What's a girl to do?"

Thirty seconds later, Dante is stripping off his clothes, climbing under the pulsing shower, and letting me lather him up: his pecs, the small hard curve of his back, his rounded glutes, his thighs.

This doesn't last long since I have to have him now. Doing the "sexy" in the shower isn't usually as easy as it looks in the porno flicks, but Dante makes it a breeze while he holds me up and braces me against the cool tile of the shower. I don't even care I'm still on the "ballooned" side—a good thing since I'll only get worse.

I focus on the here and now, like the position of my legs. My thighs are wrapped around him like a tongue around a lollipop. I have myself a lick of pleasure while he pumps me. He's relentlessly massaging my insides and teases that internal ticklish spot until he makes every muscle under my belly contract. Engorged and swollen between the thighs, I let out an unexpected wail and start bucking until I'm finished taking him for all he's worth as much as he's taking me.

And as always, all my worries fade to black.

Dante and I are drying each other off while still standing in the tub when an awkward question pops into my head. Giving in to the need for immediate gratification, I ask my burning question straight up.

"Dante, how old are you?"

He spies me, his dark brow knitted. "Does it matter?"

"I'd like to know."

"Old enough."

"Come on, I'm serious." I tousle his luscious hair with the towel. He takes his time answering, which kills me to no end.

"Twenty-seven."

"Oh."

"Too old or too young?"

"Depends. I turned thirty a while ago. There's a three-year difference."

"Three, huh? Oh man, that can only mean one thing." He sighs a long, drawn-out breath. He doesn't look too happy.

"What's it mean?"

"It means you're good at math. And if that's the only problem you can come up with, then we're doing okay. I've been through worse." He prizes my eyes with a teasing smile before grabbing my towel and draping it on top of my head.

"We're *doing* okay, huh?" I repeat while I make a turban out of the terry cloth.

Doing.

As in, "present tense" doing.

As in, "continuing to do."

As in, "no definite end in sight."

It's an odd thing to hold onto, but I'll take it.

"And you've been through worse? Do you mean, like, worse than a three-year age difference with a woman you're seeing, or worse in general?"

He shrugs; I can tell it's a defense mechanism.

"Worse in general. It might not look it from the outside, but believe me, I come from a broken home. A seriously fucked-up one. A pack of liars and thieves who think the only way to get by is to rob people blind. We got some awful-bad blood in us."

"Wow, you said you talked to them about this before, right?" While I wait for his response, I take his towel and pat the fine black damp hairs glistening on his chest. He doesn't actually need the help, I just like to touch.

"Yeah, but there's no talking sense to them. I tried plenty. Then we had a blowout. I never went home again. I've seen what their lies have done to people. Lives destroyed. I'll never live that way."

"Aw, Dante, I'm sorry."

"Living poor and happy is better than trying to get filthy rich and be miserable. No need to stick around with liars, you know? Why do people like that even bring kids into this world if they live their lives based on lies? I'll never do that. Even if the rest of my family is doing it."

He stops there. With little effort, he gathers me into his arms and kisses me. I see a small smile on his face for my benefit, but I also see the tension.

"But I won't be living at all unless I get us something to eat," he tells me.

He pulls away, steps out of the tub, and hauls on his Jockeys and jeans. Before he can get to his button-down denim shirt still on the floor, I snatch it up and slip into it. How else am I to keep him shirtless over breakfast? He good-heartedly acquiesces and leaves the steamy bath to go make us some grub.

I return to grooming by combing out my hair again. But Dante's words ring in my head. He sees no reason to stick around liars. Since I'm not mentioning the need to take a baby test today, do I fall into that category? I shake it off, chalking it up to a mental reservation. Why say anything until I'm sure? I can't even face his reluctance to bring kids into the world.

Minutes later, I'm tugging on some old boxers (yeah, yeah, they used to be Jeremiah's) when the aroma of nutty coffee accosts my olfactories.

Barely able to walk after our stint in the shower (how does he do that to me?), I stagger down the hall toward the kitchen. I round the corner and see Dante staring down at a section of the *Boston Sunday Globe* on the dinette. The tension in his face is evident.

"What is it?" I ask and approach.

He holds up the section between us, keeping me at arm's length. I stop dead in my tracks and get a good look at the headline. "Jeremiah Stone, CNN Reporter, to Wed Local Ad-Woman: Date Set For This Fall." Right underneath is an enormous color photo of Jeremiah and me, smiling, and holding hands at last night's political awards ceremony.

My eyes frantically scan the article. The feature indicates that Jeremiah and I are back together and in love. Jeremiah's got quotes bleeding all over the damn thing. One quote states we never technically broke up. Instead, we chose to take a "breather" because his career had been taking its toll on our relationship. By staying apart for a few months, we could both focus on our careers, put all our ducks in a row, and tie up any loose ends so we could get back together and focus on each other to ensure a successful marriage.

Aside from Jeremiah's lazy use of tired clichés, the article sounds unbelievably believable.

Shit.

"You should have told me you and your fiancé got back together."

"But we didn't. Trust me—"

"It's in the paper. Details and pictures."

"Dante, it's blown way out of proportion. We're not together."

"Really? Says here he's come back so you two can get married."

"We're not getting married. That's not why he's come back. Honest."

"Then why is he here? Why are you two in the paper?"

"I-I can't tell you."

He slams the article onto the dinette and heads toward the door. Just as I follow, pleading with him to let me explain, a key jiggles on the other side of the door's lock.

I'm momentarily grateful that Brooke's finally come home. She'll save my ass.

The door flies open wide.

Jeremiah bursts into the room. And I die a small death.

Brooke! Where in the hell are you when I need you?

Jeremiah is about to crash right into Dante. God, I can't look. I cover my face to brace myself for their collision. When I hear no bodily impact, I drop my hands to see the two of them staring stunned at each other.

Jeremiah pulls his gaze from Dante and narrows it onto me. I look back at him and I, too, stand there stunned and stare at Jeremiah's swollen black eye. What a butt-ugly shiner.

"What happened to your eye?" is all I can utter.

"Let's just say I had to fend off someone who'd like to see me dead."

I immediately think of the evil-guerrilla-thugs after Jeremiah's controversial footage and after his life.

Before I can ask him the details or see if he's all right, he returns his black-eyed expression to Dante. He takes in the sight of Dante's bare chest and bootless, bare feet and immediately puts two-and-two together. It isn't too difficult. Witnessing Dante hanging around my apartmentette on a lazy Sunday morning, clad only in jeans, with coffee and the Sunday paper nearby, it's easy figure out whose bed his boots have been under.

Jeremiah's face flames red with rage.

"So, this is the asshole you been seeing?" Jeremiah demands to know. "Didja tell him about the baby? Didja decide yet if he's the father? Or is it me? Didja even take the damn test yet! Huh? Tell me you did! I need to know, Nina! My future depends on it! Which of us is the father? Me or this asshole?"

FOURTEEN

Torn between two druthers

Under any other circumstance, juggling two men would be a real boost to the ego and proof that a *chicka boom* attitude really works. But truthfully, having those two men come face-to-face horrifies me.

I can't focus on my horror and humiliation, however; I'm more concerned about Dante's hand . . . the one he's balled up into a fist and is raising into the air. He's about to reach for Jeremiah and lay into him good.

I know why, too. I'm sure no one calls Dante an asshole and lives to tell about it.

I leap in between the two men and push Jeremiah off-balance to make him fall to the couch. My ploy at throwing myself in the middle must be working because Dante lowers his clenched fist to his side. He may be a bad boy, but apparently he's a good man who'd never slug a woman. With the altercation diffused, I set my sights on Jeremiah.

"Shut up, Jeremiah! Don't say another word. Your mouth has already gotten us both into enough trouble."

"*My* mouth? It's not *my mouth* that got us into this mess!"

"Hey!" I yell at him. "You want another black eye?" I point to his shiner. I figure a slug from me probably wouldn't hurt anywhere near as much as a slug from Dante, who's got forearm muscles the size of grapefruits. "I'm more than happy to give it to you if you don't put a lid on it!"

Jeremiah tentatively fingers his bad eye and shuts up, at least for now.

"What's he talking about, Nina?" Dante's voice is low and gritty and full of concern. "What baby?"

"You didn't tell him?" Jeremiah spews out to me. "Oh, that's classic! You fucked up good this time, you know it?"

Dante really gets torched at Jeremiah's remark and he moves in for the kill. Apparently, Dante doesn't defend a woman with idle threats when a good simple punch would be more to the point.

While he may not like the way Jeremiah is talking to me, I refuse to have Dante shedding blood all over the walls. I can't afford to lose my security deposit.

I step in Dante's path and press my palms against his chest. I shake my head "no."

"He's not worth it. Let me take care of this," I tell him.

"You got some explaining to do," Dante says furtively, but then eases his stance.

"I'll explain everything. I promise."

From behind, Jeremiah grumbles something almost inaudible, but a few nasty words come through loud and clear. Keeping the pressure against Dante's chest, I twist and glare at Jeremiah.

"What do you want, Jeremiah?"

"I came to get my stuff. Stuff I left in your *bedroom*."

He tosses Dante a brutal sneer. Dante takes another step toward him, clearly indicating I was kidding myself to think I could keep Dante from pounding Jeremiah. I'm no match for his size or strength, but I continue to try. Jeremiah suddenly rises from the couch, rearing to go and ready take on Dante.

"Whoa, wait! Dante! Jeremiah! Please!"

But it's not working. I take the "expectant mother" approach, clutch my belly, and cry out, "Oh, the baby!" I double over, feign unbelievable pain. It's a lousy tactic, but I'm reduced to these low blows by now.

Both men stop dead in their tracks and stare at me in panic.

I take advantage by standing upright and separating the two men with both extended arms. I give a warning glare at Jeremiah.

"Jeremiah, I mean it! Just go back and get your freakin' stuff and get out!"

He glares at me. "You were faking?"

I roll my eyes. "Of course I was faking!"

"Damn, you're good," Dante says, his expression impressed, but serious.

"Jeremiah, get your stuff and go. We'll talk when you chill!"

Jeremiah hesitates, but finally stalks down the hall. When Dante doesn't go after him, I ease up and turn toward him. He merely stands there, frowning down at me. We wait until Jeremiah passes us with a toiletry bag in hand and marches out the door. As he closes the door behind him, he yells, "You better know something soon!"

The tension, thick and unbearable moments ago, lightens to barely tolerable now that Jeremiah's gone. I'm still standing before Dante like a guilty party on trial. I'm looking all around the apartmentette, to the dying plants, the dusty picture frames, and non-alphabetized CD collection. I look anywhere I can—anywhere except into Dante's eyes. I can't. I just can't.

"Is it true, Nina? Is there a baby? It could be mine?"

"I'm not sure. If there's a baby, it could be yours. An old condom is known to break down and disintegrate, or get 'lost in the shuffle' if you know what I mean. Do you know what happened to it?"

"Can't say that I do. I was totally focused on you. The question did occur to me the next day, but—what the hell, Nina, why didn't you say anything?"

"I didn't know how you'd take it. I got scared that you'd get scared."

"I'm scared of nothing, Nina, nothing. You should have told me."

"I'm sorry. I didn't know what to do. I guess when I couldn't be sure who the—" I cut myself short. I would have cut my throat right then if I had a knife. Heck, a paper clip would do. I don't deserve to have a voice box since I never know when to shut up.

"You can't be sure who the father is? So Jeremiah wasn't making shit up?"

He jams his hands into the pockets of his tight jeans and takes a step away from me. Talk about both parties feeling the rejection right then. This must be the part where I see the bitter side to Dante. The way Jeremiah took the news and laid into me, I wouldn't be surprised if Dante does the same thing.

"I never should have come."

"Dante, please—"

I reach for him, but he steps back. He almost recoils, but he's not the type. He just makes it clear he doesn't want me touching him right now. Can't say I blame him. He stands there, waiting to hear more. I try to find the words to explain my unexplainable behavior.

"I didn't hear from you. And believe me, I waited. I figured you got tired of me and moved on, and just took off. I missed you so much I couldn't stand it."

"You missed me so much so that you slept with Jeremiah."

Ouch.

I wince inwardly at his blatant observation. I hate the fact I'm guilty as charged.

"Oh, gosh, I can't change what happened. You came into my life, and disappeared just as fast, or so I thought. You got to remember, Jeremiah was the guy I was supposed to marry. *Twice.* We'd been together for years. I was only with him one time since he's been back."

"But you wanted to get back together," he asserts.

"Honestly? A small part of me might have. Life got hard. Slipping into the 'old me' looked appealing at the time. But I realized the 'old me' is already gone. So is that way of life. And I have to do some reconfiguring."

"So you weren't gonna say anything to me today about the baby?"

"I was gonna go buy a test today, but then you showed up. I was thrown off-guard."

"So you're not sure you're pregnant?"

"I'm pretty sure I am *not* pregnant. The test is just official confirmation." I don't hide the resignation to my tone. Why bother? "But I'll get one today. I promise. I just haven't had the chance to get to a store. Things have been a little crazy, to say the least."

"I don't want to talk about this here. I want to take this outside."

"You mean, like, to duke it out with me?"

"No, to get some fresh air. It's gotten kinda hot in here."

Without bothering to ask for his shirt off my back, he grabs his leather jacket from the dinette chair and hauls it on. As he heads out the door, I tag along. At least going outside will put us on neutral territory.

He stands on the shrub-lined walkway leading to the venerable brick apartment's front entrance flanked by two Corinthian columns as grand as he is. The phallic effect is not wasted on me. Luckily, no one's coming or going in the nearby parking lot, leaving us alone to continue our little discussion.

"Are you sorry I came here today?"

I stumble back and gaze up at him in surprise. The hard edges to his frown soften to a curious look.

"Sorry? No, no. Not at all."

"But it's over between us?"

"No."

"Don't lie to me, Nina. Jeremiah's back. You screwed around with him. Your wedding day's already making headlines. He's living here with you. You could be carrying his baby."

"Well, sheesh, when you put it that way . . . but, we're not back together. He's in some kind of trouble and I just agreed to help him for a week or two. We're faking it."

"That's some faking."

"But we were. I mean, we *are*. He . . . he knows about you, you know."

"Obviously."

"No, really. Would you have come up in conversation if I really were to marry him? Did you notice the article didn't have one quote from me? We're not getting married. There's nothing going on. He's not here with me, you are."

In the morning sunlight, Dante spies me, sizing me up, staring me down, and deciding if I'm telling the truth or if I'm no better than his rotten, lying, scheming family full of crooks and thieves.

I implore him with my eyes. "While I may not know what the hell I'm doing with my life, or what the hell I want in this life, I do know I have *not* set a wedding date with Jeremiah!"

Dante inspects me further and as if using some instinctual-lie-detector radar, he nods in acceptance. He's got to see what's in my heart, he's just got to. He can't miss it, I'm wearing it on my sleeve—I mean, *his* sleeve; I'm still in his shirt and nothing else (except Jeremiah's boxers) while we stand outside.

"I have no ownership here, I know," he begins to say, "but you still could have told me he came back. Then I would have understood there would be a chance you might get back together. Then I wouldn't have . . ." He stops his words, his tone still riveted with anger and frustration.

"You wouldn't have what?" I ask.

God, I couldn't stand it if he hates me.

"I wouldn't have spent so much time having you on the brain since that first night we met."

"Really? I've been on your brain?"

I know I visibly gush. How could I not? It's about the most sincerely honest, romantic thing any man's ever said to me.

"Why do you think I keep stalking you? I've never done anything like this . . ."

He sounds more mad at himself than at me. The muscle in his Romanesque jaw pulses wildly. He's holding something back big-time.

"Go on. You've never done anything like . . . what?" I prod.

"Let's just say I never stick around long enough to stalk a woman."

Okay, as inappropriate as it is at the moment, I'm smiling up at him big time. A toothy-gummy-dorky smile, I'm sure, and so unattractive, but I can't help it. Speaking of teeth and gums, I wouldn't mind running my tongue along his in a full-blown, unadulterated, reassuring kiss. But I hold back. After all, we're in the middle of an emotional crisis here.

"Aw, you're not stalking me so bad." I touch his arm. He watches me touch him. I like watching him watch me.

"You wouldn't say that if you knew what I'm thinking when I think of you."

"What do you mean?"

A light breeze tousles his dark hair, making me want to press my lips against his. I have to keep my tonsils to myself. I simply must contain my overwhelming urge to hold him until he gets what he has to say off his chest. And only then can I impose *myself* onto his chest instead.

"When you're not around," he begins, but then takes a breath, "I still think of you . . . every way imaginable. Every position imaginable. Then, when I can't take it anymore, I have to see you. Like this morning. Like that night on your balcony." He peers up at the balcony to my place.

The memory of that sexy night floods me and I immediately grow warm. Romeo and Juliet, eat your heart out. No balcony scene in any Shakespeare play would ever compare to our own balcony scene played out that way. Well, except maybe for this one porno flick I saw last year, entitled, *Romeo Ate Julie Wet.*

Dante sets his eyes possessively on me. I swear they're changing color, like a mood ring against heated skin.

"I'm feeling all kinds of shit for you and I really didn't need this to happen. I was supposed to take off for El Dorado today." He gazes forlornly at his motorcycle.

"El Dorado?"

He nods. "I was supposed to just hop on my bike and head for Texas, but it didn't happen. I didn't get my bike tuned up in time. That never happens. And I didn't care. On account of I'm here, with you."

I never heard the guy say so much in one breath. I recognize his relay of information for what it is: an outpouring of emotion.

"Would it help if I said I'm glad you didn't go? And I'm feeling what you're feeling, too? But I was afraid to feel it, because of exactly what you just said. Let's face it, you got a shelf life shorter than a carton of milk. I knew you'd be taking off for someplace. I didn't know it would be El Dorado . . ."

"But I didn't go," he reminds me.

"But you didn't go," I remind him right back.

Unsure of what this means for us, we stand in silence. A deafening, screeching, nails-down-the-chalkboard kind of silence.

"You lied to me, Nina."

"And you caught me," I remind him. I say it in a teasing tone to keep the conversation light. "It happened because I've had no practice at this."

He looks at me sideways. "Practice at lying?"

"I mean, I've had no practice at *managing crises*. I really thought I shouldn't say anything until I could be sure about . . . everything in my life."

"Oh, right, that whole 'big plan' you been working on. Guess I forgot."

"Speaking of the life plan, there's more."

"More?"

"Um, it's sort of a change in subject. And probably not the best time to ask this."

"I'm not up for handling much more."

"It's not a bad thing. I've just never asked out a guy before, but I have this Spring Fling Gala hosted by the ad agency where I work. It's fancy, and I'm sure it's not something you'd want to do, but you wouldn't go with me, would you?"

"You're not taking Jeremiah?"

"He doesn't even know about it. My life is just that—mine. End of story. He's really got no part in my private affairs. That's what I've been trying to tell you. So, would you come?"

When he hesitates, I pull out the heavy artillery. Maybe if he understands my predicament, then he can be swayed.

"See, I work at Avalon Advertising. Remember the whole promotion plan? Well, there's this guy, Chad Gorham, who wants the position I'm after, too."

Dante lowers his gaze to me and looks me straight in the eye.

"Did you say, Chad Gorham?"

"Yeah, yeah, you heard me right. From the famous 'Gorhams' of Boston. He works at Avalon with me. Anyway, he's not above doing whatever it takes to get the promotion, and it would be better if I had someone to go with me to the Spring Fling. It's this coming Saturday night and . . ."

But Dante's already leveled me with a sobering expression.

"It's not a good idea," he announces.

"You're still upset about Jeremiah. You've got to believe me, Dante."

He rests his hands on my shoulders, simultaneously calming

me down and getting me revved up by his touch. He gives me a look so sizzlingly sexy, my insides liquefy.

"I believe you. But you got to believe me, too, darlin'. You don't want me there. A guy like me will only make matters worse."

"No, I don't feel that way."

But he shakes his head in a refusal to accept my feeling. He cups my cheeks in his hands and kisses me square on the lips.

"We've both got a lot to sort through. We can't be doing something like having me show up at a company event just yet."

"But Dante, you're as good as anyone who'll show up at the Spring Fling—"

Dante laughs, obviously comfortable with his renegade maverick lifestyle that keeps him on the outskirts of "civilized, polite" society.

"You'll be hearing from me. You can tell me news about the baby when you know more. And then we can figure out where we stand."

"Promise?" I ask.

He nods.

"You sure you won't go with me?"

"The best way for me to help you on Saturday is by not going to this event."

He gently breaks away, turns, and saunters toward his bike. He turns around once and walks backwards, all the while his arms are open wide.

"Trust me on this," he says, "the way you should have trusted telling me about the baby." He spins back around, hops on his bike, and starts it up.

He looks at me one last time. "You could have told me

sooner about the baby, Nina." He revs up the bike louder than necessary. "You could have told me."

After Dante pulls out and takes off down the road, I start to turn to head back into the brick apartment building until another car comes into view. I immediately recognize the vehicle, so I wait until it pulls into a parking space in the nearby parking lot. A moment later, Brooke gets out of her Nissan and saunters up the walkway. She's scrutinizing my body, from Dante's oversized denim shirt, to Jeremiah's baggy boxers, to my bare legs. She draws up her gaze and looks at me quizzically.

"Hi Nina, did I miss something?"

"I think I'm gonna be sick," I say through a moan for about the ninth time.

I roll over in my bed and throw the pillow over my head. The blankets are tangled in a heap at the foot of the mattress; I'm too burning hot with humiliation to need them.

"The bucket's been beside you on the floor for ten minutes, and still, you got nothin'," Brooke's muffled voice reminds me through the downy feather barrier balled up over my ear. "I think it's just the dry heaves over what you got yourself into. I really think you're probably having an allergic reaction to the confrontation with Jeremiah and Dante."

Brooke certainly got an earful when she showed up after my emotional altercation with the two men. I had to stand there pantless in the parking lot for ten minutes reliving what happened as I filled her in on the sordid details.

As I lay like a lump, I realize I haven't taken a moment to ask Brooke how her date went with the number-cruncher. I pull the pillow off my face and tuck it under my head.

"I'm such a lousy, self-centered friend. I didn't even ask how your night went. Distract me and tell me everything."

Brooke's face stretches to crestfallen. She leans toward the bucket and draws it closer to herself. Definitely not a good sign of how things went.

"Oh, I been waiting so long to go out with him. And he's such a great guy. I mean he's perfect. Absolutely perfect. What he lacks in years, he makes up in maturity," she admits sadly.

Her unexpected description surprises me. "Oh! In that case, can I borrow him? He sounds like the perfect escort for my Spring Fling."

"Oh, honey, I'd let you, but I had to let him go."

"Humph. I can see why. All that perfection can get in the way of a good relationship . . ." I wait for Brooke to explain why this perfect guy isn't right for her. She inspects her shoes, apparently stalling for time. "Hey, look at me. What happened?"

She raises her guilt-ridden eyes to mine. "Not all of him is perfection. He . . . he has a club penis."

This definitely gets my attention. I never heard of such a thing. A club foot, yes. But club penis? No. And I'm not liking the "pop-up" visual coming to mind.

"Care to explain?"

"I can't . . . it's too . . . odd. And I feel so shallow, like I'm discriminating against someone with a disability. And it's not a disability, I mean, he's fully functional, and even compensates for it way beyond the call of duty, but still. I mean, we went at it all night. But in the morning, when the lights came on, I got too freaked out. I couldn't handle messing with a guy with a . . . with a . . ."

"Club penis."

"Do you think I'm awful?"

"Hell, I dumped a pretty cute guy once because I didn't like his profile. Full frontal facial features were great. But every time I sat in his truck looking over at him, there it was. This . . . this gawdawful *profile*. Augh."

Brooke's eyes brighten and she looks relieved that I understand.

"That's how it is with me! Every time I look down at it, the tip looks like it's been gnawed off and poorly reattached, so now it bends to the side. I mean, the girth is wide enough and shaft long enough, and you'd think it woulda' added to a girl's pleasure, but it didn't. He'd be thrusting one way and his tip would be banging another way. It was too confusing. I guess I just couldn't get past it. It was a mental thing."

"Sorry it didn't work out."

"Don't be. I'm sorry enough for the both of us." Brooke rises and returns the bucket to my side. "Oh, gosh. It feels so good to get that off my chest. I really hope I'm not a horrible person."

"You are, but I still love you. We don't call each other 'co-whores' for nothing."

"I'm glad I talked about it. I guess sometimes we just have to come to terms with who we are and where we're at. How else can we move on, right?" She takes a cleansing breath. "I'm gonna go get some coffee. You want some?"

"Nah." I press a palm to my nauseous rounded tummy. "Not till this funky feeling passes."

Brooke leaves me to my funk. But her words stick to me like day-old semen.

Like Brooke, I have to come to terms with who I am. I'm a young woman trying to play "catch-up" by cramming several years' worth of experiences into a handful of weeks. Let's face it,

I decided to change my life from "apathy" to "activity" and I wanted it changed *yesterday*. Sating my needs immediately has always been my modus operandi. Can I change my nature? Alter my M.O.? Soldier on with my self-improvement kick? Or do I accept my internal wiring as it is?

I also have to come to terms with where I'm at; I'm still in a mental place where I'm relying on various men to dictate my lot. Think about it. First, a bunch of old cronies at the agency have me jumping through hoops to fit their old-boy mentality. Second, I have to find a date for the gala to appease them. Third, I become emotionally dependent on two men to help me figure out who I am.

Cripes! I haven't changed a bit!

What was I thinking?

What was I doing?

I've been going about it all wrong! Shoot, I was just about to borrow a man with a club penis! I would have been willing to go with him anyway just to continue playing the old-boy game. A game designed for me to lose no matter how long I play. A game I'll never win if the rules remain the same.

Me? Win their game? Hell, I'm barely a contender.

Man, I bungled it big time, didn't I?

But I get it now.

I need to accept that I'm probably going to go to the gala alone. Flying solo shouldn't be so bad, should it? Heck, what does having a date have to do with my competence as an account executive of special projects anyway?

Nothing.

It may look like I dodged Chad as my date for the gala, which I did, but I simply have to face the consequences of my actions. And if I don't look like a team player, then so be it. The

Trinity will have to promote me based solely on my credentials, vagina and all.

Suddenly, I feel good. Empowered.

The nausea stops.

And right then, I come to another decision. Yes, I will still go to the gala. With or without a date, I intend to make a grand appearance and look absolutely fabulous.

Cool, that's the newfangled Nina talking. She does exist!

Oh, yeah, and this newfangled Nina will have that promotion in the bag by the time she shows up at the Spring Fling.

And wouldn't you know it, my period shows up right at this moment, as well.

And so does the godawful cramping.

FIFTEEN

Men are like grapes . . . They come in bunches.

❦

It's midmorning on Monday and I'm still in my pajamas. Since seeing Brooke yesterday, I've been doubled over with some pretty bad cramps. Sure, I'm glad my "monthly" did indeed arrive, albeit, a little too heavily, which makes me suspicious about a pregnancy, but did it have to come with all the bells and whistles of a headache, fatigue, and aches? Sheesh.

It's the worst period I've had in my entire life, and I can't help but wonder . . . am I feeling this bad because the new low-dose pill is messing me up and it's not right for me? Or am I feeling this bad because the pregnancy "didn't take?" That sort of thing can happen, according to the nurse I called at the doctor's office. But did it happen in this case? I'm not sure. I guess I'll never know. The not-knowing has kinda left another ache within me—like a sense of loss of something special I'm not sure I ever really had: a baby.

But that ache and sense of loss makes me think that something was going on besides just a messed up cycle. That actually, maybe, I really was pregnant. It sure gave me a dose of much-needed reality on handling my life with a little more care. I remember Unity asking how I would feel if there really was a baby. Honestly? Admittedly? I couldn't help asking, what if? I really liked the idea of having a baby, especially if it were Dante's, believe it or not. And because of that desire and because the chance of a baby is gone, the teeny, girlie-girl part of me mourns.

After calling in sick to work, I haul my blanket, pillow, heating pad, Pamprin, and soothing chamomile tea (compliments of Unity) into the living room and hunker down to rest in front of the TV. The movie, *Sunset Boulevard*, is playing, and I can't help but laugh because Norma Desmond reminds me of Jackleen Liquori. I'm due to have a meeting with Jackleen this week, but it ain't happening today.

It's pretty quiet right now. Brooke's already gone to her job with the caterer. They're so booked up this time of year with weddings and showers, she's been making herself scarce around here due to all the overtime she's putting in. Between bumping into her occasionally here, I'll be seeing her this Saturday night at the gala, since the catering company she works for is handling the event. It's really no coincidence. Guess who recommended them to do the job?

The ringing phone breaks my movie-watching trance. I glare at the phone on the other side of the room. Damn. It's the one thing I didn't bring with me to my perch on the couch. I ease myself up and hobble over to the phone. As I hobble back, I note the "caller unknown" on the caller ID before I answer.

"Hey, it's me." Even over the phone, Dante's voice mollifies my aches and pains.

"Hey there," I manage to say while I relish the sweet treat. He's never actually called before.

"How you doing?"

"Hanging in there. Dante . . . there's no baby." I get right to the point; that's why he's called, right?

"You sound tired. You okay?" he asks.

"Honest? I'm not feeling so hot, but I'll be fine. I'm kind of a hurtin' puppy right now. But, hey, at least I'll be able to fit into a gown by this Saturday night."

"Aw, babe, I wish I could help you out Saturday . . ."

I shush him and say, "Don't you worry. I know you have your reasons. It's okay. I can handle this guy."

"You mean, Chad?"

"Yeah. Chad."

"I hate this."

He actually sounds miserable. "Don't hate it. I'll be fine. Trust me, the way you want me to trust you, remember?" I tease.

"I gotta leave town. In fact, I'm on way out. Got some business to look into. Don't know when I'll be back."

I know what his words are trying to say. It doesn't matter where he's going. Doesn't matter if it's a road trip to El Dorado. Or Europe. I get it. He's restless and he's leaving. At least he was noble enough to hang around to see if he was a father or not.

"I understand," I tell him, but then I hear a knock on my door. What the hell?

"No, Nina, I don't think you do," he says on the other end of the line. But I know what's coming and I don't "do" goodbye's well. And so, the incessant knocking on the door serves as the perfect distraction.

"Listen, Dante, I gotta go."

I hang up on him. I can't start crying on his ass when we both knew that our *rendezvous* would have to end. Without a baby, we have no attachment; no reason to say anything anymore. It's the fastest breakup I ever had . . . maybe because the conversation couldn't be construed as a breakup, since we never technically had any real official "relationship." Therefore, a quick good-bye is the best good-bye. Quick? Yes. Painless? No.

The knocking on the door continues and keeps me from dwelling. I rise to see who it is. Something wet tickles my cheek. I wipe it away. A freakin' tear. It's exactly why I had to hang up. No crying, I remind myself.

The knocking turns to a pounding. With one hand on my abdomen and the other wiping my cheek, I stumble over to the door and look through the peephole to see who's at my door.

"Ah, cripes, Jeremiah! I'm not pregnant! So you can go away!"

I swagger back to the couch, but he starts pounding again. And I start with the tears again. Freaking hormones! They're chaotic when you think you're pregnant and they're chaotic when you're not! And they're freakin' chaotic even when you're on the pill! To hell with this low-dose crap confusing me and my body!

"Nina! Let me in!" he yells through the door. "I have a key! Don't make me use it! I'm trying to be polite by knocking!"

"What do you want?" I cry out as I try to march back to the door.

"I came here to apologize! I'm such a jerk! I got insanely jealous. What can I say? I went out of my mind because I thought I was losing you!" he calls out through the door.

"You *were* losing me! In fact, consider me lost. Now go

away!" I shout back through the door, but then I wince. Even my lungs have cramps.

"Don't say that! Please let me in!"

I hesitate. How much more crap should I allow myself to take from him? Letting him in would go way beyond being a glutton for punishment. Besides, I can only think of sprawling out on the couch in peace. But Jeremiah won't go away. Oh, hell.

"Use your damn key!" I holler back and fall back onto the couch. I damp-dry my soggy face with the corner of my blanket before wrapping myself in it tighter than a cocoon.

Jeremiah eventually comes through the door and trudges into the apartmentette. I look up at his sorry ass. It's my guess he hasn't slept any better than I have.

"You look like shit. Where'd you buy that look? All Wrong Dot Com?" I remark and go back to my movie. Norma Desmond waltzes down her grand staircase, ready for her close-up during the grand finale.

"I feel so lousy," he says.

"Yeah? Well so do I," I snap back.

I stare blankly at the television, trying my darnedest to forget my painful phone call with Dante and trying to forget the pain in the ass hovering near me. Jeremiah moves to stand in front of the television and get my attention.

"Do you mind?" I glare up at him.

"I tried you at the agency. They said you called in sick. I came right over. What's going on?"

"I already told you."

"Were you not pregnant? Or did you lose it? Or what?"

"I don't know. But I'm definitely not pregnant."

"But do you think you were?"

I drag my expression up to his and look solidly into his gaze. "I . . . I don't know. I'll never know."

"I'm sorry."

"No, you're not."

"Yes, I'm sorry you had to go through this. But when it comes to having a baby right now, I'm definitely not sorry. I can't bring kids into this world for them to watch me get killed."

I inspect his face and notice the bruising around his eye has morphed to an ugly greenish-yellow welt.

"I see your point. Honest. While there's probably never a 'best' time to have a family, right now would probably be the worst time for you, with killers after you and all."

"I got scared," he mumbles and pulls his gaze away.

His words register slowly. I'm awful good at reading into things, but this sudden revelation blows me away. I never saw it coming. Jeremiah Stone? The globe-trotting journalist? Admitting to getting scared?

"You?" I ask, but he won't look at me. "So that's what this is about? You got scared? Scared of which part? Babies or bombings?"

"All of it. I was scared of so many things. Losing you to another man. Not seeing my baby born, if it was my baby. The possibility of leaving behind a pregnant woman I never married. The possibility of leaving behind a son or daughter who would never get to know me . . ."

He turns his back to me. I don't think he's crying, but he hates to have someone witness him in a weak moment. I'm unsure if I'm in the right frame of mind to contend with Jeremiah's raw emotion. But I might as well face this.

"It's one thing to be scared. But you got downright mean

and nasty to me. Don't worry though, you don't have to be nasty or scared anymore. There's no baby and it's over between Dante and me." I feel the threat of another round of tears, but swallow them back.

He turns back around and faces me. "Nina, listen to me. Things will be different. You gotta believe me. I know I've screwed up some, but I'm still working on it. Just you wait and see." He pulls off his jacket and marches toward the kitchenette.

"What are you doing?"

"I'm gonna take care of you. I don't see that creep here taking care of you, now do I?" he says and disappears out of the room.

He's not a creep!

I want to scream the words but I'm too worn out.

"Anyway, I'm here," he calls out from the kitchen, "and I'm gonna take care of you. I'm gonna make the biggest batch of chicken soup for you. The one I learned to make from that old Peruvian woman while I was hiding out in the jungles of South America."

I've had his Peruvian chicken soup before, and it's damn good, but no way am I eating any of it. I always end up bloated from the salt he dumps into it—

Wait a minute. *Jeremiah. Cooking. Ballooned body parts. Pure Salt.* But not just any old salt. He uses the good stuff.

"Don't you dare make me another meal! Soup or otherwise! I saw what you put in my cabinets! All those exotic spices. They've wreaked havoc on my system. You were using pure MSG instead of salt, weren't you?"

"You know I do. It's no secret," he responds.

"No wonder I bloated up to twice my size. You made a frightening situation worse, mister! You and your damn cooking!"

"You don't like my cooking?" he calls back to me. I hear pots and pans clatter and crash.

"I do like your cooking. But with your highly-concentrated pure sodium additive, you turned me into a waddling salt lick. I'm still peeing my brains out from all the retained water I'm shedding! Do you know what you put me through? Augh! That's it! I want you and your spices out of my life!"

"Come on, you don't mean that. You're upset. You've got to let me take care of you," he insists and suddenly reappears in front of me. "If you won't let me cook, then what can I do to help?"

Did he not hear me? Fine!

"You can pop this in the microwave and reheat it for me before I throw you out." I hand him my mug of cooled tea.

Apparently happy to oblige, he takes the mug and bounds off. I settle back, reach for the hot water bottle, and lay it on my abdomen. When he reappears, he gently places the mug in my hand. I take a sip, it's just hot enough. I sip some more while he sits down next to me.

"Before you throw me out, I've come to a decision. I'm taking you to your Spring Fling this coming Saturday night."

I choke on the tea and the hot liquid spurts out my nose.

"You're what? How'd you know about the Spring Fling?" I ask and wipe my nose on a dry part of the blanket.

"We were engaged before, remember? I know a thing or two about you. The summer solstice is coming up, right? I take you to the bash every year at this time."

"You were overseas every time."

"But I'm not overseas now. And I remember the pictures you sent me. It was like I was there with you."

"But really, how'd you remember the Spring Fling?"

"Actually, when I called your agency this morning, the receptionist complimented me on the *Time* article I was in and asked if she would be seeing me with you at the gala."

I was about to attempt another sip of tea, but stopped myself. I put down the mug before it could slip through my trembling fingers.

"What did you tell her?"

"I told her it depends on whether or not I'd be away on assignment. I have to keep up the journalist mystique, and never commit to one thing."

"Nothing ever changes with you," I utter.

"I should have remembered the gala. I'm such a jerk. No wonder you're so mad at me. But don't worry, I'll go with you."

Now, I'm fully aware of my vow to keep him separate from my personal life. And while he's doing all he can to be nice to me, it doesn't mean I'm gonna fall for him. It's been hot-cold-hot with him and I can't handle it anymore, not in this emotional and physical state.

I'm also fully aware of the irony here. I just broke things off with a guy I wanted to stay but who won't, and now I'm stuck with a guy I want to *leave*, but who insists on staying.

"Ah, about the Spring Fling. I'm not going with you," I tell him. I'm blunt, deciding not to tap dance around the issue.

"Oh, hey, I'm sure you're still upset with me. You need time. I've been through a lot, er, I mean, *you've* been through a lot. I understand. Just let it sink in and you'll be fine."

"You don't understand. I'm going alone."

"What?" He leans back against a cushion and looks surprised.

"Oh, I get it. You're punishing me. I deserve it. I've just been so crazy lately with the nationalists trying to kill me." He points to his bad eye.

"Guerrillas," I mumble.

"Huh?"

"You told me they were guerrillas."

His brow furrows. "Guerrillas? Oh, yeah, that's right . . . nationalist guerrillas."

"Look, I'm sorry you're in trouble, but I promised myself to live my life without you—"

"Unless you need child support, is that it?" he remarks as he springs up from the couch.

"You're such a shit. That was a lousy thing to say."

"What more do you want from me, Nina?"

He stands before me, arms spread wide, waiting for a response. Hell, I'll give it to him.

"Would it hurt for you to think of someone else other than yourself for change?" I ask.

"Funny, I was about to say the same about you."

"What?"

"I've bent over backwards to show you I want to be forgiven and be back in your life. You've made it so hard for me." He paces in front of me. "All you do is focus on my screwups. You don't see how hard I'm trying. I'm willing to fight for us, but you gotta meet me halfway."

"Halfway? Are you kidding me? I've tried to meet you all the way before, but it didn't exactly go so well. We've never both tried at the same time, halfway or full-way. And it ain't happening now. Can't you see that? I know you have eyes and you can see it for yourself, so why do you keep trying?"

I really want an answer because I have no idea why he's still hanging around.

He stops pacing.

"Because I believe in us. Oh, sure, at first maybe you were merely helping me out. But now, I know what we have is special. Now it's your turn. Believe in us once again. Give me an ounce of faith. Half an ounce. Yeah, I got some growing up to do. And I'll start right now. But you have to start, too. Let me go with you to the gala so I can make it up to you."

"No. Unlike you, I *have* done some growing up. And that's why I'm going alone."

He leans back and stares at me like I'm some stranger. In a way, I *am* a stranger to him. I'm really, truly no longer the old Nina. Took him long enough to figure it out. Hell, it took us both long enough to figure it out.

"Let me get this straight, I take you to all these events for over a week and you can't take me to one little gala?"

"Why is this one night so important you?"

"The biggest media event of the summer and you have to ask me that? My livelihood depends on it!"

"Your *livelihood*? Don't you mean your life?"

He momentarily stares at me. "Right! That's what I said. My life. But my livelihood, too. How can I live my life if I'm dead? Think about it. And . . . and if I don't have my livelihood, how can I help people?"

"Come on, we've been in the spotlight all week. The society columns have us pegged to be engaged. You've gotten more face time this week than the president. Don't you think you're off the hook now that you've been in the public eye so much? Surely the guerrillas have assumed you're not their guy. Like you said, a guy in possession of the tape would be on the run or hiding out. You certainly haven't been doing that."

"True, but for me not to be in the spotlight with you now when we're down to the wire with this tape is a risk. It'll look suspicious. I'm afraid you and I did too good a job. They know the tape is due to surface any day. And they'll wonder why I'm not with you on this one big night of all nights. They'll definitely think something's up. If I'm not with you that night, those nationalist guerrillas will come after me."

I hear him loud and clear.

"Oh, this is a mess," I say, suddenly conflicted.

"A mess? No it's not! It's a no-brainer. I'll go with you."

"Dante, please . . . I mean Jeremiah . . . oh, you're confusing me! No. You'll just have to hide out for the night. I'm not taking you. It'll only end up in disaster."

Jeremiah glares at me and for so many reasons. First, I'm standing my ground, something he's not used to. Second, he's not going to the gala, and so, he's not getting his way. And third, I just called him by my lover's name in a fit of confusion.

"Did you ask *him* to the gala?" he snaps.

"Him?"

"That guy you had here. I assume he's Dante. You know, the name you just called me? Did you ask him to the Spring Fling?"

"Yes."

"And he wouldn't go, right?"

"He has his reasons."

"I can't believe you asked him to go and not me. He dumped you, didn't he?"

Okay, I hate talking about this with Jeremiah. It's just not natural. "We had a mutual parting of ways. Now lay off. It doesn't matter. I'm going to the Spring Fling alone. End of discussion."

"I can't believe you'd pick that scum over me to go to the Spring Fling. Talk about taking a step down."

"Shut up about him! Now go!"

"Oh, take his side when he's the one who dumped you while I'm the one still around taking care of you."

"Taking care of me? You've got the bedside manner of a cactus plant! I'm tired of you judging every little thing I do."

"Pregnancy is not little!"

"That's it! No more events with you! I'm done. I'm not taking another minute of this."

"Wow, you really are in knots. I can't talk to you when you're like this."

"I was fine until you showed up. And I'll be fine once you leave." *Fine* being a relative term here.

"Okay, have it your way. You're hysterical. I'll go. But you mark my words, I'm not giving up on us. And my offer still stands. I want to take you to the gala. It's the least I can do for you after all you've done for me as I face death."

I roll my eyes. He actually believes he's doing me a favor! "Don't you get it? I've made up my mind. I'm not going with you or Dante or anyone else! I'm going to rest now. Leave the key to the door before you go."

"You'll change your mind, Nina. You'll see." He tosses the key onto the end table and heads for the door.

"Have a nice life!" I holler.

"Yeah, what's left of it."

SIXTEEN

A true labia of love

In a nutshell, things haven't been going so well. It's now Tuesday morning and I'm alone in the elevator heading up to the second floor to my desk. Since I'm feeling a little better and have gotten by with a little help from my friend Pammy (my pet name for Pamprin), not to mention the perks of Percocet leftover from dental surgery a few months ago, I decide to face going into work.

This morning, I'm arriving earlier than most of the employees. I'm fearful of the pile of work that's probably magically manifested itself on my desk by now and will require a head start if I'm to catch up. I also want to appear fabulously efficient and get out of work at a reasonable hour tonight.

I hate that I had to miss work for a totally Kotex reason, but my day yesterday was awful. And if you're gonna miss a day of work, then it might as well be a Monday.

One thing is certain. While I'm not having a baby, the

non-birthing experience still made me grow, figuratively speaking. I really have to come to terms with who I am at this point. I will simply have to learn to accept it and be done with it.

Soon. I'll do it soon. I promise.

For the short term, I'll accept my dateless status for this coming Saturday night.

With a sigh, I drop my purse into a desk drawer, turn on my new computer, and stare down at the mound of paperwork, just as I expected. Nothing too horrific, at least. Mail. Memos. Call reports. Job estimates and schedules. A few budget updates. According to the scattered work, people obviously had to go into my drawers to retrieve docs needed to do their jobs. Lucky for them, I'm surprisingly organized with my file folders and computer files.

"Well, good morning. We missed you around here yesterday."

By now, I'm seated at my desk, so I spin my swivel chair around and look up at Chad. "The company didn't crumble to the ground while I was gone, did it?" I ask.

He smiles at me. It's the worst kind of smile . . . a charming one.

"It caved in a couple times, but we managed. What are you doing here so early?" he asks.

"Oh, I figured I better get a jump on any busy-work I might have. What are you doing up here on the second floor?"

"Just thought I'd leave you a note to remind you about the monthly Creative meeting we're having first thing this morning."

"Right. That's today." I push through the pile-up of papers and inspect my schedule. Good thing I came in early.

"I figured with the load of papers on your desk, the reminder would get buried. And John personally asked me to remind you."

"Really?"

"Yeah, is that so hard to believe?"

When I don't answer fast enough, Chad ambles over and sits on the edge of my desk.

"I care about you. I do. In fact, I've been meaning to ask you to go grab some lunch . . . and I don't mean to talk business."

"Then what?"

"Boy, you are a company girl, aren't you? All work and no play." He laughs and he isn't coming across so harsh right now. "I thought we'd talk about you and me. We both want the same things in life, and we're both taking the same route to get there. Personally, I don't think it's necessary."

I have no idea what he's talking about. I can't even translate this one because he's being so damn vague.

"I'm not following."

"You know, wanting marriage, family, career."

"Still not following."

"I've heard you talk. It's no secret you were hooked on Jeremiah Stone. But honestly, I think you ought to get over him and move on. Face it, you and I would make a great team if we work together."

"Team?"

"Come on, Nina. You don't really want the Special Projects job, now do you? Isn't this a delayed reaction to your broken engagement? It happens all the time. If you take a deep breath and see that, then you'll remember how content you are in your current position and will drop going for the promotion."

"You really think that, don't you?"

"Yeah, and then you and I can go to lunch, and talk about us, without the pressures of our jobs hanging over our heads. It makes sense."

"So you're trying to reason with me to drop out?"

"Look, all I'm saying is let's go out for lunch later. Instead of competing, let's just reassess our strengths and see where our relationship goes."

"Are you telling me to drop out of this race and *date* you instead?"

"Is that so appalling?"

I cannot figure out men! And they say that women are the fickle, fiendish, foolish, manipulative, passive-aggressive ones! Worse, he's using psycho-babble logic on me. It might have worked at one time, too, because in a sense, he's right on the *dinero*. Only, he doesn't know how much practice I've had with men lately.

Question is, why is he using this route to keep me from going after the job? After a quick mental scan of reasons, I can only come up with one.

"You're nervous you won't get the job, aren't you? I'm serious competition, aren't I?"

"I'm just trying to figure out what's best for all parties involved. Why not simply fast-forward to the inevitable?"

"By the term, *inevitable*, you mean, sleeping with you."

"Careful, there, Nina, talk like that can be construed as you sexually harassing me. And you don't want me pressing charges."

Okay, cue the inward groan.

"Okay, then, define *inevitable*."

"Let's see." He takes a deep breath and crosses his arms in front of his white, button-down, Tommy Hilfiger shirt. "If you get the job, you'll find putting up with the chauvinistic behavior of the senior management grueling. Your work won't be up to par in their eyes no matter what you do, but you'll slog through until the man of your dreams sweeps you off your feet, marries you, and you both live happily ever after, babies and all."

He doesn't know how much his chatter about marriage and babies kinda hurts right now. I can't let him get to me. I can't. I hide my hurt by putting on a false bravado and wearing it like a new sequin bustier.

"Oh. I see your point. But worse, when I do get the job, where will that leave you?" I feign despair over his bleak future . . . left alone with his millions in family inheritance.

"Like I said, I like you. I'd rather see us getting along. Maybe even go together to the Spring Fling. This promotion means more to me than it does to you."

"How can you say that?"

"You don't know what I go through. I come from an esteemed family. It's not about our wealth. It's about our Puritan roots. My family has this amazing work ethic."

"And you can't let them down, right?"

"I've already had one brother turn his back on them and three sisters who have already married into other families and are having babies. It's up to me now. Will you help me?"

I pause to contemplate his plea. I understand where he's coming from and his reasoning for cajoling me into backing down, but—

I feel something on my skin. I look to see him tracing a solitary finger along my arm.

You gotta be kidding.

I suddenly feel like I'm in one of those poorly made short corporate videos that demonstrate to employees what sexual harassment looks like in the workplace.

"Are you happy, Nina? I don't mean in your job, but I mean, in your life?"

I pull away.

"Of course I'm happy!" I snarl. "What kind of question is that?"

He drops his hand, along with his sultry expression that would have probably worked on any other woman on the planet. "I just don't see you as happy. I can make you happy if you let me."

"In what way?" I snap.

"Any way you want. Any way you need."

He doesn't make a move. But he's certainly testing the waters. I feel my hands balling up, either in restraint or to ready myself to slug him. As I try to think of something witty yet professional to toss back and tell him to buzz off, I see Ray make an appearance behind him.

"Oh, good, you're both here. The Creative meeting's got to start on time today because John has to make a plane to New York shortly after. Be sure you're both there on time."

Ray then heaves me a stack of magazines.

"Round up an intern to go through these for tear sheets. Anything with upholstery, fabric, furniture. We're already gearing up for the High Point furniture show in a few months."

"Um, sure, right." I take the magazines and place them on the desk beside my other piles.

As Ray disappears, I pull out any folders, notebooks, and schedules I may need for the Creative meeting. Chad is still standing there, even though I'm keeping my back to him.

"So, Chad, thanks for coming by and reminding me about the meeting. I guess I'll see you there."

I still don't look at him. Instead, I mindlessly shuffle papers into organized piles and wait for him to get the hint to get lost.

I'm not afraid of the guy, I just fear what I might do to him if he says one more inappropriate thing to me.

"Right. The meeting." He groans and still hesitates. "Consider my offer, Nina. It's better than the alternative."

"Oh? The alternative?" I ask innocently, but I still don't turn around.

"I play to win. You need to understand that."

Translation:

No more Mr. Nice Guy. Consider yourself warned.

I hear his footsteps plod along the carpeted floor until they finally fade into silence. I expel a breath. He plays to win? I could hear the unhealthy competitive edge to his tone. But I also heard the desperation of a man trying to keep up with the impossibly high standards of an upright family in the public eye. He's definitely feeling cornered.

With nine o'clock fast approaching, I collect myself and make it down to the first floor to the big conference room. A few people are already waiting around the table, including Chad, who sits at the right hand of two Trinity members. I assume the left side, across from him, and sit beside Ray. As the minutes pass, more employees, along with Ned the Network Guy, and John's executive assistant, Marilyn, drift in and take their seats.

At one minute before nine, John Avalon waltzes in and assumes position at the head of the long oval table. He begins the meeting with the ceremonial clearing of his throat and reviews some old business.

Ned discusses network security on the company web site, reviewing confidentiality procedures to protect clients. He also reminds everyone never to download anything off the Internet. I shrink in my seat despite my innocence.

Occasionally, I train my eyes on Chad and watch him closely. He catches me once or twice, but his stony expression remains unaffected. I can't imagine he could possibly have anything up his designer sleeve to squash me. Yes, he may play to win, but he also just pleaded for me to back down, right? And don't forget how he attempted to woo me, to put it politely. Sexual harassment is more like it. But his language harbored no hard-core words to nab him officially on that charge.

If he had to resort to those lengths, then he surely can't have any more wild cards left to play. Makes me think his "play to win" insinuation is an empty threat. But, man, I've got to watch this guy either way.

"Nina, are you with us?" John's voice sounds far away, humming somewhere in the back of my head. But the stern tone shakes me back to the reality of the meeting.

"Huh? Excuse me?"

"I said, you're up at bat. Tell me your thoughts about any new affinity card ideas you've been working on."

"Affinity cards? Oh, you mean for that bank's new business pitch, on, um, credit cards, er, affinity cards, right? For that bank?" *Stop repeating yourself. Stop repeating yourself.*

He looks at me as though I sprung a third boob. "Right," John says. "You know, 'that bank' is the one willing to fork over thousands of dollars if we win the account."

I nod. "Yeah, yeah, that's the one." If only I could remember the damn bank's name. But I can't, so I continue, despite the sweat tickling my forehead. "Well, um, let's see. Affinity cards have finally grown in popularity by, oh, thirteen percent in the past year. Whatever organization you belong to, or whatever sport you follow, or whatever hobby you do, you can get a credit card with that organization's logo on it. To proudly show you're part of something special, or a special interest group."

"Thank you for the rehash, but have you got anything else for Creative?"

"Oh, right. I've got a point. To get people to sign up for a new affinity card, or use their existing one more often, I propose a campaign promoting a contest."

"A contest?" Chad's face goes sour. "You mean like every other sweepstakes or bonus-points contest out there?"

I ball my fist under the table and keep myself from knocking out this takedown artist. Before he can suck the junk out of my idea, I continue.

"Not just any contest. This one's got a slant. It's tied in with television trends. We see so many makeover shows involving our homes, our lives, our bodies, but only those lucky few on TV get to participate. I propose the contest to be a ten-thousand-dollar, make-over-your-life contest. The more you use the card, the better your chances of winning."

"So, go with the tried-and-true contest but appeal to the user by what's become important today," John Avalon reiterates, then nods in understanding. "Gone are the days of champagne and caviar and cruising on yachts. Today, people want to improve their everyday world. The one they know."

"People want to remain the center of their own universe," I say, fortifying John's notion. "No sense cruising on a yacht unless you get yourself a tummy tuck to wear the latest designer bikini, now is there?" I ask the faces around the conference table. When no one objects, I decide to continue.

"Bottom line, people want to improve their quality of life. They just don't have the time or money. But the grand-prize winner will have ten thousand dollars to play with. From lipo-suction to Merry Maids, they can get it all. As for the other two runners-up, they'll get three grand each."

"It's appealing," Ray says next to me, "definitely something to form a game plan around."

His two-bits prod me on.

"And don't forget the cross-branding. The campaign will have the home improvement stores chomping at the bit to take part in this. Furniture stores. Car manufacturers. Jewelry mak-ers. Famous spas. The cross-promotion potential is endless, not to mention the print advertising we could do, and even place TV ads on all those home and beauty makeover shows, with both networks and cable stations."

"It'll take some further brainstorming with Creative," John says while he dips his head over to the other two men who make up the Trinity, "and a handful of focus groups will be needed, no doubt, but it's a viable slant."

John looks pleased and taps his fountain pen on the white pad of paper with no writing on it. His assistant-slash-fiancée, Marilyn, sits halfway down the mahogany conference table, and takes notes in shorthand. I can tell she's writing furiously be-cause her diamond engagement ring keeps glinting in the light with each stroke. The rest of the meeting is brief and goes with-out incident.

"Anything else we need to cover? Last up," John says like he always does when he wants to wrap up the monthly meeting. "No? Any report on trends? Competitor news?"

Although John asks this final ritualistic question, he usually already knows whatever anyone reports. With these monthly round-up meetings, it's a good way for him to see who's going above and beyond the call of duty and really doing what he or she can for the team. He loves things like research analyses, hearing which ad agency follows our lead in print campaigns, or copycat ad placement in publications outside the usual target market.

John scans the faces of the meeting attendees, from the manager of the media buyers, to Ray, to me, to Chad, to Marilyn, to the Trinity, to the art director, to Ned, and to the rest of the staff. The room stays quiet.

Just as John's about to end the meeting, Chad holds up a pen to call attention to himself.

"I stumbled across an intriguing notion the other day," he announces. "It's a new, untapped advertising opportunity to provide information to patrons as a whole."

Translation:

I figured a new way to cram unwanted advertising down the throats of unsuspecting victims who can do nothing about it.

Don't get me wrong. I love advertising, marketing, and public relations, but I don't like being overly bombarded with too many ads any more than the next guy.

"We're always open to new opportunities. What have you got, slugger?" John asks.

Chad pauses thoughtfully as he relishes center stage. "How about every time a person picks up the phone to use it, he or she listens to ten seconds of advertising before even getting a dial tone."

I'm hearing the words, but they're surreal. My jaw drops. Had I heard him right?

Oh my God—that was my idea!

It's a total textbook move on Chad's part, not to mention the standard victim's response on mine. Is he so vile, useless, and lame that he's actually using the clichéd corporate move of stealing someone's intellectual property? I'm telling you, he really, truly stole my idea, the one I haven't presented to the group . . . for obvious reasons.

I feel a stinging heat creep up my neck. I guess that's what happens when your blood pressure escalates until it pushes against the walls of your temples, which are now throbbing. My eyeballs are suddenly heating up and throbbing, too.

But it can't be real. I can't be hearing him right. I need to calm down before I have a stroke. I can't have a stroke, because it'll leave me paralyzed down one side. Then I won't be able to speak or use one whole side of my body. I can't have that, because if I'm slurring when I curse Chad out, then no one will understand me. And I need both sides of my body fully functioning for when I tackle him, hold him down, and slug him hard. I count to ten and do a reality check to see if this is really happening.

John Avalon's eyebrows raise and he tosses a curious look to the other Trinity members. One clears his throat and says, "Well, if that ain't a 'Why-didn't-I-think-of-that?' concept, I don't know what is."

"Hmm," John hums from his throat, "you'd have yourself one captive audience, no doubt. But would Americans be ready to give into listening to an ad or two every time they pick up the phone?"

"If they want their dial tone, they will. Think about it, the concept's not all that new. It's merely an extension of what we already experience today. When you're on hold at a company, or on hold for ordering information, what do you listen to? Instead of elevator music these days, you listen to a recorded advertisement about the products and services that company provides.

It's my guess they put you on hold on purpose to make you listen to it before you get through to anyone."

Chad crosses his arms and leans back to let his ingenious idea sink in and simmer. He appears triumphant that he's turned this dial tone, hostage-taking injustice into a moneymaking opportunity for Avalon Advertising.

As for me, I realize I've slumped lower in my seat, my spine gone flaccid, still in absolute shock over what I'm hearing. It's like he's taken my notes and rationale for the concept and used them verbatim.

"You know," the manager of the focus group studies says, "if you capture the spending habits of a particular household, you could route specific ads to the phone line, to meet the needs of that family. Think of it as using the Nielson rating mentality for television viewing, only the telephone line is the vehicle here."

The Trinity nods in agreement. They seem to like what they're hearing. They're actually considering the idea! It's preposterous!

I hate this! And I'm not taking it!

I spring from my chair, which goes flying back against the wall, slam my palms down on the table, and lean across to Chad.

"Chad Gorham, you're a thief! You tell them right now where you got your alleged"—I lift my fingers into the air and use snide "air quotes" to make my point—"*brilliant* idea!"

He looks at me innocently surprised. "Actually, I was offsite and called here to talk to someone in the Traffic Department. The receptionist put me on hold. I heard Avalon's recording on their services and thought, if only we could charge people to advertise over the phone lines."

"Augh! That's exactly what happened to me! I was the one

on hold listening to Avalon's recording when I had the thought. I was out with a client at the time! You could have at least tweaked your recited explanation for the sake of copyright law!"

"Nina, what are you talking about?" John asks.

"Hellooo! He stole my idea! It was mine!"

"That's a serious accusation. Now sit down. And calm down. Then you can explain," John says.

I look down at my hands on the table and only then did I realize I was standing up and had almost physically attacked Chad. After a few sharp breaths, a final glare, and a last-minute sneer at him, I compose myself. I do as I'm told and lower myself to my chair. Once seated, I capture Chad's attention once again.

"How'd you do it, Chad? I mean, I'm just curious. How'd you pull it off? Do you read minds? Did you go to a psychic? You couldn't have had my phone tapped, or maybe you did, but I never discussed that idea with anyone."

"Nina, if you never brought up the idea, then how can you say it was yours?" Chad asks me while he appears hurt over the accusation. "Are you trying to sabotage me? Or put doubt in their heads about me? Because if you are, it's pretty low. And unprofessional."

"No! I'm not sabotaging anyone. *You're* sabotaging *me.*" I look to Ray for support. He's sitting there staring at me, but he really doesn't know what to make of it. "Ray! John! You've got to believe me. There's no way we could have both come up with the same idea, at the same time . . . it defies all logic."

"Simultaneous ideas happen all the time," John explains. "Two advertising execs in different agencies in two different parts of the country can have the same idea for a campaign and have it come out in print. Whatever creative energy is sweeping people at the time can overlap in their projects. It's synchronicity at its best."

John finishes his explanation and pours himself his usual glass of water for a thought-provoking pause. After taking a sip, he sets his frown on me. The frown can't be good. I brace myself.

"Synchronicity can also bring out the worst in people. People who don't know how to be a good sport. Based on what I've just witnessed, I gather you're accusing Chad of stealing your idea without thinking this through."

"I've had that idea for weeks, but I can't prove it. I have no printed notes, or handwritten notes, no memos, no voice mail, no e-mail. Hell, I didn't even grumble my thoughts into the phone while on hold." I lower my gaze, fully aware of just how much I've made a fool of myself without any evidence to support my claim. "But I got that idea over a month ago. It's the truth."

"So why didn't you ever share it with the team?" John asks.

I look up at him and shake my head. "I couldn't do it. Sure, advertising before getting a dial tone is a great way to capture an audience. But as a consumer, it's a bad idea to take away what little privacy someone has in his or her own home."

"So you decided it wouldn't be fair to the consumer to abuse their dial tone privileges?"

"It's not fair at all. They're paying for that dial tone."

"Yet, you admit, the idea is good."

"Good? It's genius. Evil genius, to be specific."

"And you decided this for yourself, without bringing the idea to our attention?"

"I couldn't bear the thought of having every American hate me because I was the one responsible for invading the home's final frontier of privacy. I'd probably wind up getting some award sponsored by *Ad Age*, make all the headlines, and live with death threats the rest of my life."

"But Nina, who's team are you on? And who are you to decide what's good for American consumers or for this company? What the hell do I pay you for?"

"Huh?"

"You're salaried to bring ideas to the table, both good and bad, which means we own the ideas you come up with for Avalon. Look, I don't need a song and dance with every fleeting thought for an idea, but when you come across anything with potential, you take your idea to Ray. You can hurt this company's future by intentionally *not* sharing ideas. Consider it a passive form of sabotage, something not tolerated at this agency."

"Isn't sabotage grounds for being fired?" Chad pipes up.

"I don't think Nina meant to sabotage anyone." Ray comes to my rescue. "She simply didn't use good judgment."

"No one's getting fired here today," John announces. He sets his sights on me. "I'm not happy to hear this. Understand something, Nina, when an idea is presented, it might be right or it might be wrong. Or it might be the springboard to an even better idea. But if an idea is never presented, it can never get to the best end result. Got it?"

"Got it," I mumble.

"See you all next month."

As the employees rise and gather up their things, I scoop up copies of my typewritten thoughts about the affinity credit card makeover contest and hand them to the Trinity assistants and close my notebook. From there, I simply sit quietly and feel stupid. This recent turn of events has knocked me senseless and I have to take a minute to calm my nerves.

"Nina and Ray, come to my office in five minutes before I leave for New York." John barely looks at me as he turns to leave the conference room.

So much for calming the nerves.

After hearing John's directive, Chad looks over his shoulder at me and shakes his head, not spitefully or sadistically, but sadly. He pities me, I know, because he intends to pummel me into the ground. He even warned me, but I didn't listen. He turns and leaves the conference room with the rest of the employees.

Ray and I are left alone, quietly sitting at the very dark, very polished, conference room table.

"I blew it, Ray."

"You certainly did."

"Lemme ask you, can Avalon lay claim to my creative thoughts? They don't really own them, do they?"

"Let's see. You said that you're the one who heard the recorded advertising message while on hold, right?"

"Yes! Yes! Me!"

"Okay. You were off-site doing Avalon business. You call Avalon with a question. You're on hold with Avalon. You hear Avalon's recorded message, which triggers your idea for Avalon to create more advertising opportunities. What do you think?"

"I think you made your point. Any advice?"

"Yeah, don't do that again. I'll see you in John's office. Don't be late. In fact, be early."

"Ray, please don't be mad."

"I'm not. I'm disappointed. You had a great opportunity and you lost it."

He rises, gathers up his folders, and heads out of the conference room. Before I get up to go, I take a final moment to decipher what happened during the meeting. How did I get put on trial and found guilty for something I literally didn't do? And how did Chad Gorham get rewarded for his unethical behavior? And lastly, how could he have known my idea?

Synchronicity, my ass.

Then again, I have no proof of his stunt. Therefore he gets to remain innocent, at least until proven guilty. And I intend to prove his guilt . . . somehow.

SEVENTEEN

Self helpless

❧

I make the strut-of-shame toward John's office. Before entering, I pass John's assistant, Marilyn, and her breasts, both poised pertly at her desk.

"Oh, hi, Nina. John will be back in a minute. Hey, I liked your credit card contest idea in the meeting. I'd sure love to win that makeover."

Her kind words lift my spirits. "Oh, thanks Marilyn. Yeah, too bad agency employees wouldn't be qualified to enter. It's standard procedure."

"Too bad. Oh well, and hey, did you decide who you're bringing to the Spring Fling? I've got to get the list to Creative to have programs printed."

"Um, sure, I guess you could say his initials are TBA."

"Too many men to choose from, hmmm?"

I wink at her but say nothing more as I enter John's office. I sit in the maroon leather guest chair next to the one occupied by

Ray. He's sketching something onto his pad of paper. I look over to see a rendering of a cottage with a small garden, on a cliff overlooking the ocean. He's obviously got retirement hot on his mind and can't wait to cultivate his garden.

"You could have lied," he says without looking at me. "You could've said your dial-tone idea got lost when your computer crashed. You could've said you were letting the idea simmer before presenting it."

"Forgive me for not thinking on my feet as fast or as deviously as Chad can. He caught me off guard."

John Avalon blows past us and sits at his enormous black leather chair behind his desk. My stomach turns and my heart sinks. Or does my heart turn and stomach sink? I only know, I'm twisted inside because I wonder if he heard everything Ray and I just said.

"Whether Chad or anyone else uses or steals your ideas is irrelevant, Nina. In fact, 'stealing' is good in some occupations, take baseball for instance." John laces his fingers together and lays his hands on the top of his desk.

Yep, he heard us all right.

"Creativity is public domain inside the walls of Avalon Advertising, both figuratively and literally. Chad understands that; you can learn from him. I don't care if he dug through your trash bin to get the idea or if he pulled it out of your ass, he did the right thing by letting the agency decide the fate of the concept."

John seems a lot more mad about this than he did at the meeting.

"It's like Ray said, I used bad judgment. I'm so sorry," I offer.

"Oh, you're gonna be a lot sorrier in a minute."

"What? Why? What happened?"

"I have to catch a plane. I'll make this quick. For starters, I just had a chat with the manager in Traffic. It seems a job estimate for a photo shoot for the Curly-Girl spring apparel line was signed-off with a decimal in the wrong place."

"And?" Ray prompted.

"And due to the error, over two thousand dollars has to be knocked off the price. We didn't have much markup on the campaign's photo shoot to start. Worse, with some clients having to pull their accounts due to the economy, it means it'll cut even more into the employees' profit sharing."

"Oh, man, that's gonna tick off a lot of people," I murmur mindlessly. "But I can't imagine having an error on a job estimate. I triple-check my work and everyone signs off."

"I can't tell you how it happened, but it did. Add to that, your crashed Pentium from a downloaded virus, the lost manhours because of your misuse of equipment and time lost at Avalon, and your corrupted computer files—it's adding up. Too many errors, not enough hits."

"It wasn't my fault." The pathetic words gurgle out my lips and limply flop forth. What kind of useless response is that? But I have no other recourse.

"I called your clients yesterday to see how things were going. Two complained how you sent them print ads with typos you should have caught, just before going to print. Don't you know what four-color separation costs by now? And I just got off the phone with Jackleen Liquori."

"Oh, no. What did she say?"

"She's not too happy with you."

"But I kill myself for that woman!"

"It seems you get mouthy with her."

"She needs it."

"She said you showed up drunk for work on your first day with her."

"I was not drunk. I was hungover. I distinctly recall, the hangover had already kicked in by the time I saw her. I even—"

"Nina, you're not helping yourself here." Ray lays his hand on my arm to keep me from saying more. "In fact, you're in the direct path of getting fired if you're not careful."

But everything seems to be crumbling down around me. I know my work is good; I know it's error free, so what the hell is going on? Could I really be that distracted lately? My world is spiraling around me and I can barely hang on.

"Damn it, Ray, I'm in a catch-22. If I say it's not my fault, I look pathetic. If I say I'm being shanghaied, I look like I'm dodging responsibility and blaming others. What am I supposed to do?"

"I'll tell you what you're supposed to do," John cuts in.

"Tell me. I'll do it. Anything."

"Fix these problems and keep any more from happening. And no more sick days until this crucial time is over."

His sick-day remark makes me wanna cry. "But you have no idea what I've been through. And I can't control—"

"You'll have to. I can't pull you off the accounts, because that'll look even worse and I can't get anyone up to speed fast enough to take over."

"Okay, okay. I can do it. If that's what it takes. Trust me, I can do it. I can."

"No, you *will* do it. If you want a future here at Avalon, you better clean up these disasters. Consider yourself on probation for the next thirty days. You have until then to turn things around. Chain yourself to your desk if you have to and stay there until every one of your clients flips with joy over you. But whatever you do, don't move from your desk."

Just as John rises to leave, his office door bursts open wide. We all sit stunned and watch a whirlwind-of-a-woman make a grand entrance. She's dripping in gold jewelry and Chanel-everything-else.

"Yoo-hoo! Jackleen Liquori has entered the building!" she announces.

"Jackleen? What are you doing here?" John asks. "I was just on the phone with you."

"Yes, I know, dear, I was there. I was pulling up to this monstrosity you call a 'manor house' at the time."

"Why didn't you say something to me?"

"Because my business here doesn't concern you, my sweeeet-baby-doll-dahling." Jackleen graciously smiles at the two men, but then turns toward me. "I'm here for *her*." She points a scarlet talon at me; her extra long, extra black, false eyelashes flutter in my direction for dramatic emphasis.

"Me? But I didn't do anything wrong, I swear!" I cry out.

"Relax, dahling. You're fine."

"Then why are you here for me?"

"Why, my dear, I'm here to take you away from this horrid place." She gestures to the dark paneled walls and bookcases.

"Take me away? Away where?"

"Shopping, of course!"

"I'm dead. I'm dead. I'm so fer-reekin' dead."

I can't stop saying the words because I can't believe my fate to-day. One minute, I'm warned that I better keep my sweet-apples in my chair at my desk; the next minute I'm holding on for dear life in Jackleen's Mercedes convertible with the top down, zipping along the highway heading into Boston to go shopping. Jackleen heard that Newbury Street is a fun place to shop, so she's driving in that general direction.

"I'm so dead."

"No, you're not. Now stop saying so. You sound like a broken record. Do you know what a broken record is?" She looks down her nose and through her dark Donna Karan sunglasses at me. She's got her hair in a leopard-print pink scarf to protect it from the wind.

"I know what a broken record is. I can't help saying it . . . I'm so dead."

"You're not dead. You heard Ray. He reminded John that you're supposed to do whatever it takes to make your clients jump for joy. In this case, 'jumping' translates to 'shopping.'"

"Why me? Why me? Why me?"

"Because you're the one who needs a gown for the Spring Fling, that's why."

"What?"

"Yes, dahling. It's all you ever talk about on your cell phone with your girlfriends. And you're right. If you're representing me, you'll have to play the part to the hilt. Based on what I've seen you wear, I've arrived in the nick of time."

"You know I need a new gown because you eavesdrop on my phone conversations?"

"Of course! In fact, we both need a gown."

"We? As in, 'us'? You mean, you're coming to the gala?"

"John invited me personally."

"I can't do this today. I have way too much to do at work. You have to turn around and take me back."

"I'll do no such thing."

"I mean it, Jackleen. Turn this jalopy around now."

"I'm buying you a gown."

"Oh, no you're not."

"Oh, yes I am." She presses her foot to the accelerator. I slam my hands onto the seat and door to brace myself against the increasing speed. "Either I buy you a gown or you're fired."

"I'm practically fired anyway! No thanks to you!"

Obviously, she's not turning around anytime soon. The speed whips my hair into my face, but I don't care. I'm hanging on come hell or high water. Why is it every time I try to stay on the straight and narrow, I get totally derailed?

"You have got to lighten up, young lady. I liked you better when you showed up for work drunk." She leans over and pops open the glove compartment, not too concerned about her straddling two lanes on the highway. After rummaging around inside, she pulls out a silver flask.

"Oh, no, you don't. You're not drinking and driving, you hear me?" I yell.

"Who said it's for me? It's for you." She thrusts the flask against my chest. "Besides, I'm already drunk."

After hearing this, I clutch the flask. It's barely lunchtime, but quite frankly, I need a swig. I open the cap and guzzle. I think I'm drinking scotch, but it's anyone's guess. I only know my throat burns. Kinda like it did the night I shared drinks with Dante while we chatted about my grand plan for a new sense of direction in life. When did my compass go so haywire?

But it's the memory of Dante that makes me guzzle the stuff. I haven't allowed myself to think of him—his smile, his thighs, or his good-bye—until this moment. Heck, even Jackleen fell head over heels for him by the time she hopped on his motorcycle that first day I met her. Speaking of that first day with Jackleen . . .

"While we're on the subject of drinking, why'dja go and tell John Avalon I showed up drunk for work the first day I met you?"

"He asked me how things were going with you. I wasn't about to lie."

"But didja hafta tell him I was drunk?"

"Weren't you?"

"Well, yeah, but still . . ."

"For someone in the business of public relations, advertising, and publicity, you are terribly green, aren't you?"

"Whassat supposed to mean?" I yell into the wind as she careens down the highway.

Jackleen takes the flask from me and has herself a healthy gulp. She swerves lanes, not because she's so visibly drunk, but because the raised flask in front of her face is blocking her view. A few cars veer off and honk, but they're wise enough to get out of the way of the speeding convertible.

"I did you a favor by telling them you showed up drunk."

"And how do you figure that?"

"You can be so straight-laced. I had to get them jazzed about you. They need to know you can be wild and still handle an account like mine. Just imagine, they now know you can do a fabulous job, even while drunk. And I told them so. Simply fabulous."

"Fabulous? Really? They neglected to tell me that part. But still, what you did was awful. I'm in so much trouble now. Couldn't you have just given me rave reviews? You know, I scratch your back, you scratch mine. Isn't that one of the golden rules?"

"Oh, fuck the rules!" Jackleen laughs while the convertible swerves between an eighteen wheeler and a black pickup.

I have to settle her down and bring her to her senses before she gets us both killed, and before my brain starts sloshing around my skull with the alcohol I'm chugging.

"Aw, Jackleen, come on, without some rules, there would be utter societal chaos." *Sounds like something I would have said to Dante.*

"You make it sound like chaos is a bad thing."

"I mean it. Sometimes you can be so well intentioned, but you do everything bass-ackwards and it makes more trouble for people."

"Speaking of bass-ackwards, where on earth are we?"

"I have no idea, I wasn't paying attention." I stare at the signs with city names and routes leading to the more northern parts of New England. "Oh, hell, I think we're heading north into New Hampshire instead of south into Boston. Please, Jackleen, just turn around and take me back to the agency."

"I'll do no such thing. Now look in the glovey for a map. The company that shipped my convertible here graciously put one in there for me."

I roll my eyes, but do as I'm told. My hand reaches in and out comes another flask. I hold it up, then jostle it to see if it's full. It is.

"How many of these things have you got?"

"Not nearly enough. Now, hurry, where's the map?"

I return the flask, then pull out what appears to be a map, but the top portion is singed and brown. While I unfold the giant paper, Jackleen looks down her nose at the browned edge.

"Oh dear . . . that's right. I burned it."

"What?"

"I had to see what my facial expressions would look like at night by a fire just before filming a scene for *Cacambo!* So for practice, I burned part of the map and watched my reflection in a mirror. I specifically burned New Hampshire. I didn't see the need to keep it."

"That's just terrific. It doesn't matter where we end up because this little adventure is gonna get me fired anyway. And it's all because I'm a big fat hairy puky loser! Augh!"

"I've had just about enough from you, young lady," Jackleen yells haughtily and swerves over to the slow lane. She veers off the highway and into a small rest area. "You and I are going to have a little talk." She throws the Mercedes into park, turns off the ignition, and gets out.

"Fine."

I attempt to reassemble the map by folding along the creases. But with the singed parts, the task is practically impossible. With a growl, I crush it into a giant messy ball and toss the wad of paper onto the console between us.

Jackleen marches to my side of the car and pulls open my door. "Come on, let's do this and get it over with."

Just as I get out and stretch my legs, Jackleen bends her knees and puts up her dukes. "You and I are going to have it out once and for all."

"Jackleen, please, you look ridiculous. You can barely hold up your arms with the weight of all those gold bracelets and rings you've got on."

"These gold rings can do a lot of damage! Think of them as brass knuckles." She starts bouncing and dancing on her well-heeled toes like a badly trained boxer. "Come on, let's get it out of your system."

I'm not about to hit anyone in old-school, head-to-toe

Chanel. There's still a thing called brand name reverence. While I don't exactly genuflect before fashion designers, I do cross my arms and refuse to get into it with her.

"I touch you and I get fired on the spot, not to mention jailed for assault and battery. Now take me back to the agency. I fail much better there."

I turn to get back into the car. I feel a slender but gnarly hand curl itself around my arm.

"Oh, no, you don't. I will not have you blaming me for your demise for the rest of your life. And I will not have you continue with your self-effacing attitude. Now, put 'em up. Time to face your demons, Nina Robertson!"

She starts wobbling on her skinny heels, bouncing around me. She fakes a couple jabs to my gut to scare me and provoke me into a fight. Once, she pokes me right in the chest.

I stare at this aging movie star who has more guts and glory in her little pinky finger than I do in my entire body. I really must be pathetic if this woman has had it with me and is actually taking the time to try and punch my lights out. She's right. The time has come to face my demons. But where do I begin? Which demon haunts me the most? Professional life? Family life? Love life?

While I try to decide which tragic flaw has got my G-string wedged up my butt crack the most, I keep my arms by my sides. Of all the times I've wanted to slug this woman, I'm now given the chance, and I don't have the heart. Doesn't irony ever take a day off with me?

"I hate the thought of being alone," I blurt out. There. There's the demon of all demons.

As if momentarily stunned by my admission, Jackleen freezes. She lowers her bony fists and plants them on her hips.

"Alone? You think you're all alone? Oh, dahling, you're not alone. You're surrounded by people who care about you. Why, you're always on your cell phone with a friend or your mother or someone."

"Maybe, but I'm talking about my future. I have no one in my life to share it with. I dunno. Life shouldn't be this hard. If I had someone special in my life, maybe I wouldn't feel so bad about everything else."

"You mean, as in, a man? Why is it so important to you to have a special man in your life?" she asks.

"Someone like you wouldn't understand."

"Try me."

Where do I begin? I never dreamed I'd be facing my future solo and I'm terrified. My bottom lip trembles pathetically while I try to find the words.

"Oh, come on, dahling. Talk to me. Why is it so important for you to have a man?"

"Because I can't fold a map," I cry.

Her eyes widen, then her false eyelashes flutter up and down as she nods.

"I understand. So, you can't fold a map. Well, I can. When push comes to shove and you have to do it alone like I have these past few years, then believe me, your sense of direction becomes sharp as a tack."

"You've gone without a man for that long? Sheesh, according to the tabloids, if you go without a mate, you go into withdrawal."

"I was in prison, dahling, remember? I learned to do without, and so can you. We'll do it together."

"I'm glad you can do it, but I don't think I can. Sure, I can be adventurous . . . just not on my own. I'm already used to getting sidetracked by you, taking some crazy scenic route instead of the straight and narrow. What am I supposed to do when you go back to California? What am I going to do when my friends go off and get married? My mom won't live forever. I'll be alone."

Jackleen's expression softens with sympathy. She places her hands on my shoulders.

"Then come with me."

"To where?"

"California."

"And do what?"

"Do what you're doing now. Be my executive assistant. My publicist. My public relations specialist." She cocks her pink-scarved head to one side; her hair is still perfectly hair-teased and sprayed underneath, despite the drive from hell. "Be my *friend*. That's right. I said it. *Friend*. Now close your mouth. You look like you're catching flies." She drops her arms from my shoulders and plants them back on her hips.

I do what she instructs and clamp my unhinged jaw shut, but it does little to alleviate the shock that has me more paralyzed than the effects of a stun gun.

"Well, Nina? What do you say? You can start a new life in LA. Meet a whole new crop of men in Beverly Hills. You can work for me in Hollywood. Red carpets all the way. I pay top dollar. I need someone like you to tell me off when I need it. Someone who can stand up to me and my demands."

Wow. California. I'm tempted. I'm so tempted. A new life. Big bucks. Total girl-glam. All the sequined bells and gold-dipped whistles I could stand. Not to mention a whole slew of new diamond-studded studs I'd meet. The vision of beginning a whole new life clear across the country accosts me in one spine-tingling blow. I would be starting over. Starting from scratch. Starting from square one. How exciting. How wonderful.

But more to the point, how exhausting.

"I can't do it. Your offer sounds terrific. Honest. But as lousy as my future looks right now, I'm just getting settled here, right where I am. I've got to give it a shot here."

"Just getting settled? Dahling, you've lived your whole life here."

"What I mean is, I'm getting settled with who I am and what I want. Even though I may not know where I'm headed, I want to stay. Here. On my own turf. I'm sorry."

Jackleen frowns. "In that case, you leave me no choice for what I have to do. I simply must insist that you be pulled from my account. Effective immediately."

EIGHTEEN

Today's horror scope is . . .

Mom's villa sits smack-dab in the middle of her retirement village, North Shore Acres, clear across the other side of the city of Salem. The buildings on the compound are quaint enough; they look like little cottages and really aren't too depressing, considering most people are on the brink of death here; I never see anyone under the age of sixty roaming around.

As I pull in, I notice the swimming pool has officially opened for the summer months so everyone can gather 'round to gossip like high schoolers. Apparently the rumor mill runs rampant through the place faster than a bad case of dysentery. I'm not looking forward to living that sort of life. But facing obstacles like Jackleen's constant histrionics makes me feel like I'm already living a junior-high-like lifestyle.

Lucky for me, Jackleen downgraded her demand yesterday from "effective immediately" to "as of midnight of the summer solstice," which means she hasn't changed my "probation" status to "fired" status yet. She's going to wait until the night of the Spring Fling in three days to make a scene and fire me on the spot in front of the Trinity. I know how she operates. She loves crisis. She loves attention. She loves the bad publicity; it's all she can get these days. Unfortunately, it's coming at my expense.

Through the windshield, my mom's villa comes into view. After I park my Honda, I make my way up the tulip-lined stone walkway to her front door. Why did my mother insist I come over for supper tonight immediately after work? I've got so much already on the brain, like the possibility of losing my job, I really don't think I can handle another hassle to weigh me down, which is exactly what I expect from her today. I dunno why. Just a hunch.

I still feel kinda lousy, so I've changed from my work clothes into something casual; a pair of denim overalls, a gray Old Navy jersey, and my favorite kick-around hiking boots. My hair is pulled back in a messy ponytail, just the way my mother hates.

I ring the doorbell. A moment later, the door flies open. My Auntie Carolyn—as in, the mother to my arch rival cousin, Celie—peeks her head out. Uh-oh, only pain and anguish can come of this.

"Nina! Hello!"

Auntie Carolyn grabs at me, hauls me into the house, and hugs me to her low-slung bosom. We're standing in the intimate foyer (really just a teeny tiled entrance with a bunch of decorated red hats on a coat rack), smiling like goofs, and trying to appear pleasant.

"How are you, dear?" she asks graciously.

"Doing okay. And you?" I respond just as graciously.

She lets out an exasperated sigh and glances around the corner toward the kitchen. She folds her hands as if in prayer and levels me with a grim stare.

"We've been through a lot, but we're doing much better now."

We? We, who? What does she mean "we?"

A thousand thoughts whir through my mind; did Ma fall? Did she have a spell? Some sort of angina attack? I silently hope my mother's plight has nothing to do with her indulgent consumption of alcohol.

"You mean, you and my mom? Is she all right? What happened?"

"Oh, your mother's fine, dear. She's on the toilet. That's why she didn't come to the door herself." She stuffs her hands in the pockets of her denim romper with apple appliqués all over it.

"So, what's going on?"

I wait for an explanation, until my good ol' cousin Celie appears down the hall and stands beside Auntie. She looks peaceful. Serene. Sedate. Mom told me about the new-generation antidepressant she went on following her broken wedding date. Maybe that's the reason she appears so reserved. I definitely don't feel daggers shooting from her eyes the way I did the last time I saw her after I sneaked into her wedding gown.

"The 'we' means my mom and me," Celie announces. "Hi, Nina." She stuffs her hands in her pockets the same way her mother does, except Celie's got on low-rise jeans and a black, midriff-revealing jersey.

I stand guarded and say hi back. From there, we file into my mother's little living room and patiently wait for her to come out of the toilet. Auntie talks about my mother's irritable bowel, then quickly moves on to my mom's green thumb. All the while, Auntie admires all the ferns and ivy in macramé plant holders hanging from the low ceiling. She wends her way all around the room stuffed with colonial-style brown furniture and various tchotchkes, including a few Hummels and porcelain figurines.

A moment later, my mom, dressed in a purple T-shirt with a picture of a big hat in red glitter on the front, makes her grand entrance into the room. She's got a large shopping bag in one hand while she balances a platter of sandwich meat in the other. She lowers the platter of ham and bologna to the dark brown coffee table. She then thrusts the large shopping bag onto my lap and spins back toward the kitchen.

"I've got rolls coming," she says from down the hall.

"I'll help you." Auntie scurries out of the room after her.

Why do I get the feeling I've been set up?

"So," I begin to say to Celie; I couldn't feel more awkward, "I didn't expect to see you here." I keep the shopping bag in my grip, unsure of what I'm supposed to do with it. It'll be a good barrier if Celie takes a swing at me.

"Well, I'll level with you. I planned it this way. I worried if you knew I was coming today to talk to you, you'd be too embarrassed to face me after what you did."

"After what I did—" I'm about to remind her who started the wedding wars by stealing *my* chosen wedding gown, but my mom shows up with a plate of bulky rolls, cheese, and mayo.

"I broke out the Chinet," Ma announces.

"What's the occasion?" I ask.

"The occasion is we're all here together," my auntie says as she follows behind, juggling paper cups and plates, a two-liter of D.C. under her arm, and a pitcher of Bloody Mary's, complete with celery stalks.

I bite back fighting words. I still grip the shopping bag's handle tightly and try to be cordial. Gracious. A decent human being.

After all, I'm a guest in my mother's home and I remind myself to behave like one.

"Well, aren't you gonna open it?" Mom asks me.

I glance between her and the shopping bag in my white-knuckled clutches. The shopping bag must be the "thing" mom wants to give me. I nod to her and say okay. I spread apart the handles, remove the white tissue wrap stuffed at the top of the bag and peer inside.

I see fabric. I puzzle at this. What do I want with fabric? I can't sew. Never could.

"Go ahead, pull it out. Go on."

I reach in and pull out the heavy material. As I pull, I realize it's not just fabric. It's a quilt.

I hold it out and admire the pattern sewn with fabric in all my favorite pastel colors; pale pink, light green, and cream. The pattern has all these interlocking circles all over it, topped off with a soft green border.

Admittedly, it's beautiful.

"Ma, I didn't know you took up quilting again."

"I didn't. I've been saving it for you."

She glances down at her handiwork, but isn't gushing with pride the way she used to when presenting someone with one of her handmade quilts.

I'm still puzzled. I know she quit quilting about five years ago because she didn't get along with the members of the quilter's guild and didn't want to quilt alone. So she upped and left. I don't ever recall her mentioning a quilt she made for me.

"Saving a quilt for me? All this time? Why?"

She points to the pretty pattern of circles on the quilt. "See that? It's a wedding ring motif. I was saving this for when you got married, but I'm tired of it taking up space in the closet. So,

I'm just giving it to you now, seeing as you're not getting married." She takes a long gulp of her Bloody Mary, then points to the platter of meats and cheese. "Sandwiches anyone?"

My auntie and cousin act unfazed by what they've just witnessed and dive into the food, right along with my mom. As for me, I have no appetite. I can only sit in shock and stare blankly at my mother. It's bad enough to give up on your daughter and unload an old wedding gift to make space for storage, but to do it in front of this particular audience goes too far.

So, that's it, huh? That's the "thing" she had for me? Has my potential for marriage expired in my mother's eyes? I didn't even know marriageability had an expiration date. Has my own mother decided I'm past the "use-by" date in the areas of marriage and child bearing?

"You gotta be kidding. Is this what you think of me? That I'll end up as some spinster and wind up living . . . here?" I ask, still holding up the quilt in shock.

My mother looks at me perplexed. "What are you talking about? I don't have the room to keep that thing anymore and you don't have any wedding plans. So, you might as well just make good use of it."

She truly doesn't see how she is crushing me, especially in front of Celie and her mother. Unable to face their stares, I glare down at the quilt. Perhaps I *could* make use of it—as a drop cloth while painting furniture.

"Things happen in life, Ma. People change. I can't just snap my fingers and determine when I'll get married."

"Yes, you can. But you won't. You go and tell me Jeremiah is staying with you and you don't fight to keep what's yours?"

"He's not mine. Jeremiah's moved on. So have I. I'm over

him. You'll have to accept that. I'm only helping him while he's in town. Besides, you can't force someone to love you."

"She's right," Celie pipes up. "You have to wait for the right man to come along. If he doesn't love you enough to want to be with you and marry you, then I say, screw him. You don't want him anyway. Right, Nina?"

My eyes bug out at Celie. Did she just come to my defense?

My mother throws down her sandwich. "Well, I say bullshit! Maybe if you tried, Nina, just tried, even once, I could have had grandkids by now! You shoulda married Jeremiah when you had the chance. You know they either die or defect on you anyway."

Celie chokes and coughs before horking up a chunk of ham. "Oh, no! Please don't say that," she cries to my mom. "I hate to think of any man dying or defecting on me, or poor Nina, for that matter." She places her hand over her heart; she's acting as if she's truly concerned. I'm confused as hell.

My mom doesn't respond, but she does pull the celery out of her Bloody Mary and bite down with a defiant crunch. At least she says what she really has on her mind; that she's greatly lacking in the grandchildren area and she's hating it.

Obviously, this is about her, not necessarily me. My nonexistent love life must reflect poorly on her within her circle of friends; as though my shortcomings as a daughter reflect her shortcomings as a mother. How do I argue with her when she's believed this about herself since as long as I can remember? Now is probably not the time to announce that I actually thought I was pregnant just days ago. I'd be downright cruel to throw that in her face now. Oh, how I'm tempted, though.

I grip the quilt and stare down at it. "I-I don't know what to say about all this," I mumble.

"Saying 'thank you' always works when receiving a gift. Whether it's a quilt or someone's opinion," my mom snaps.

"Right. Uh, I got to go. I'm sorry."

I smile feebly and stuff the quilt back into the bag. I grab my purse and stand up calmly, which is kind of hard since my heart's pounding and I'm really primed to cry right now. Celie lowers her sandwich to her Chinet plate and looks up at me. She rises, too, and touches my arm.

"Wait, Nina. Please. I have something for you, too."

"What could you possibly have for me? Matching pillow shams to go with my new quilt?"

"I wanted to see you today so we could have a little chat," Celie says as we stand alone in my mother's bedroom with the door closed.

Just moments before, she pulled a, "Will you excuse us?" to my mom and auntie and tugged me into this room.

I sit down on the mauve floral bedspread and try to ignore the mothball-scented air. But I can't ignore how being alone in tight quarters with Celie makes me nervous. I try to recall if I have mace in my purse in case she tries to lunge for my throat. I can't imagine she's gotten over the fact that her wedding has been destroyed by me.

"What's this all about, Celie?" I ask.

"I've done some thinking. See, I realize how silly it was for us to get into that little squabble during my bridal shower."

"You put me in a headlock, then hurled me down your staircase. I don't think 'squabble' is quite the word I'd use."

"Neither here nor there. What's really important is, after

much soul-searching, I've come to a decision. I don't think we should let this little recent unpleasantness destroy our relationship. I think the time has come to get past all this and move on."

I remain silent and allow her words to sink into the ol' noggin. First, I try to accept her left-of-center definition of *squabble*. I mean, I'd hate to see how she'd define the term *fight*, but I'm pretty sure it would involve mutilation or death. I then contemplate the other part she said about getting past all this.

What could possibly be the catalyst for her attitudinal turn-around? Did she recently experience some sort of emotional growth spurt? A spiritual spurt, perhaps? A penal spurt? Maybe she realized what she'd done when she stole my chosen-gown in the first place and now has come to apologize. Even so, what could have possibly brought on such an epiphany?

"What's gotten into you?" I can't help but ask.

Celie clasps her hands together in front of her pelvis the same way a frigid schoolmarm would when addressing her students. For emphasis, she takes a deep breath during her dramatically pregnant pause.

Pregnant?

I wince inwardly at my own word choice.

"Come on, fess up. What's this about?" I press.

"I've decided to forgive you."

"Forgive me?"

"Yes, I forgive you for ruining my wedding, my future. I forgive you for sneaking into my wedding gown, something I considered so sacred and beautiful."

"That sacred and beautiful wedding gown was originally mine, so if anyone tainted it, it would be you."

Celie's eyes flutter closed, and she takes another deep breath. I swear she literally has to restrain herself from putting me in another headlock.

Once she opens her eyes, she says, "I didn't come here to argue. I came to forgive you, and I also want to thank you."

"I can't imagine what for."

"I met someone. It never would have happened if I didn't call off the wedding." Celie's eyes glisten and she really does seem to be floating on Cloud Nine. "We're in love."

Ahhh. I got my answer. Her epiphany came in the form of a new man. She found a replacement for her ex-fiancé; traded in the old dog for a brand new puppy. True love would certainly explain her behavior earlier in the living room when she came to my defense. Falling for another man would be the only explanation.

But how'd she do it? And so fast? I mean, I just started on my dating rampage and while it started off with a bang, it's fizzled out faster than a plug-in vibrator during a blackout.

For the moment, I decide her lucky-in-love status happened so fast because she has extremely low standards in a mate. But that doesn't jive; I have *no* standards in a mate and still I have no real potential candidate for a life-mate to speak of. What gives?

"I'm happy for you," I say brightly, "honest."

"We're eloping. Soon." She gives me a serious nod. "I'm not taking any chances this time. I can't let you or anyone else ruin this engagement for me."

"Celie, come on, I know I tried on the gown, but don't you think you overreacted by not marrying the guy? Nobody put a gun to your head and demanded you call off an entire wedding."

This quiets Celie. She raises her chin and nods. "Yes, I overreacted and ended the engagement and I have you to thank."

"Celie, come on, stop 'thanking' me—"

Celie holds up her hand and shushes me. "Hold on a minute. You might as well know, I wasn't ready to get married. He wasn't the right guy for me. I guess I got caught in a race to the altar with you and soon needed an 'out.' That's where you came in."

"Me?"

"Oh, I was furious with you when I saw you in my dress. But you also gave me the perfect excuse to bow out of my wedding. I just told everyone I was so traumatized by what you'd done that I couldn't wear the gown and I couldn't go through with the wedding. I did tell the truth, at least to a degree."

My jaw hangs loose at this information. "So, you used me as an excuse to bail on your wedding?"

"I had no choice. Didn't you see the mountain of wrapped gifts piling up in the formal living room? And everyone was so excited. I didn't know how to get out of the engagement and still save face."

"Let me get this straight," I begin, attempting to quell the mounting anger simmering through my blood. "So, you didn't end the engagement because I tainted your wedding gown? And you don't think I have some social 'singles' disease after all?"

"Oh, well, I don't know about that. I was furious when I saw you in my gown. I wanted to kill you. It was only after I threw you down the stairs I realized I had the perfect opportunity to break the engagement."

"You know, all this time, I felt like a louse for what happened. And to think, you were just using me." My voice rises right along with my ire.

"I should have told you sooner, but to be honest, I never really cared how I made you feel. No more than you cared about me."

My anger deflates. She's got me there. It's true. I've never cared about her feelings. I shrug, guilty as charged, but I can't look her in the eye. She already knows I agree with her.

"Anyway, I let things go too far," she continues. "When I broke the engagement, I hurt a man who didn't deserve it, and I feel awful. Maybe if I didn't get so wrapped up in caring what the family thought, I never would have said 'yes' to a man I liked but didn't love just to beat you to the altar. And I probably never would have chosen the same wedding gown as you, just to add insult to your injury. I can see that now."

Celie pauses thoughtfully and shakes her head. She doesn't say anything more. It's as if she's waiting for me to respond.

What am I supposed to say here? She's not apologizing for stealing the gown out from under me, which triggered the disastrous events at her bridal shower; she's merely "explaining." But she's *forgiving* me, remember?

I guess I ought to "explain" without officially apologizing, too. It's the least I can do. "Okay, Celie. I'm not exactly innocent, either. I got carried away, too, when I tried on the gown at your bridal shower."

"I'm not surprised you got snagged in it. Serves you right. What made you think you could fit into it anyway?"

"Celie, you know—" I bite my lip. No sense in arguing with her about dress sizes, weight issues, or any other numbers game.

She doesn't even realize the magnitude of her insults and I don't have the inclination to convince her I'd actually had a lot of breathing room in the "size eight" gown. I decide to leave the petty, shallow task of splitting pubic hairs to her. She'd claim I was the one in denial anyway. I can't be worrying about her warped reality right now.

"Never mind," I say brightly, "what was I thinking trying on that dress?"

"I don't know, but I need to give you something."

Celie rises from the bed and goes to my mom's closet. She retrieves a large rectangular box wrapped in royple-colored wrapping paper and shoves it into my hands.

"What's this? I couldn't stand the thought of another wedding quilt."

"Oh, will you open it already?"

As she sits beside me, I tentatively pull at the flaps and slowly tear off the paper. Celie grows impatient and assists in ripping away the wrapping.

I lift the lid to the box and peer inside.

I gasp.

There, in all its opulent glory, is my wedding gown, folded around a protective cardboard mold and preserved in its original pristine grandeur. I blink in disbelief at the radiant dress shining into my eyes, its glowing rays of celestial light beaming brightly up from the box. It's blinding. Absolutely blinding.

I tear my gaze away and gape at Celie.

"Why?" I ask.

"I couldn't keep it. I know I'll never wear it and I know how much you love it. I had the back hooks fixed and the whole thing boxed for you. And you know what? I'm okay with it. Good things have happened in my life lately. And to be honest, they happened because of you. Funny how fate works."

"A freaking riot," I say dumbly. My eyes soak in every detail of the fabric, from the sewn-in pearls, to the ornate beading, to the lacy latticework.

I force my attention away from the gown again and train my

eyes on Celie. Despite her bizarre words of forgiveness and blaming me for her ruined wedding, I decide to rise to the occasion. This moment serves as the perfect opportunity to end the rivalry between us once and for all. I must tell her what she so desperately needs to hear.

"Thanks for the wedding gown, Celie. And, thanks for . . . um . . . forgiving me."

"You're so very welcome."

"I guess you won the marriage race after all."

NINETEEN

Does marriageability really have a shelf-life?

❦

I plop the large box containing the wedding gown onto my bed. When I can't stand it anymore, I lift the lid, cast it aside, and stare down at the white lacy bodice all plumped up and formed nicely within its carton.

In the background plays a suicide-set: a terrific compilation of big-eighties, big-haired love ballads. Steve Perry's oddly soulful tone fills the bedroom; he's just so damn fitting for my melancholy mood right now.

Brooke's been hovering in the doorway, dumbstruck at seeing the cursed wedding gown again. She finally screws up the courage to venture into my room and stand at the foot of the bed.

With her officially by my side, I pull the gown from the box and flounce it across the bedspread.

"How . . ." she begins to say, as shocked as I am by my new possession. "How'd you wind up with this thing?" She points down at all the lace and tulle, until something else on the bed catches her eye. "And what the hell is *this*?" She moves her pointed finger to the mound of handmade wedding-ringed-motif fabric, compliments of my mom.

"It's a wedding quilt. I learned today that being 'marriage material' has an expiration date. And apparently mine is up. Hence, the gown from my cousin and the quilt from my mother." I hold up the quilt and strike a pose that would make Vanna White envious. "She's been saving it for my 'big day.' But just like sour milk or rancid meat, I'm past my expiration date. I've 'gone bad.' So she just unloaded it on me."

"Holy shit. Why do you go visit her?"

"Hell if I know."

"And what's the story with the gown?"

"Since I'm tainted and got my 'single' cooties all over it, my cousin doesn't want it. She's got someone new in her life and refuses to have this diseased fabric anywhere near her new man."

Normally, now would be a good time to cry, but I'm so numb by all that's happened in the last few days, my shock absorbency has already reached maximum capacity.

I tell Brooke about my disasters with Jeremiah and Dante, my horrors at work, and the snafu at my mother's place. While I relive all these events, reality hits me like a ton of brick chocolates.

"I'm crying uncle," I announce. "I'm done with all this. I want to go back to living safe and quiet. It's for the best. If I'm lucky, maybe I could crawl back to my old job, if the agency still plans to keep me. Maybe I can learn to accept that a big-time job and halfway-decent relationship just ain't in the cards for me. Shoot, even Jackleen recanted her job offer."

Brooke angles her head and stares at me. She frowns down at the gown lying limply on my frilly pink bedspread.

"Are you kidding me?" she asks. "You're crying uncle? Admitting defeat?"

"What's wrong with admitting defeat? I'm just not junior-executive material. And I'm not marriage material. People are turning in their wedding merchandise, looking for a refund on me." I point to the gown and quilt. "What will it take for me to see the writing on the wall?"

"But look at who's doing the writing. Your left-of-center mother? And your competitive-jealous cousin? Don't get me started on the evil rival at your job relying on cheesy tactics to get you fired. You really want them as your barometer of success? You're gonna let them determine your fate?"

"Look at the evidence. I've got the gown, but no groom. I've got the quilt, but no husband. I aimed for a promotion, but got a probation instead. I have to step back and take inventory."

"Not if it means seeing the inventory as only half-empty. What about the positives? You had two men demanding your attention. One took you on the adventure of a lifetime, not to mention great sex, according to you. The other had you rubbing elbows with the rich-and-famous. You got to hang out on a Hollywood movie set and work with a movie star who wanted to hire you."

"Yeah, but—"

"No buts. Sure, there were downsides, but we call that 'life.' Life's ups and downs."

"Sheesh, I expect this sort of talk from Unity—"

"Nah, she'd explain your *next* life, not *this* one. All's I'm saying is, you may not have what you want just yet, but give yourself more time."

"Time? It's been *weeks*. I'm talking an eternity. Cripes, I go nuts waiting for the popcorn in the microwave as it is."

"I know you want everything right here, right now, tied up in perfect little bows and at your disposal. But when it comes to life, some things take time to fall into place. And I believe they're worth waiting for."

"But I've been trying to fix so many things at once, you'd think one of them would have turned out all right by now."

Brooke laughs. "Hello! I tried to warn you about juggling so many life changes at once. Admit it, you've had way too many balls in the air—Jeremiah's, Dante's, Chad's. No wonder you're overwhelmed and can't see you're way out of this."

I listen hard to Brooke's well-meaning tirade. I do remember how she tried to warn me. But did I listen? Nah. Is it too late to listen now? I'm not sure. But she's onto something. Maybe I do need to catch my breath. I've always been a sprinter when it comes to attaining goals. I guess I ought to pace myself. What an odd concept for someone like me.

"You're right about a few things. I admit, I did have some fun with Dante and Jeremiah and Jackleen just before crashing and burning. Tell you what, I'll start chilling out a little better. And I'll stop freaking out so much over every little crisis, like going to the gala."

"The Spring Fling is a good place to start."

"It certainly is. In fact, I'm not going at all."

"What?"

"I'm picking my battles. And I pick not to fight this one."

Brooke lets out an exasperated sigh. I know she's trying to be patient with me, but what the hell did I do wrong now?

"You have to go, Nina. You're the reason my boss got the catering job there. You're on probation and might not even have your old job anymore. If you don't go, it'll look like you're afraid. Then your big bosses will believe they're justified in giving the promotion to Chad."

"Oh, for Gawd's sake, are you saying I should still fight for what's mine?"

"I always believed you were fighter in your own funky way. I've seen you shop in the trenches at Filene's Basement, remember? You let no woman get in your way of a good bargain."

"Yeah, I got the battle scars to prove it."

"This whole job thing is no different. You can do it."

Brooke gives me a thumbs-up. She then turns her thumbs down at the gown and quilt before heading out my bedroom door. "I've got chocolate penis-pops to make for a bachelorette party. I'll be in the kitchen if you need me, or if you want to sample one . . ." she says as her voice trails down the hall. "Don't let me down, Nina. Don't let yourself down, either. You go to that gala with your head held high."

My head held high?

Could I go with my head held high but with no one on my arm? I ponder this notion. I think back to the past three galas and recall one crucial detail; I went every year with no one on my arm. Jeremiah had never been there when I needed him. My four-year anniversary with Avalon Advertising is the day before the Spring Fling. This Friday, to be exact. In all those years, was Jeremiah ever there for any event? A picnic? A gala? A Christmas party? Never.

I'd always played the understanding girlfriend, then became the understanding fiancée. I'd always have to explain how Jeremiah was in Africa doing a story on the illegal ivory trade or something. My audience would *ohhh* and *ahhh* and say how lucky I was to snag a man with such an exciting life.

Yeah, a life that didn't include me.

Well, it seems I just answered my own question.

Yes, I can go to the gala with my head held high and with no one on my arm. Hell, I've been doing it for years. No more excuses for an absentee fiancé. No more relying on another person to make me feel whole. No more relying on another's adventures to make me feel special. Over the past few weeks, I've had my own adventures: a death ride in a convertible, a pimp-and-ho party, a whirlwind sexcapade with a motorcycle-wielding rebel. Oh, the list goes on.

My blood rushes through my veins and rekindles my sense of purpose, my sense of adventure. The old feeling of "I can do this" bubbles up within me. I even look forward to the rush of finding a gown on short notice.

Oh, I know I've tried a few times to pursue a gown hunt, but it's been a dreaded task. Now, it's an opportunity to try something new on for size . . . namely me. The new me. Not quite the new me I was aiming for, but it's better than the old me. I need a special gown to reflect my new status.

Call me Goldilocks in a G-string, but I simply need something that fits me just right. And it's got to look fabulous, just as I'd originally planned.

I don't need a white, froo-froo gown because I'm not a bride. I don't need a simple black cock-and-tail dress because I'm not schmoozing with dignitaries while on Jeremiah's arm. And I don't need a short little number with easy access because I'm most definitely not aching to have Dante's hands all over me.

Okay, okay, yes, maybe I am still aching to have Dante's hands on me! I don't think that particular feeling will ever go away, but I can't be flitting around in a flirty dress flaunting my horniness, now can I?

My gaze falls to the wedding gown. Time to say good-bye. Before I do so, I mindlessly finger its folds, admiring its craftsmanship. But I quickly realize it represents lost dreams and dashed hopes.

And don't that just piss me off.

I stand up, hover over the gown, and sneer. I'm tired of mourning who I'm not. Time for me to get angry. Anger gives strength. Anger can be cleansing. Anger is impetus for change.

I grasp the shoulders of the gown and hold it into the air. With a rush of strength, I rip a rosette off a shoulder. Then another. And another. The sound of tearing fabric slices through me like fingernails down a chalkboard. Yet, it's thrilling. And admittedly, it hurts, just a little. I don't care. Still too mad. Besides, tearing at the gown helps me to bid *fondue* to my broken dreams. While that part does feel good, I allow a small part of me to grieve the loss. Just a teeny bit.

Don't matter. Don't matter. Don't matter.

The need to tear up my past intensifies. I flip the bodice over and rip away the three rosettes on the bustle. This loosens the light white layer of tulle stitched against the waistline. And so I tear. I pull at the tulle until yards and yards and yards of it unravel and I'm engulfed by the mountain of delicate fabric.

I flip the gown back over and inspect the front. All that's left is the white satiny core of the gown; its low scalloped neckline, its superstitched, super-structured form.

It'll take more than my bare fingernails to rip these threads, as I've previously learned. I grab a pair of scissors and lay them on the bed. I return to holding the gown into the air, deciding where I should start destroying first.

And right then, it's as if I see the gown for the first time; I see it for what it is.

Under all the wedding-cakey, gooey-sweet fluffy fabric, is a simple dress with great "bones." Amazing structure. Sure, it had great *crafts*manship on the outside—at least before I tore it all off—but underneath it all, is the *work*manship.

The gown is made so well, with a shape so terrific, it flatters my body every which way. I can say so, because it's the very reason why I chose this gown to begin with. I felt it emotionally the day I found the dress. I felt it physically the day I snuck into it. I feel it this day. It's not all the froo-froo that I love, it's the amazing strength of the gown's fundamental structure underneath that makes me feel fabulous.

And haven't I been saying all this time that I wanted to go to the gala looking fabulous?

A fat, satisfied grin spreads wide across my jawline.

By golly, I believe I've found my gown for the Spring Fling Gala.

In precisely twenty-four hours, I'll be making my grand entrance into the Tenth Annual Spring Fling Gala Event of the Avalon Advertising and Public Relations Firm. Until then, I'll have to get through the rest of my workday mentally preparing for it.

So what if I don't have the perfect date for the event, or *any* date, for that matter? So what if I lose the promotion to Chad, or don't fall back into Jackleen's good graces before then? So what if I don't even get to keep my current job and I get escorted from the premises? At least I will have arrived with my head held high and I'll know that I tried. And I'm gonna look damn fine in that gown.

The gala is to be held on the manicured grounds of the

agency. John Avalon hosts it here on the estate so he can show off how a top-notch operation is run.

I can't help mentally reviewing my tah-dah-like "coming out" into Avalon Advertising's grand foyer (pronounced *foy-yay* around here). With my head currently in the clouds, my body physically sits through one of the agency's more fun meetings.

On the last Friday of every quarter, the agency hosts a pizza luncheon in the elaborate dining hall we fondly refer to as "the caf." The term couldn't be further from the truth with its stained-glass windows running to the top of the cathedral ceiling, not to mention the collection of impressionist paintings on the walls.

While we shovel our faces with pizza, each member of the Trinity gets up to speak. The bigwigs introduce new employees, discuss awards, and dazzle us with new business accounts. They always end with the announcing of birthdays and employee anniversaries for that quarter.

Between wiping the pizza sauce from their mouths and gulping down Coke, fellow employees politely applaud each little milestone. They're all especially polite when it comes to applauding the four-year anniversary of one employee who's managed to get herself on probation while going for a promotion.

Thankfully, most staff members barely pay attention as they continue to shovel in their lunch. I, of course, don't shovel in as much as I usually would . . . I've got me a gown to fit into tomorrow night. And as we've all learned from Jeremiah's cooking, too much sodium—like the gastronomical amounts in pizza—can wreak havoc on a gal's already borderline figure.

Toward the end of the pizza fest, John Avalon announces the list of the top celebs and media stars attending the soiree tomorrow evening. This year includes a European prince, six baseball players from the Boston Red Sox, two hotel heiresses, a bubble-gum pop singer to perform her one-hit blunder, and lastly, a movie star.

The term *movie star* makes me cringe. I can't imagine what Mean-Jackleen Liquori will have up her sleeve for when she throws me off her account tomorrow night at midnight.

John Avalon then announces for all employees to "get out of here" as soon as they can this afternoon. A major cleaning service, along with an events-and-entertainment company, need to come in and make the manor house sparkle with decor.

Just as I rise to leave, Ned, the network security guy approaches. "Hey, Nina, looking forward to tomorrow night?"

"Yeah, as a mattera' fact, I am."

"Oh, good, um, I've got something to ask you. It's kind of personal."

I freeze. He's got this oddly nervous look on his face, almost quizzical, as he stands there and prepares to ask his big question. I think I know where this is going.

Ned is sweet, and helpful, and even kinda cute in a nerdy sort of way, right down to his bottom-only braces. He really deserves to be spared rejection. But I already made up my mind to go dateless to the gala and I intend to keep it that way. After my trysts with Jeremiah and Dante, I can't be adding another guy to my sexual "repertwat" anytime soon.

"Oh, look at the time. Gee, I really have to run. Can your question wait until, oh, say, Monday morning?"

If I even have a job by then, that is.

"I guess it could, but then it would defeat the purpose of what I have to ask you."

"But I really gotta run . . ."

"I'll make it quick." He stands in my way of escaping him

and his big question. He's pretty adamant for a pocket-protector type. "Are you going with anyone to the gala? Anyone at all?"

I suck in a deep breath. "No. I'm not going with anyone. I'm going alone."

"So you're not going with Chad?"

"Boy, word really gets around. No. I am not going with Chad. And I don't intend to."

"I know it's none of my business, but, are you involved with him? As in, like, dating?"

"What?"

"Maybe not officially dating, but maybe coming in with him at the agency on the weekends by any chance? Or late at night? Like, secretly?"

"Again . . . what? Hey, if there are any rumors flying around about us, it's just a ploy of his to get the upper hand on the promotion. Is he starting one about me?"

"No, not so far."

"Well, then I'd say you covered your bases. Now, I really have to go. So, if you're gonna ask me out, then I'm sorry, I have to say my answer is no. I can't. I just got out of a couple of relationships and—"

"No, no, that's not it, either. I'm trying to figure something out, put the pieces together."

"Oh," I answer, feeling silly. "Um, what sort of pieces? What gives?"

Ned looks around to ensure no one's listening to us. He leans against the wall by the doorway and sets his puzzled gaze on me. "I was trying to uncover your virus and backtrack it. I like a good challenge, you know?"

"What have you found?"

"There were some odd times when you were signed in on

your computer. I checked them against the times you used your ID badge to get in and out of the building. They didn't all match. It was like you weren't even here at times when your computer was being used."

"I tried to tell you!"

"I know that now. Oh, man, wait till you hear what else."

"Tell me!"

"The only other name consistently in the building every time you were allegedly logged on to your computer but not into the building was—"

"Chad Gorham," I finish for him.

"I'm not surprised, Nina. Your password to your computer has been on a yellow sticky note on your phone for the past four years. You're so trusting, and now you know the worst that could possibly happen. You gotta be smarter about security, like I am. I'm sure Chad had a field day once he got your password and rummaged through your computer stuff."

I recall John Avalon saying he didn't care if Chad had dug through my trash bin to get my ideas. I quickly make the mental leap from an actual trash bin to the virtual recycle bin on my computer.

I also recall typing a few short notes on the dial-tone advertising idea on my computer. I saved the document, but then quickly deleted the whole file, hating the idea of abusing people's telephone lines. I forgot how a deleted document goes to the recycle bin and simply sits. Chad must have retrieved the file from there. Son of a bitch.

"I'm such a fool. How am I supposed to win out over an evil genius?"

"Technically, Nina, he's only done something mildly unethical. And it looks like he did it for the good of the company. Still, it would be a shame for a guy like that to get the promotion over you."

"I don't see myself getting the promotion either way. But I'll be damned if I'm gonna let this guy come up smelling like roses. Say, Ned, would you do something for me? Can you print out a report of the times when Chad and I were in the building and on our computers?"

"It'll take some time."

"You think you can get the info in time for the gala? Would that be enough leeway?"

"Plenty."

His answer is Muzak to my ear canals. The guy's pulled through for me once again. "Aw, Ned, you did all this for me?"

"Just doing my job ma'am. I just did it a little faster for you 'cause you're pretty cool. And I love the investigations process." He pats his pocket protector.

"You're sweet. And I'm sorry I jumped to the conclusion that you were going to ask me to the gala. I don't usually make assumptions."

"It's okay. You're great, but you trash way too many computers. You'd give me too many heart attacks. We just wouldn't be compatible. But I'm glad you're willing to fight this guy."

"To the finish."

TWENTY

Show time!

The evening of the Spring Fling has finally arrived and it is a particularly balmy summer solstice. The sunset tonight offers the promise of a spectacular show. You know what they say, red sky at night, sailor's delight.

Wait a minute.

Or is it, red sky at night, sailors take fright?

I only know what I see in the summer sky. Just enough rippling clouds float along, showing hints of a glow from the low-lying sun's rays. It's only dusk, and already the evening has taken on a golden, incandescent hue. The only things piercing the glow of dusk enveloping Avalon Advertising are the searchlights crisscrossing into the air, which adds a Hollywood-like glamourama to the event.

With a thudding heart, I'm sauntering up to the majestic entrance of the ad agency. After four years, I still can't help but admire all the fieldstone workmanship of the manor house, which looks like it came from an English fairy tale. Various vehicles, including Porches, Bentleys, and Ferraris occupy the spaces closest to the entrance. I, of course, had to park my Honda in the regular employee parking.

I smooth the candlelight-white satin gown that fits me just right. Draped over my shoulders is a pure silk, white-on-white damask wrap with an intricate floral motif and fringe that swings in time with my confident stride—my *chicka boom* stride, that is. My touched-up highlighted hair (Golden Angel Number 69), is worn long and loose in a Veronica-Lake coif, following an extensive pin curl session with Chloe, my hairstylist. The shoes, Prada. (What else?) My white clutch, a bargain from Mah-shálls, is encrusted with Austrian crystals, making it heavier than the contents inside.

To overshadow any nervousness, I walk casually toward the building's portico, silently chanting *chicka chicka boom chicka boom* to keep a slow rhythmic stride. I nod a gracious hello to Ray and two other employees who have chosen to go stag as well. They're standing near a limousine and are chatting with the CEO of a Fortune 500 company that they've been wooing as a client.

And so, I turn and face my grand entrance alone. Too bad Brooke couldn't be with me, but she had to arrive on the grounds much earlier to work with her caterer boss. She dragged Unity (kicking and screaming) along to help, since this is such a busy time of year for catering companies.

But honestly, it would have been so cool to have Dante here by my side. We could have pulled up on his rumbling hot-rod Harley. He would have looked so hot and debonair in his rented tux. His helmet hair would have been impossibly tousled . . . the kind of hair you grab and haul closer to your sweet spot when he's diving down—

Okay, so it's been a while since I did the "sexy" with him, or anyone else for that matter. Can I help but get a physical hankering for him occasionally? I certainly developed a penchant for the guy, that's for sure, even if the breakup did hurt. But I've got to shake off any meandering sexual notions. I've been good about not pining away for him.

I gulp down a deep breath, ready to sashay in so I can go hunt down the nearest martini station. Since John Avalon is looking to catch the attention of the *Sex and the City* crowd who monopolize editorial in the publications residing on Sixth Avenue, he's made damn sure to provide twenty different kinds of martinis for tonight's event. Talk about yer target marketing.

I step under the overscaled portico illuminated by a blindingly brilliant chandelier. I wait for an entertainment staff member to open the enormous wrought-iron door imported from England.

But when the door opens, it's not a waitstaff member who beckons me to *entrez-vous*.

"Chad! What do you think you're doing? I, oh, grrr, never mind!"

Deflated, I brush past him; he doesn't dare touch me or stop me.

"We need to talk," he says and adjusts his perfectly fitted tuxedo.

"Now?" *In the middle of my collapsed moment?*

What happened to my grand entrance? What about the *ohhs* and *ahhhs*? And where is everyone?

"Please," he says, his tone laced with a cold urgency. He

steps into the foyer, turns right, and stalks partway down the secluded hallway of the new wing, leading toward the media room, the library, and a couple of small conference rooms.

"Why isn't anybody here?" I demand. I don't know why, but I'm following him.

"They're down at the gallery, showing a few *Wall Street Journal* columnists the new print ad campaigns." He stops abruptly and faces me. "Have you thought about what I said? About backing down from this promotion? It's a wash for you. So why not make it easy on everyone involved and withdraw?"

"Withdraw? Chad, this isn't one of your family's political campaigns. I'm a candidate for a job, not for office. I don't just 'withdraw.' Besides, the last thing I'm going to do is make it easy on you. You've made my life hell; you jeopardized my rep and livelihood. I intend to return the favor."

His eyes widen in surprise. Apparently, he's not accustomed to people standing up to him, at least for this long.

"Didn't you hear anything I told you the other day? Don't you realize how important this gig is to me?"

"Ditto. And if you're still approaching me about this, you must be running scared. A little healthy competition got you worried, hmmm? Let me guess. You couldn't earn the promotion on your own, so that's why you resorted to below-the-belt tactics."

"Tactics, huh?" His eyes slit thin as coin slots. Is he actually mentally calculating which tactics I'm referring to? Trying to decide which ones I've got figured out? "Which tactics might those be?" he asks, confirming my suspicions.

"Oh, you'd like that, wouldn't you? To have me hand over a nice tidy list of the dirt I have on you? Why? So you can attempt a little damage control in time to save your ass tonight? I don't think so."

"I know what this is about. You still resent me because I got the dial-tone ad idea to the board first, huh?"

"I resent *how* you got the idea. There was only one way. You broke into my computer and stole it. It might not be enough to get you fired, but this company will see you for what you are and no employee will trust you."

"You got anything to back up your claim?"

"Still fishing for that list, hmmm? Don't you know by now, every move you make inside these walls is documented and on file somewhere? That's all I have to say."

I hope my threat is enough for him to quit pestering me. I tuck my crystal purse under my arm and turn to leave.

"Yeah, I figured you might get your hands on some computer log and point your finger at me. But I don't think you will."

"I'm not saying another word about it, except that I've got nothing left to lose, Chad." I stomp unladylike down the hall; I'm not here to impress him. "Nothing to lose!" I yell again over my shoulder.

"Yeah, but Ned does."

I stop dead in my designer tracks. I slowly pivot and glare at him. "What did you say?"

Chad crosses his arms over the lapels of his tuxedo and saunters toward me. He's already gloating, but hasn't filled me in on a single thing. He's got me nervous, though.

"What's Ned got to do with anything?" I demand.

"Oh, I know all about Ned's investigative instinct. He's good at it. But he's not quite as good at network security . . . you know, the one skill he got hired for."

I feel my stomach turning at the looming threat. How brilliant of Chad not to threaten me, but to drag an innocent victim into this mess.

"Seems your little friend, Ned, has a tiny oversight in his 'secure' programming, which allows hackers *outside* these agency walls to access all the servers and gain entry to all the accounts, credit cards, web site info, you name it."

"That's impossible."

"I've already hacked my way in and I'm primed to pounce. You're not the only one with precious documentation to get someone fired."

"Have you told anyone about this?"

"Don't have to. They can find out for themselves. It's simple. You make me look bad by revealing the data you obviously got from Ned and I'll make Ned look bad when I go in and hack the hell out of the system. Since I can do it from the outside, no one will know it's me. Nor will they care. They'll be too busy scrambling from the security nightmare, oh, and firing Ned in the process."

"All I have to do is tell them what you just said to me. They'll know what you did."

"Awww, but how will that help Ned? He still screwed up. Are you willing to let him get fired for your cause? The one guy who's helped you? Ball's in your court, sweetheart. What's it going to be?"

I've never had the feeling of being cornered before. It's awful. You can't breathe. The walls close in. A panic attack hovers, ready to swoop down on you.

Looks like I was right after all. I can't fight evil genius. It's one thing for me to get the boot, it's another to let Ned lose his job. Everyone's allowed to screw up once, even if his is a doozy. I almost laugh to myself when I think back to Ned's mini-lecture on how I should be less trusting and more smart like he is.

Oh, Ned, welcome to the poor, poor fool's club.

"Why, Chad? Why are you doing this when it's all gonna come out eventually? Maybe not today or tomorrow. And maybe not even by me. But if I don't catch you, someone will. Someone will nail you red-handed right in the middle of one of your rotten schemes and you'll get fired. You'll see."

"Yeah, but with my family name, I'll always get another job. You really need to worry about yourself. And Ned."

"I just want to know why. I thought your family had a strong work ethic. Why do you have to take these shortcuts?"

Chad stands there, his thin lips firmly set. I see a flicker of vague emotion in his eye. Fear? Pain? It's almost a familiar flicker, like I've seen that look before. Yet I can't place it. But I know I definitely stomped on a nerve.

"What is it, Chad? Tell me why," I press. "I'm just so damn curious. Maybe if I understand why, then maybe I'll make it easier on all of us. Tell me *why*."

"Because I'm a Gorham," he sneers through his perfectly white teeth. "A family of super-achievers. We not only do everything big, we do it fast. You *fall* behind in this family, you get *left* behind . . . in disgrace. I won't do it."

"So it's not the whole Puritan work ethic thing, but it's family pressure, the demand for perfection, that pushes you? Got something to prove to the family, eh? Well, no wonder you resort to cheap tactics. God, at least it makes you human, a little," I remark and roll my eyes.

"I told you before. I have no intention of letting down my family. I've got plans, big plans, and I'm not going to let anyone destroy them. Not even you."

Chad's really letting loose now. Seems I've opened the floodgates of some pretty nasty familial issues. He continues to yammer away, letting out his anger and frustration, furious that a little assistant, a woman to boot, can keep him from what he wants. I guess therapy is out of the question for a "public" personality like Chad. He's really glaring at me now, and even the classy tuxedo can't dress up his ugly side.

"And I've worked too hard to let someone like you get in my way." He points a finger in my face. "I'm not going to end up with nothing from my family and get stuck panhandling my way through Europe on an old café racer."

Europe? Café racer?

Oh, no. Although his emotional outburst runs together in one major-ass temper tantrum, these few words strike a chord. They're too unusual, and too familiar to leave them alone.

"What did you say? Something about cafés and racers?"

"Forget it," he growls.

"You have to tell me."

"Look, all I'm saying is I'd rather play to win than hang onto some ideals, living hand-to-mouth, riding a motorbike."

Motorbike!

And there's the magic word. My pulse picks up. I can actually hear the blood roaring through my ears. I look into Chad's eyes and fear I recognize the flicker of emotion that I'd seen only once or twice before; in the eyes of another man who used to ride a café racer through the streets of Europe, picking up odd jobs to make ends meet.

"You did say, *café racer*, didn't you? And *Europe*? And *motorbike*?"

Chad cocks his head. "Wait a minute. Sound like someone you know? Someone, as in Nathaniel Gorham?" he asks through clenched incisors. "Is he back in the country?"

"What? Who?"

"Nathaniel. My brother."

Quickly, I'm relieved. As odd as the coincidence appears, at least Dante's name is not Nathaniel Gorham. "Oh, for a minute, it sounded like someone I used to know. I don't recall his last name," I confess.

Because I don't recall him ever giving me his last name.

"No last name, huh? It sure sounds like Nathaniel. My brother doesn't recall his own last name, either. But I guess when you disown your own family, and call them a bunch of liars and thieves, you don't need a last name."

"Oh, God," I gasp noisily and double over. My hand flies to my heart to keep it from bursting through my sternum, until my purse drops and spills all over the floor. Quickly, I bend at the knees and scramble to gather my lipstick, license, car keys, and my wits.

Chad doesn't bother to assist me with my contents scattered on the floor. I think he likes to see me on my knees before him.

"You seem upset, Nina. What is it?" he asks, suddenly calm. Boy, this guy can turn off and on his emotions faster than your average manic-depressive.

I pop up to my full height and level him with a confident stare. "It's nothing. Nothing. I'm just a little light-headed."

"Do you want something to drink? Are you all right?" Chad watches me with a loaded smile. He's gloating again, calculating again, like he's already figured out something I haven't yet. "Could it be something I said? Or *someone*?" he asks.

"No," I snap way too defensively. "Not at all."

"Whoever this guy is, who happens to sound exactly like my brother, he's got you worked up. I mean, since we're sharing, care to share?"

I withhold my glare and try to shrug it off. Getting heavy doses of Dante's memory is throwing me off, making me dizzy, that's all, or so I tell myself.

"I think I've shared enough. Besides, I told you, I don't know your brother."

"Well, most people don't. He probably goes by his middle name now. Nathaniel got it from our great grandfather. *Nathaniel D. Gorham* got banished from our family years ago."

I clamp up my crystal purse, but nowhere near as fast as my throat clamps up. I gasp for air.

"Nathaniel *D*. Gorham?" I blurt without even realizing it. Does the middle initial have to be a "D"?

"Yep," Chad continues to gleefully torture me, "my great-grandfather made his wealth in the shipping trade with China. Generations later, Nathaniel comes along and forsakes the last name 'Gorham' yet keeps his middle name, *Dante*."

Chad *tisks* as if ashamed over the event. But it's obvious he really doesn't mind. As for me, I wouldn't mind paying tribute to the porcelain goddess right about now.

Chad sighs and rubs his chin. "Well, I guess it's easier for my brother to have no last name, you know, with all the broken-hearted women he leaves in his wake. But, nah, it can't be the same guy you know, Nina, now could it?"

"No," I utter on a poorly stifled choke, "it can't be the same guy. It can't be."

TWENTY-ONE

You had me at nice ass.

❦

I'm alone, making sure I'm as far away from Chad as I can possibly get. I head toward another wing of the manor house. I know I'm walking, but honestly, I can't feel my legs.

I can't believe it. Oh, my stomach hurts. I'm gonna wretch, I just know it. But I can't. I have to get through the rest of the night and couldn't possibly afford to have vomit spattered on my look-at-me gown.

I hear swing music echoing through the chambers of the manor house, which thankfully drowns out my windstorm thoughts. I also smell hors d'oeuvres, shrimp wrapped in bacon, I think. Not helping the desire to wretch, people.

Oh, Dante, how could you?

All his talk about growing up in a family of liars and thieves. He made it sound like a band of gypsies raised him, not one of Boston's leading clans. And to think I spilled my guts to him about Chad and he didn't say anything or offer to help me. But why? Was he a coward? Couldn't be. The guy saved my life the first night I met him.

Maybe since he "withheld vital information" about the identity of his family (*translation: an indirect lie, in my book*), he knew I'd find out the truth if he came with me tonight. The desire to wretch transforms into the desire to cry. Dante didn't turn out to be the man I thought. Good thing he broke things off when he did.

I round the corner down a corridor, passing clusters of people chit-chatting, and I march into the grand assembly hall with the staging area. I force myself to adjust to the dim lighting of the ballroom-like atmosphere. Only candles on the small rented four-top tables cast a glow extending to the dance floor and swing band. Overhead, hundreds of black and silver helium balloons fill the entire ceiling. They've got streamers of ribbons hanging down from each one adding to the festive mood of everyone . . . everyone but me.

Near a station set up as a chocolate martini bar, Brooke is concentrating on overseeing the stock of glasses. Next to her, Unity is stirring a chocolate martini and handing it to Anna Wintour. She's heavily "conversating" with the super-editor about the importance of a harmonious metaphysical composition of one's wardrobe. Anna appears pleasantly intrigued.

Brooke looks up from restocking the martini station with Godiva chocolate sauce and white chocolate stirrers. "Oh, Nina, hi! Oh, wow, you look gorgeous! Let me see. Turn around."

I whine and offer a pathetic twirl; even Unity and Anna nod with approval.

"I just can't believe how pulled together you look! The shawl-thing, the purse, my God, those shoes." She points and then shoves a white chocolate mousse martini into my hand. "I don't want any dark chocolate near you tonight, you hear?"

"Yeah, yeah, yeah. Oh, Brooke, I heard something awful."

"What is it, honey? Are you all right?"

I take a gulp of the frothy white chocolate drink and set down the martini glass.

"Dante's real name is Nathaniel Gorham, as in, Chad Gorham's black sheep brother. Oh! If I see Dante one more time! Oh! The things I'd say to him!"

"Oh, shit, Nina," she utters. She's looking over my shoulder and out into the makeshift ballroom. "Looks like you're gonna get your chance."

I must say, this is one of those moments where you would love to have your "ex" see how gorgeous you are when you're all dolled up. Let's face it, we girls live for this kind of moment. But it's too soon and I have way too much on my plate to add a heap of he-man named Dante Gorham.

"Here he comes. Good luck, Nina." Brooke grabs a tray and scurries off to tend to her catering tasks.

I can only stand there cemented to the spot. Alone. Abandoned. I dread having to turn around to see him head my way. But I don't have to turn around. I sense the heat he's throwing me. I smell sex and candy. His scent grows stronger. I know he's near. Too near. I even feel the warmth of his breath suddenly splay onto my bare neck. Knees, don't buckle on me now.

"Nice bum, where ya from?"

Augh! I spin around and glare up him. Oh God, he's so beautiful in his tux. Does he have to clean up so good? Too bad he's a lying, conniving, scheming, son of a bitch. But he's a beautiful son of a bitch.

"Don't you 'nice bum' me, you bastard! How could you do this to me, Dante? Or should I say, *Nathaniel*!" I push him and push him hard. Of course, he doesn't budge. Then again, one-hundred-percent unadulterated muscle never does.

Dante nods with guilt. "I was afraid of this. That's why I came. I couldn't let you go through tonight alone."

"Alone? I've been going through everything alone! I've been dealing with Chad on my own and the whole time, he's your brother! And you don't tell me?" I'm baring my fangs at him while I talk; I mean business. "You lied to me. You should have told me."

"Would it have mattered?"

"Oh, please!"

"Knowing or not knowing wouldn't have helped you. It was better you had no idea and that I stayed away. I didn't want to blow your chances of getting your promotion."

"Then what are you doing here now? You changed your mind and want to witness me blow it? Hey, why not get a ringside seat while I duke it out with your brother and lose."

"That's not why I'm here. I hated the thought of you facing Chad alone. I realized I couldn't do it. I was halfway to Texas when I turned around." He gives me one of his manly, irresistible, lopsided grins. "I don't know what the hell you did to me, girl, but I couldn't let anything happen to you. It's the truth. You have to trust me, Nina."

His smooth words tear through me like a rusty serrated fingernail file. Learning Dante's true identity is still too painfully fresh to get over so quickly.

"Trust you? I've been through too much to trust you. You've

lied to me all along. Your brother is trying to destroy me as we speak. Hell, you're probably in on it with him."

Dante actually squints hard at me in disbelief. Oh, as if I care if I hurt his feelings.

"You really believe that?"

"You're a *Gorham*, aren't you?" I snap and spin away.

He grabs me by my shoulders, spins my body back to face his immense tuxedoed chest, and squares off with me.

"See, this is why I have nothing to do with my family. They're a pack of liars and cheats. Chad's no different. They hurt everything they touch."

His hands stay pressed against my skin and his fierce energy zaps through me. Good golly, his very touch has got my vagina waging war against my brain. *Make him go. Make him stay. Make me come. And then make him go.*

I shrug off the combatively conflicting thoughts as I reluctantly shrug out of his hold. "Dante, let me fight this battle on my own. I've come this far—"

"Let me help you. Bring me to Chad and—"

"No, besides, you have your own battle to fight," I say to him as Jackleen floats across the dance floor toward Dante. She sinks her manicured tentacles into him and sweeps him onto the dance floor. If I didn't know any better, I swear she's got her hand cupped against his ass under his tuxedo jacket. But it's hard to confirm because the gold lamé and reflective sequins on her gown are absolutely blinding.

I swallow a tearful lump so big, that if it lodges in my throat, it would look like a third breast on me. I can't have that, how would it make the dress look? I swear, when this is all over, I'll have a good cry, or laugh, or both, depending on my mood.

For now, I've got to stay focused and find Ned. I've got to

warn him about Chad's plan to ruin him. I can't let that happen. Plus he'll have the generated report of sign-ins I need to nail Chad. Or at least put a chink in his armor. Just as I'm about to leave, I see Ned engrossed in a chat with Brooke. I approach them. They're talking about the molecular properties of chocolate and how she can manipulate it for her chocolate-pop adult-basket business. I'm not sure who I'm supposed to save in this case. I invade the sliver of space between them, trying to act calm, cool, and collected.

"Are we doing all right here?"

"Nina," Brooke playfully elbows my side, "where have you been hiding him? You keeping him to yourself?" She bats her eyelashes up at Ned.

"Um, I see you two have met. If you don't mind, Brooke, I've got to cut in here for a minute." I turn to Ned. "I have to tell you something. Chad's got some big plan to ruin you if I try and take him down. I can't let that happen."

But Ned merely smiles as if humoring me. "Don't worry about me. He can't touch me." He looks back to Brooke, ready to continue his fascinating conversation with her.

"No, Ned, you don't understand," I tug on the sleeve of his black tux. "He's lined you up to take a fall if I get him in trouble. You'll get fired."

Ned grips me by the shoulders and gently squeezes, indicating for me to get a hold of myself. "It'll never happen. So, don't worry. I'm in the middle of a very important discussion with the most beautiful woman ever, so give me a minute, okay?"

He's right. When will he and Brooke ever get to have a magical first-meet again? I should at least let the guy have this one fleeting moment of glory before they fire him and throw him out on his ass. All because of me.

"So, you two were, like, discussing your peeny-pops and adult baskets, huh?"

"Oh, yes," Brooke coos. "Ned here has been more than helpful. He's even offered to demonstrate a little chemistry with chocolate on me—I mean *with* me—one day. I'm thrilled." Brooke's face is lit up so much, she's casting a glow that radiates farther than the candles in the ballroom.

"What a surprise you two hit it off. Who knew? I'm sorry I came in to break you two up—"

"Break us up?" Ned cuts in. "To do that, we have to go on a date first, if that's all right with you, Brooke."

"I'd love to. I want to know every quality about chocolate that I can," she purrs.

Okay, I can't take it anymore. Brooke is a sure thing; Ned's got the date. But he isn't going to be able to afford any date with Brooke if he loses his job on account of me.

"Hey, this lovefest is great and all, and I'm rooting for you both, honest, but Ned, we really need to do a little damage control, remember?"

"Right," he says to me, floating down from his cloud and coming back to the here and now. He turns to Brooke. "Damn, I left my superhero cape at home tonight. I guess this penguin suit will have to do." He fondles his authentic seventies retro tuxedo and offers her a dashing, computer-guy smile, despite the bottom braces.

Brooke's so damn smitten, she doesn't notice the braces or doesn't seem to care. Good for her.

"Go save the world, big guy. I've got a room to work. I'll see you later?"

The moment he nods and she smiles back, I hook my arm around his and haul him off.

"Ned, things are getting awful complicated tonight. Bizarre. Odd. Please, focus here. Where's the computer log?"

"Log? Oh, right," he says, coming back down to earth completely. "I misplaced it. I mean, I had it, and *boom*, it was gone."

Keep breathing.

"What do you mean it's gone?" But I already know it means Chad probably swiped it. "Never mind, no time. Can you get me another one? Please. As in, like, now?"

"That's not so easy to do. Upstairs is locked. I'll have to get to a computer somehow, but I'm working on it. Don't worry." He looks over his shoulder to catch Brooke bending and retrieving some napkins from the floor. I'll be damned, she's watching him watch her.

Just then, Ray appears and announces to the guests that John Avalon is about to begin a tour of the new wing of the manor house.

"Oh, Ned, I'd feel better if you worked on it now. I know how the Trinity operates. We'll have a tour. And right as we sit down to eat, everyone gets up to say a few words. That's when they'll announce promotions. Time's a-ticking."

Ned seems to understand my dire circumstance. "I hear you. And thank you for having such a gorgeous friend. I owe you big."

"Let's call it even," I say. After Ned dashes off, Ray appears by my side.

"How you doing, kid?" he asks. "Look, I know the moment of truth is coming, but, don't worry. Just accept—"

"I can't," I blurt, "I won't."

"Nina, it's the biggest party of the year. Whatever you have up your sleeve, don't do it. Don't do anything to cause a scene tonight."

"Ray, my livelihood is on the line. I've got dirt on Chad. He has to be stopped. His name matches the times on my computer when the problems started. I'm just waiting for a report—"

"All circumstantial. Doesn't prove a thing. You'll put your ass in a sling for nothing tonight. Bring it up on Monday."

"Monday'll be too late. The promotion is tonight. Honestly, it's more than just a dumb promotion, it's about stopping a really rotten person. Ray, Chad Gorham hurts people."

Ray visibly falters. My hopes lift. Will he be on my side?

"Let him hang by his own devices another day. Even if you reveal something murderous about him, John Avalon will not forgive you for doing it tonight."

"Surely, John wouldn't—"

"If you pull any stunt, I will have warned you and cannot stand behind you. I'm not going to jeopardize my retirement because you're so impatient that you refuse to listen. It's your biggest downfall, young lady."

A train of guests pass by and form a group ready to take a tour of the castle-like manor house and see all its newest renovations. The crowd includes reporters from the *Globe*, *Herald*, *Boston Magazine*, a few television network reporters, and even a rep from the *Entertainment* channel on cable.

Jackleen whisks by in a glory of gold. She's got Dante on one arm which makes my heart sink momentarily, until I remember I hate him. I hate him. I hate him. She slips her other arm through Ray's and whisks him along. She's threatening Ray to save a few dances for her later on . . . or else.

"Come along, Nina, if you know what's good for you! I want you right there for when I make my grand announcement tonight," she says with both Dante and Ray still on each arm.

Like a puppy dog, I follow along. Might as well get all the rejection out of the way in one fell swoop.

Just as we approach the wrought-iron gated door in the front reception area of the building, flashbulbs go off and a small raucous ensues. I'm at the rear of the pack, but judging by the hoopla, I already understand what the commotion is about. Of all people to make an appearance here tonight, this is the last person I need to see.

TWENTY-TWO

I'm about to climax, what's <u>your</u> excuse?

✦

"You gotta be kidding me," I groan. The small group surrounds none other than Jeremiah Stone. Soon after, the crowd continues on tour, leaving me to glare up at Jeremiah, who's standing there waiting for me.

"Oh, this night just keeps getting better!" I snap at him.

He ignores my comment and opens his arms wide to receive me. I merely stand there, until he gives me a pleading look. I notice a magazine photographer hanging back and still taking his picture. Oh, right, the whole life-or-death image issue with the guerrillas. The things I do to save people's lives.

I give him a big fake hug and air kiss around him, dodging a plump juicy one meant for my lips.

"So, Jeremiah," I say through the gritted teeth of my smile. "What the hell are you doing here?"

"I couldn't let you go through tonight alone."

Where have I heard this one before?

He gestures to the individuals mingling about down the hall. "See, I let you and everyone believe I really wouldn't show up tonight."

"To throw off your stench from the bad guys."

"Right. The revolutionaries."

"You mean, the nationalist guerrillas."

"Yes," he nods to amend his explanations, "nationalist revolutionary guerrillas."

Whatever we're calling 'em, where are they anyway? I haven't heard of any official death threats. No car bombs have gone off. No building's burned down. Aside from Jeremiah's black eye, the threat has been rather minimal.

"You know me too well, Nina. Despite the risk of the bad guys, I'm here now, just as I promised. I'd never let you down."

"Oh, joy. Lucky me. Look, ah, I'm doing fine on my own. So you can turn around and go back from where you came. I'm on a tour right now."

"Come on, Nina!" Jackleen screams out from the pack down the hall.

"Tour? I'd love to take a tour," he bellows and smiles into the video camera of a cameraman walking by.

I roll my eyes, but have to take into consideration what Ray said. After all, if I'm to make a raucous tonight, and get thrown out, I'm certainly not going to waste it on Jeremiah. I've got to pace myself.

I growl in frustration and trudge down the hall with Jeremiah in tow.

Everyone's filing into the new media room. The crowd *ohhs* and *ahhhs* over the fine walnut paneling. Oddly, it's Ned giving the guided tour of the media room. He personally claims responsibility for the programmable controllers and cool hi-tech toys of the room. He pushes on panels to reveal hidden telephones and uses his wizardry to show off his gadgetry. He presses a button on a control panel and the blackout blinds close. Dim lights cast us in a warm glow.

He then points to the large imposing bookcase occupying one entire wall. He explains it's a faux bookcase. With a press of another button, the bookcase rises and disappears behind a panel in the wall to reveal an amazing movie screen behind it. As if on cue, the lights dim further and a series of the agency's award-winning television commercials play out.

The staff on the tour, including John Avalon, all gush with pride while media members and guests watch in awe. Ned then strolls over to a walnut chest beside a leather club chair, removes the top to reveal a hidden computer.

A computer?

Hell, I thought the walnut chest was just for show all this time. Even I'm intrigued . . . and I *work* here. Ned explains how the secret projection room behind the faux bookcase runs the movie screen. And he can control all functions from where he sits with the newly installed computer.

"Say, Nina, I'd like to show some computerized features and use a few of your clients as examples. Would you do the honor of explaining what you see on-screen, in layman's terms?"

Looks like Ned got a computer after all! Yeah for Ned! And yeah for me!

When he winks at me, I jump into professional mode. "Why yes, Ned, I'd be happy to go through the process, from creating a schedule right down to *generating a report.*"

As the images display on the screen, I describe the activities we see.

Ned then brags about his amazing network security, especially on-line and has the great idea of demonstrating it live on the massive movie screen. Okay, I was good for a minute, but now I wanna cry. Poor, poor Ned. So proud. Worked so hard. And he's being so set up. Worse, he's asking me to help get him in trouble. Why didn't he listen to my warning? Why? Why? Why? I can't let him go through with this.

"Ah, Ned—"

Before I can stop him, he's clicking away and accesses the Internet with amazing speed. He explains what he's doing as it appears on the giant movie screen.

I have no choice but to offer my take on what I do for the client to make my job and theirs easier. My lecture is brief and to the point.

Ned picks up where I leave off. "On the Internet, we've got maximum security. Confidentiality is crucial. We take it to the highest level, not only for ourselves, but for our clients."

He clicks his way on-screen, demonstrating the security of the Avalon Advertising web site. He even shows paths hackers could take and how they would not only be thwarted, but traced so they could be prosecuted to the highest extent of the law.

His confidence makes me sweat. I pray his demonstration won't blow up in his face. I also pray his job-interviewing skills are up to par.

"As you can see, I'm a little different from most network security types. I focus on keeping hackers out. But I also try to know their mindset. Call it a game of cat-and-mouse. But if anyone even attempts to break in, although they *won't*, I still want to know about it. I live for this. For example, why, here is a hacker now! Let's do this live."

I swallow hard. The crowd looks at some web site images on the movie screen and then sees the coding of a hacker who's been trying to break into the system. Ned traces the path of the hacker.

"Why Nina," Ned says, "it appears a hacker tried to obtain your confidential information on one of your clients on-line."

I gasp. "Oh, Ned! No!"

With every click, my breath grows more shallow. I'm terrified for when Ned and the entire Avalon staff discover the hacker has come anonymously from the outside and has indeed broken in. Ray's warning words of not causing a scene ricochets through my head. I bite my lip until I taste blood.

During this demonstration, I briefly watch the crowd, until I inadvertently catch Dante's eye. He's being molested by Jackleen, but his stare is on me. He mouths the words, "You look beautiful."

I whisper back, "Bite me."

He chuckles and raises an eyebrow as if actually considering biting me. He then returns to observing the screen—pretty gallant for a biker-guy-slash-dynasty-guy.

While I'm sweating, drenching my gown, Ned's still center stage. He spits out words like, "follows a maze," "falls into my trap," and "trace it back to . . ." He's clicking through this live demonstration. Everyone's waiting to see the capture of this hacker. Collectively, we hold our breaths.

"The Internet is public property," Ned continues, "but any corporate piracy we discover can and will be prosecuted within accordance of the law and the official Internet commission." Ned pauses pensively and regards what he's viewing.

"This hacker hasn't broken in, although he believes he has. And that is the trap I set for him. And the hacker is . . ."

No one breathes yet. But they're smiling as they wait for the name to be revealed.

A dialog box pops up like a massive window. The words glow into the room. Every member of Avalon Advertising gasps.

"Chad Gorham?" John Avalon asks aloud. He breaks through the crowd and stands in the center of the room. He stops in front of the giant movie screen and gazes up at the name.

I try to stifle a giggle of relief. I cover my mouth and try to hold back my screams of delight.

John glares at Ned. "I hire you to keep hackers out. Not seek them out, bait them, and trap them."

"No, sir." But Ned looks guilty as charged. "But I don't set bait. A hacker has to come into the back door of the site on their own recognizance. If he does this, then he's playing hard ball and it's my goal to stop him for good."

"But when did you set up traps? Is this what you spend your days doing?"

"No, sir. I do it on my off time. For fun. It's a hobby. I love the investigations process. So I just apply my techniques to Avalon. After hours, so there's no confusion."

John hangs his hand on a hip; his other hand cups his chin. He's shaking his head, unsure of what to do with this information.

Ray steps forward, with Jackleen on his arm, who's still clinging to Dante and drags him along, too. Ray gazes at the awestruck faces of the crowd. "I'd like to state for the record that you all have witnessed just how protective the Avalon staff is of all our projects."

Good for Ray! He's saving face for the sake of the crowd. He's so darn awesome at his job. No wonder he's in so tight with the old boys.

"And when it comes to loyalty and protection, I believe Nina Robertson has something she'd like to share. And John, whatever she has to offer, I stand behind her one-hundred percent."

All eyes settle on me. When flashbulbs go off in my direction, Jeremiah lays a hand on my shoulder to slip into the picture, until I shrug him off. I step through the crowd and approach John and Ray—and Jackleen and Dante by default.

"I was going to wait until Monday morning to talk to you about this, when it would be a more appropriate time," I lie to him. I look to Ray for support before continuing. He beams back at me in pride over my blatant fabrication.

"I'd like to hear it, Nina," John says with a grim expression.

"It appears as though our 'hacker' has also been attempting to sabotage, um, a fellow employee's work and computer."

"Is that so?"

"Yes," I say, then turn to Ned. "Can you call up the recent sign-in roster for the company as well as computer users in a generated report on the network? I'd like to use it to back up my claim. Would you do the honors?"

"Be happy to."

Ned does a little fancy footwork on the movie screen, highlighting times and dates when Chad was in and out of the building and how they coincide with questionable actions going on with the computer network. I, of course, narrate this whole scenario, filling in the pieces, but never mentioning the victim of this sabotage, namely me. It's all for the sake of the media.

"Where the hell is Chad?" John asks.

Ned looks around. "Last I saw, he went into the library."

John Avalon turns to address his tour with a smile. "Ladies and gentlemen, you've seen excellence at work here tonight, and the evening's still young. If you'll excuse me for a few minutes. Ned here will finish demonstrating the features of this room before leading you to the next stop, the library. I'll see you there."

The light in his eye dims slightly while he sets his sight on me. "Nina, come with me. Ray, you too."

We follow John, which includes Jackleen and Dante, too, since Jackleen won't let go and Ray is loving his half of the attention. Our little group marches down the end of the hall to the great double doors leading into the library.

John grabs the large iron doorknobs, pushes open the massive library doors, and barges his way in. The rest of us follow behind him.

The moment we enter and see Chad, we all freeze at the horrifying sight before us.

At least, I think it's horrifying. I'm not exactly sure what I'm seeing, but if I'm not mistaken, Chad has got John Avalon's fiancée, Marilyn, pinned against the floor-to-ceiling bookcase. He is pawing and groping her frantically and her body language indicates she's not exactly liking it.

TWENTY-THREE

Don't defecate where you dine.

Chad's really smooching it up with Marilyn, sucking on her neck and shoulders. Marilyn's hands are braced against his arms; she's facing away from us and she's squirming. Chad is so hot into his pursuit, he doesn't even realize an audience has busted in on his private party.

I can't believe my luck! Chad Gorham is getting caught with his hand in his big boss's cookie jar! As I watch the dramarama play out before me, I have only one thought.

Thank Gawd it isn't me getting mauled.

Just as John Avalon and the rest of us realize what we're witnessing, Marilyn raises her left arm into the air, her hand balled into a fist.

"Chad Gorham, get the fuck off my fiancée!" John bellows, reverberating through the entire cavernous room.

Chad looks up to see us all standing at the doorway, which

means he doesn't see Marilyn's left fist come swinging across his chops.

I gasp, cover my mouth, then cover my eyes, but realize I gotta see this, so I cover my mouth again. This way, no one can see me smile, and I get to watch with delight while Marilyn punches the daylights out of the guy.

Once he's punched in the face, Chad's head snaps back. Blood spurts from his jaw, compliments of Marilyn's diamond engagement ring gashing him.

Marilyn pushes him away, knocking him off balance while she wails out a slew of cussing at him. When Chad falls hard to the floor, she goes after him again. She's about to kick him in the junk with her spiked heel until John leaps into the melee and embraces Marilyn. She breaks down into sobs and falls into his arms. Between her tearful cries, she spits out words like, "bastard," "pervert," and "rapist."

Boy, Chad has sure earned his share of labels this evening. I did try to tell him his dirty doings would catch up to him. Who knew they'd all be in the same night?

Ray picks up the library telephone and calls security. By the time Marilyn explains what happened and John confronts Chad, security arrives. They're about to haul him away when John tells them to stay for a moment.

"I want Chad to hear this," John says. He's been more than merciful this evening, I must admit. I'd say it's for the sake of the gala, but he always keeps a level head in any crisis.

Speaking of the gala, the crowd on tour shows up, right on time. While Ray assumes his position next to John, Jackleen goes to Marilyn and with gentle coos, she comforts her, much to my surprise. And yes, Dante snakes his way charmingly through the crowd and stands beside me. I brace myself for the onslaught of hormones I endure whenever his aura invades my personal space. Oddly enough, he says nothing, but offers mute support. Good thing he's mute or he'd get a pointy elbow to the rib.

"Nina," John turns to me. "I was going to save this for after dinner, but I believe I have an announcement to make. Sometimes, it can be tough to decide which team player to promote within a company. But in light of recent events, the choice in this case has become quite clear."

With a broad grin to the crowd, John Avalon makes a grand gesture my way. "Ladies and gentlemen, I'd like to introduce the new Account Executive of Special Projects, Nina Robertson."

The crowd breaks out into applause. I hear a few girlish cheers in the background. I'd know those squeals anywhere. Brooke and Unity have been eavesdropping the whole time.

Through the applause and congratulations and hugs and kisses, my heart keeps leaping and doing a jig. On the outside, I do my best to be calm, cool, collected, and sophisticatedly delighted at the promotion. As the small crowd dissipates to move onto the next big event on the tour, I hang back momentarily to let everything sink in. I watch Jackleen hook Dante and Ray in her arms and lead them out of the room. Dante turns to look back at me helplessly, but I offer no assistance. John, who has Marilyn snuggling close to him, now approaches me.

"Nina, I'm sorry it had to come to this, but you handled yourself like a pro. I assume you'll accept my offer?"

"Accept it? Hell, I'm going to keep everyone so busy, you'll wish you never hired me in the first place."

My wicked retort earns a satisfied grin from John. "I'd expect nothing less from you. I'll see you at dinner in the assembly hall." He gently escorts Marilyn out of the library.

At some point, police officers showed up with a real-live detective. They're interrogating Chad and filling out paperwork.

The crowd thins and the glitz of the media and paparazzi have followed everyone down to the makeshift ballroom. I lag behind, but by the time I make it back to the front reception area, Jeremiah and Dante are standing there waiting for me by the wrought-iron door.

"Congratulations," Dante says, throaty and proud. He's watching me and doesn't even seem to notice Jeremiah several feet from him.

"Right," Jeremiah chimes in, "congrats."

I pull my gaze from Dante and nod a thank-you to Jeremiah. He takes this as an opening to talk before Dante gets the chance. He steps forward.

"Nina, I'm happy for you and all, but you have got to decide."

"Decide?"

"It's either him or me." He kicks his head in Dante's direction.

I'm stuck between choosing a self-absorbed, selfish, camera-hungry man who has never been there for me in the *past*, and a lying, rich, wanderlusting man who will never be there for me in the *future*. Oh, it's a toss up.

"I choose *neither*. I'm kinda happy with how things are right now. Alone. So I think it's best for both of you to go."

Dante's stands stonelike, while Jeremiah's face drops.

"So that's it? You want nothing to do with me? *Me?* Jeremiah Stone?"

"Oh, Jeremiah, I tried to tell you."

"And I tried to tell you . . . I-I did love you, you know." His eyes lower while he tells me this lie. A classic gesture. "And all I asked was that you keep your mind open to other options in this world."

"You didn't want me to keep my mind open, Jeremiah, you wanted me to keep my legs open."

Chad passes us with security and hears me. "That's a good idea, Nina!" he yells and sneers. "You better keep your legs open if you plan on getting ahead in this shit hole!" He struggles against the security officers escorting him toward the wrought-iron door.

Dante leaps through the air, tackles Chad, and keeps pounding his brother, until a security officer tries to pull him off. Jeremiah merely stands there on the sidelines and does nothing.

I'm yelping out a scream and I dash over to Dante, who's now being restrained by the officer.

"Please, stop! That's enough!" I beg the officer to leave Dante to me. Since he's aware that Chad deserved the belting, he entrusts Dante to me and assists the other officer with hauling Chad out the door.

"Dante, give me a minute alone with Jeremiah, then you and I can talk. All right? Please?" I smooth the folds of his tuxedo, rubbing my hands down the slopes of his chest, hoping to calm him down. I can feel he's still tense. He reluctantly gives me a brooding nod.

I walk Jeremiah to the door. I guess this bad-ass reporter decided not to defend my honor the way Dante did because he can't afford another black eye to that pretty face of his. He was right when he said earlier that I know him too well. But just standing there and not sticking up for me was still a cowardly gesture in my book.

"I deserve a woman who wants me to be the center of her world. I'll settle for nothing less," he rants.

"I know, I know," I tell him in a motherly, under-standing manner as he skulks out the door. "You'll find her someday."

Time to brace myself for what needs to be done next. I turn and walk up to Dante. I must say, he's shown greater chivalry and dignity than any of the men I tangled with tonight.

He takes my hand and holds it. He's still brooding, but he's taking this whole good-bye thing like a man. "So, like Jeremiah said, that's it, huh? I'm sorry I lied to you and I don't blame you for never wanting to see me again."

I feel awful. He really looks torn up. "Oh, Dante, it's so much more than that. We both know we don't have a future. It wouldn't work. We never even expected to try. I mean, I have to think about my kids."

He knits his brow at me. "Wait, you already have kids?"

"No, silly. Not yet. But I will. And what am going to I tell them? 'Sorry, kids, your dad chose the open road over his re-sponsibility to you.' Or how about, 'Oh, sure, your dad loves you, but he loves his chrome and wheels just a little more.'"

"Is that how you think?"

"No, Dante, it's how you think. And that's what worries me. You told me earlier that you were 'feeling all kinds of shit' for me right now. But what about tomorrow? How will you feel about me then? You come and go. I stay for the duration. That's where you and I are too different."

"For the record, when you thought you were pregnant, I didn't hate the idea."

"For the record, that does make me feel better."

"But I can't change your mind?"

"No more than I can change yours."

"Then I guess it's back on the road to El Dorado, Texas, for me."

The thought of Dante riding on his Harley in a tux makes me smile. "By the way, what's in El Dorado?"

"Paradise, I hope."

Setting Dante free has put a real damper on the evening I think as I enter into the transformed ballroom. Dinner has been served, and the entire audience is applauding Jackleen Liquori while she glows in the spotlight beaming on her. She's blowing kisses to everyone.

"Nina!" Unity shouts and drags me aside. "You musta' been awfully good in a previous life. They've been looking all over for you! Jackleen just handed over her entire PR account to you! Oh, hey, I gotta go, I'm chatting with some people about a yoga-inspired line of cruisewear!" Unity kisses my cheek and bounds off to serve dessert to a table of fashion editors.

The audience keeps applauding and they're all looking at me. Oh, God, another congratulations. Looks like I finally got my grand entrance after all. A spotlight beams at me. Through the glare, I see Jackleen blowing more kisses my way.

She then gathers everyone's attention to finish her announcement by saying, "And thanks to Nina Robertson, I believe I found my future husband number five!" She hugs Ray, who's gushing unbelievably. "And this wonderful man has agreed to write the great American novel . . . all about *me*!"

A gasp and laugh spill out of me. I'm so overloaded right now my head is spinning. I'm thrilled, I'm sad, I'm overwhelmed. I smile again at everyone, say a few almost-truthful words about what a pleasure it's been to work with such a fine movie star, and then slink out of there.

Exhausted, I fall against a wall. It's over. All of it. Thank God. I close my eyes and catch my breath.

"Okay, Nina, where is he?"

I hear the voice, but I can't believe it. I open my eyes.

"Celie? What are doing here? Where is *who*?"

"Jeremiah. I couldn't stand knowing he was here with you another minute. You might as well know. We're getting married. I came to tell you in person so I could see the look on your face."

TWENTY-FOUR

The Princess Diarrheas

I know who I'm looking at. And I know what I'm hearing. But her words are simply not sinking in. "Ah, left field, here. What are you talking about?" I remain against the wall for support.

"You want to know? Jeremiah was using you. And I happily agreed to it. After your breakup, his reputation got damaged due to some rumor. At first, he tried not to involve you because he wanted to spare your feelings."

"My feelings about what?" I'm truly curious.

"Of finding out he dumped you because you couldn't keep up with the hectic life he leads." She flips her light brown hair over her shoulders and juts out her jaw at me. "It takes a certain caliber of woman to keep up with a public personality like him. And you're not it."

"Really? I seemed to hold my own the past week or two. In fact, it looked to me like he came crawling back."

"Oh, that. He just needed to be seen in the spotlight with

you a few times. His job assignments started to go down when some lies started that he'd been involved in some overseas kinky sex ring. The sex ring scandal was bad enough, but they said he had a *male* concubine. He denies it and I believe him."

"So, ah, you don't know anything about any sexcapades of his?"

"Come on, Nina. You and I both know a guy like Jeremiah isn't gay. And I keep him *satisfied*. Breaking off your engagement was simply bad timing. It made the rumor look true. So appearing to get back together with you seemed the best way to do damage control."

"Why couldn't he do damage control with you and spare me all the grief?"

"Because people would have said we were faking it for him to save face. Since you two were already engaged, no one would have questioned it. Besides, you apparently really do have some modicum of talent in the PR department. That certainly helped. And I just relished the idea of you thinking you had a chance to be with Jeremiah again, only to be disappointed."

She's got to be kidding me. So during his little disappearing acts he was seeing Celie? I knew something was up. Then again, Celie could be lying.

"But what about the nationalist guerrilla revolutionaries? I saw his black eye. They wanted him dead."

Celia nodded. "The black eye was from me. I wanted him dead after he thought he got you pregnant. I figured you blew it for me once more, but you didn't. I'm not about to let you blow it for me ever again. So we're eloping. Tonight. Now, where is he?"

"Whoa. Wait a minute. I don't think I like what I'm hearing. He was my fiancé first," I tell her.

"Yeah, well, the wedding gown was *mine* first."

"Technically, no. I found that gown."

"Yeah, but I bought it! Oh, it doesn't matter, that rag was nothing but bad luck!"

"Oh, I don't think it's so bad. Of course, I had to *take it in a few inches*, but I think it turned out pretty well." I point down at the gown.

Celie squeals in horror and she stumbles back. "What did you do? That's a four-thousand-dollar wedding gown! Don't you know it's the beadwork and lace that make the gown!" She hyperventilates and does some self-talk to calm down.

I don't have time to debate the gown's true architectural makeup, I just need to clear her out of here. "Come on, Celie, now is not the time. Let's go."

"No, I'm not leaving until I find Jeremiah. We're eloping. Tonight." She stamps her foot and doesn't budge.

This has gone too far. "Ah, Celie, about marrying Jeremiah, are you sure you know what you're getting into?"

"Absolutely. After we elope, we're jet-setting across the world. He told me you never wanted to travel with him to all the exotic places he visits."

"He was right about that."

"Your loss. But my gain. He needs to do research overseas, so we're tying our honeymoon into it. An entire whirlwind tour!" She crosses her arms and glares at me smugly. "That's right, Jeremiah's taking me away from here. First stop, Thailand."

Oh, poor poor Celie! Someone should tell her!

"In that case, I wish you a world of luck," I say. "I really mean that. Honest. You two deserve each other."

Translation:

You two really, really deserve each other.

She's wise enough to read into my feigned well-wishing and

glares at me in confusion. I tell her Jeremiah's already gone and I send her on her way.

The time has come to head home. My work is done here. It has to be. What else could go wrong? Or right, for that matter? I make my way back to the front reception area, picking up my crystal clutch and silk shawl along the way. I saunter along the spit-shined tile floor and head out to the illuminated portico.

My thoughts settle on Celie. She truly believes she's won out on all levels. It's okay. Maybe she'll finally leave me alone. But I can't help but laugh about Jeremiah's plight. So, the media took a machete to the guy's machismo after he bagged out on me. He became desperate to rectify his rep so he plotted the public appearances with me. He played me like a G-string. Imagine! Going through those pains all in the name of a job!

I trudge out into the cool night. The searchlights are still crisscrossing into the black sky, as if dancing to the faint swing music filling the air. The ground is wet and glistening from a recent shower. The brightness of the portico chandelier reflects against the shiny limousines, Beamers, and Mercedes.

I pass the vehicles, looking forward to the stroll toward the boonies where my Honda is parked, even if these heels are starting to hurt. I'm appreciating the night . . . and the solo time. I start taking mental inventory of my personal status quo.

I lost my wedding dress, but got a great evening gown. I've lost Jeremiah for the third time, but I'd say it's the last. I had a sex-stuffed whirlwind affair with Dante, but no prospects for a future mate. And yes, I got the promotion . . . but at what cost?

Surprisingly, my sense of urgency to have it all has subsided.

My need for "immediate gratification" has been downgraded to "impatient perseverance." Hey, it's a start.

I owe a lot of my new attitude to Dante. I've learned that being too rigid on achieving an end result can be hazardous to your health. My battered emotions fully support my lesson. I may not totally agree with Dante's completely non-directional ways, but he's shown me I don't have to take a one-way road toward extreme societal convention. Living life falls somewhere between the two. If only I had the chance to tell him.

I pass through the pillars with lion statues guarding the entrance and round the corner of the curved driveway.

There, in the middle of the long winding driveway, a black silhouette of a man on a motorcycle captures my attention. I can't help but smile. Okay, my heart's a-racing, too.

Dante waits in the half-shadows between the lampposts lighting the drive. He's straddling his motorcycle, oozing sexuality in that suave rented tux of his, and waits for me to come to him.

"Dante." *Need I say anymore?*

"Neeeh-naah." His trademark throaty purr is delicious and smooth, like warmed gooey caramel drizzled over French vanilla ice cream.

"Bike broke down?"

He gives me a look to indicate no bike of his ever breaks down.

"I hate to say it, but I'm happy you showed up tonight," I tell him. "And I'm impressed you stuck around after. It says a lot about your character. And that you're truly concerned for my career."

"I don't give a rat's ass about your career. I only care about you."

Aw, don't you just love this guy?

"Good to hear."

"But do you realize what you've done tonight? You dumped me for something I never did."

"But you will. The open road will take you away. I have no doubt. You called me and told me yourself."

"Yeah, and if you gave me the chance, I'd have told you I'd be back. But you hung up."

"You wouldn't have come back to me."

"I came back."

"This time."

"Okay, so it's true I like to go *thataway*. And you like the straight and narrow. No matter who we are, the future for us is still the same . . . unknown." He pauses and knocks his knuckles against the gas tank of his bike. "I hate losing something so important to me because I can't predict the future."

"What are you losing?"

"You."

"Are you kidding me?"

"You know, people talk all about love and shit like that. But honest to God, Nina, with you . . . I'm feelin' it. I mean, I'm really feelin' it."

That's got to be the most romantic thing he's said to me since the last romantic thing he said. I choke back a girlie yelp. With a deep breath, I prepare to say exactly what's in my heart.

"I'm feeling it, too." My voice quivers and I can't help but let out a small cry. I'm just so damn happy right now. "And I'm sorry about so many things. Not giving you a chance to explain yourself earlier, or that day on the phone. Sorry for not having faith in you." My shoulders drop in surrender. "We might lead different lives, but apparently you're living life the right way. You taught me a lesson."

"I don't recall teaching any lesson."

"You teach by example, going where the wind blows."

"Yeah, but digging your boot heels in and streamlining your focus ain't all bad, either," Dante confesses, almost shyly.

Holy cow.

I blink twice up at him. I'd rub my eyes to be sure I was looking at "thee" wanderlusting Dante Gorham, but the three coats of mascara prevent me from doing so.

"Oh? You now think focus isn't so bad? What happened to heading for *thataway* and getting there *whenever* if the whim hits you?"

He says nothing. But he does shake his head at me, glints of brightness from the nearby lamplights flicker against his ebony hair.

"You know the other reason I came to see you tonight?" he asks.

"Another reason?"

"I been thinking. Speakin' of digging in your heels, it might be time to stick around for a while."

"Define 'a while.'"

"Longer than the shelf life of milk."

My toothy grin spreads on my face even wider. I can feel it through my long-lasting lipstick.

"Uh-huh," I say. "Go on."

He sniffs. "Been wanting to open a vintage motorcycle shop and motorbike touring club. Give an outlet for yuppie bikers and weekend warrior types."

"You been wanting to do this? For how long?"

"Too long. But it would take a lot of marketing and advertising to get the venture off and running. Know any cute little ad execs stupid enough to take on such a project?"

"*Stupid*'s not the word. Try, *insane*."

"Oh, and the exec would have to be female. Beautiful. Smart. And willing to sleep with me at a moment's notice."

I sigh with resignation. I saunter over and look him straight in eye, something I still find so impossibly overwhelming to do.

"You know, I think I might have someone in mind. But she's very busy. I'll have to pull a few G-strings."

"Tell her it could turn into a really long-term project. Long days. Longer nights." His low tone cloaks me in heat. I hear the promise of a thousand tomorrow's in that tone.

"But I have a couple questions," I begin.

"Oh, man, lay it on me."

"Um, what do you think of Thailand?"

"Never gone there. Never intend to."

"How good are you at folding maps?"

"Never really needed one. But I've never had an issue with them."

A mild sense of peace consumes my insides.

"Did I pass?" he asks.

"Good enough for me," I say through a grin.

He hooks one arm around my waist and hauls me closer.

"One more thing . . ." he says.

I fall into him and gift him with a kiss before asking, "What's that?"

"I need to know. Do I have something worthwhile to stick around for?"

"You mean, as in a long-term relationship, exclusive only to each other? Hmm, let's see."

I ease away from him and stroll to the back of the bike. I strap on my designated helmet and tighten the strap under my jaw. All the while, Dante's body contorts to watch my every move. I unceremoniously hike up my white satin gown, straddle the back of his motorcycle, and throw my arms around him in a tight, tight squeeze.

"Whoa, can I take that as a yes?" he asks. "You think we got a shot at a future?"

"Hell if I know," I answer happily, "but for now, let's just ride."